ETHNIC WARFARE IN SRI LANKA
AND THE UN CRISIS

About the author

William Clarance first became interested in Sri Lanka and the United Nations through South Asian friends and reading history at Oxford in the 1950s. But it was not until 1988, when he was posted to Colombo to head the UNHCR monitoring and reintegration programme for Tamil refugees repatriating from South India, that the two interests came together professionally. This is where the narrative in the present book begins; it continues throughout the critical early part of *Eelam War II*, during which as an outsider he had exceptional exposure to all levels of Sri Lankan governance and to the problems and potential for a UN agency protecting civilians in conflict. He now lives in retirement with his wife – also a UN staff member – on a small farm between the Jura and the Alps, writing on protection in conflict and following the drift of international events with concern, of which the present book is a logical outcome.

Ethnic Warfare in Sri Lanka and the UN Crisis

William Clarance

Pluto Press
London • Ann Arbor, MI

Vijitha Yapa Publications
Sri Lanka

First published 2007 by Pluto Press
345 Archway Road, London N6 5AA
and 839 Greene Street, Ann Arbor, MI 48106

www.plutobooks.com

British Library Cataloguing in Publication Data
A catalogue record for this book is available from the British Library

Hardback

ISBN-13 978 0 7453 2526 2
ISBN-10 0 7453 2526 2

Paperback

ISBN-13 978 0 7453 2525 5
ISBN-10 0 7453 2525 4

Library of Congress Cataloging in Publication Data applied for

Sri Lanka Edition published by

Vijitha Yapa Publications
Unity Plaza, 2 Galle Road, Colombo 4, Sri Lanka
Tel: (94 11) 2596960 Fax: (94 11) 2584801
e-mail: vijiyapa@gmail.com
www.vijithayapa.com
www.srilankanbooks.com

Paperback

ISBN-13 9789551266547
ISBN-10 955-1266-54-4

10 9 8 7 6 5 4 3 2 1

Designed and produced for Pluto Press by Curran Publishing Services, Norwich
Printed and bound in the European Union by Antony Rowe Ltd, Chippenham and
Eastbourne, England

*To the victims of civil wars,
who deserve better protection
from the international community
— and to those fieldworkers
who strive to provide it.*

Contents

Contents

[ix]

CONTENTS

CONTENTS

Maps

Plates

Acronyms and non-English terms

Acronyms

AU	African Union
AMIS	African Union Mission in Sudan
BSA	Bosnian Serb Army
CGES	Commissioner General for Essential Services
CIS	Commonwealth of Independent States
CPA	Comprehensive Peace Agreement in southern Sudan
DFID	Department For International Development (UK)
EEC	European Economic Community
EHED	Eastern Human Economic Development
EOKA	Ethniki Organosi Kyprion Agoniston
EPRLF	Eelam People's Revolutionary Liberation Front
EROS	Eelam Revolutionary Organization of Students
GA	Government Agent
IASC	Inter-Agency Steering Committee
ICES	International Centre for Ethnic Studies (in Colombo)
ICRC	International Committee of the Red Cross
IDP	internally displaced person
IPKF	Indian Peace Keeping Force
IRA	Irish Republican Army
IRO	International Refugee Organization
ISGA	Interim Self Government Administration
JHU	Jathika Hela Urumaya
JOC	Joint Operations Command
JVP	Janatha Vimukti Peramuna
LTTE	Liberation Tigers of Tamil Eelam
MSF	Médecins Sans Frontières
NGO	Non-governmental Organization
NORAD	North American Aerospace Defense Command
OCHA	UN Office of the Coordinator for Humanitarian Affairs
ORC	Open Relief Centre
PFLT	Popular Front for the Liberation of the Tamils

PLO	Palestine Liberation Organization
PLOTE	People's Liberation Organization of Tamil Eelam
RAO	Refugee Affairs Officer (UN)
RPG	rocket-propelled grenade
SCF	Save the Children Fund (UK)
SLAS	Sri Lankan Administrative Service
SLFP	Sri Lanka Freedom Party
SLMM	Sri Lanka Monitoring Mission
SPLM/A	Sudan People's Liberation Movement and Army
SRSG	Special Representative of the Secretary General
TDDF	Trincomalee District Development Foundation
TELO	Tamil Eelam Liberation Organization
TNA	Tamil National Army
TNT	Tamil New Tigers
TUF	Tamil United Front
TULF	Tamil United Liberation Front
UDI	Unilateral declaration of independence
UNAMIR	United Nations Assistance Mission for Rwanda
UNCCP	United Nations Conciliation Commission for Palestine
UNDP	United Nations Development Programme
UNF	United National Front
UNHCR	Office of the United Nations High Commissioner for Refugees
UNMIS	United Nations Mission in Sudan
UNP	United National Party
UNPK	UN Peacekeeping
UNPROFOR	UN Protection Force
UNRRA	United Nations Relief and Rehabilitation Administration
UNRWA	Relief and Works Agency for Palestine Refugees in the Near East
UPFA	United Peoples Front Alliance
VVT	Velvettiturai

Non-English terms

cadjan   matted coco-palm leaves used for thatching

Eelam   the independent Tamil state for which the LTTE and other separatist groups have been fighting

Gam Udawa village awakening project

goigama   high Sinhalese landowning caste comparable to the Tamil *vellalar*

grama sevaka village headmen

jawan   ordinary soldier in the Indian Army

kachcheris government headquarters in a district headed by the Government Agent (GA); figuratively, the provincial administration

kadalodiekal *karaiyar* elite: enterprising merchant seafarers, some of whose families own temples in VVT; prominent in the struggle for *Eelam*, most notably in leadership of the LTTE

karaiyars coastal dwellers, particularly in the Vaddamarachchi and VVT, traditionally fishermen, pearl fishers and seafarers

karawa   Sinhalese caste comparable to the Tamil *karaiyars*

kovil   temple

maha   the first annual paddy harvest

Sangha   Buddhist clergy

tosai   Tamil for *dosa*, riceflour pancake with vegetable filling

vanni   literally "the jungle": usually used for the mainland area in the north south of the Jaffna peninsula and north of Vavuniya, where much of the action in this book takes place

vellalar   high Tamil landowning and farmer caste

yala   the second annual paddy harvest

Acknowledgements

Acknowledgements appropriately start with my wife, Suzanne, who put up with a UN commuting marriage during my Sri Lankan years, Binod Sijapati, who shared much of the thought and action and without whose insistence this book would not have been written, and Anton Verwey, another former comrade in the field, with the widest experience of UNHCR operations over the last 30 years.

In Sri Lanka, my closest counterparts in government, Bradman Weerakoon, Devanesan Nesiah and Charita Ratwatte, have all been supportive and helpful with comments and advice on particular aspects, as was Neelan Tiruchelvam, with whom I originally discussed the project in mid 1999 – shortly before he was assassinated. Also in Colombo, General Nalin Seneviratne and Ananda Chittambalam helpfully commented on early drafts.

In Europe, those who have kindly commented on various drafts at different stages have included David Gladstone CMG, former British High Commissioner in Colombo, Dr Nicholas van Hear of the Refugee Studies Centre (RSC) in Oxford, Dr Cathrine Brun of the Norwegian University of Science and Technology (NTNU) at Trondheim, Austin McGill, former legal officer in UNRWA and Simon Springett of Oxfam. As regards libraries and other institutions, particular thanks are due to Vije Vijayapalan of the unfortunately discontinued *Sri Lanka Monitor* project in the British Refugee Council, Ponnudurai Thambirajah, librarian of the International Centre for Ethnic Studies in Colombo (ICES), and the RSC library staff in Oxford, as indeed their colleagues in UNHCR's Documentation Centre in Geneva before, in an act of misguided economy, it was closed down. Finally, Chris Carr, my editor at Curran Publishing Services, has provided shrewd guidance and patient assistance in preparation for publication.

Preface

Why another book on the Sri Lankan conflict? Why now, in 2006, a decade and a half after the events which the core narrative relates? Why the international protection theme? Why the reflections on terrorism? Why the fieldworker standpoint? Why the preoccupation with the United Nations, UNHCR, the refugee agency, and the UN system in general? The answers to these questions are complex, inter-related and cogent.

Why the Sri Lankan conflict?
Relatively little has been written about this for a number of reasons including security, difficulty of access to the war zone and military censorship. Moreover, owing to the complexity of the historical background, the storyline often lies buried in the detail of a long chain of intricate events. And as regards media coverage, until the breakthrough in the peace process in early 2002, the conflict had the status of an all-but-forgotten war, with reporting limited to the most sensational incidents.

The present book, however, draws on a personal journal made at the time day-by-day as events unfolded on the ground during 1990–91, beginning with the withdrawal of the Indian Peace Keeping Force (IPKF), which was followed by the three months of President Premadasa's promising but in the event abortive peace initiative. The journal continued thereafter during the critical first 18 months of *Eelam War II*.

Why now?
Because for many years it was not possible for outsiders who had been closely involved in sensitive humanitarian work in the war zone to write about their experiences without fear of prejudicing the fragile preliminaries to the peace process. That changed with the more relaxed and open atmosphere after the ceasefire of 2002; now in mid 2006, with the deadly drift of events, an outsider's view of the grim reality of frontline conditions during an acutely critical period of the conflict can provide a timely reminder of the price of returning to civil warfare.

International protection?
Eelam War II was important for international protection because its complex ground situation put to the test the Office of the United Nations High Commissioner for Refugees' (UNHCR) traditional perception and practice of its role – to deal with the outflow of fugitives from internal conflicts only as and when they arrived in countries of asylum as refugees – and found it to be wanting.

The situation was all the more challenging in that, while there was a clear moral responsibility to protect within Sri Lanka, there were no precedent models in agency field practice to guide the shape of appropriate response. In the event, the agency field team already present, which had earlier experience from the now defunct programme to monitor the reintegration of Tamil refugees returning from South India following the 1987 Peace Accord, devised a small but innovative programme of protection-orientated relief – the concept and mechanisms of which is best described as protective neutral engagement. This new programme supported an active protection role within the country of refugee origin as an alternative for displaced and endangered civilians who for various reasons did not want to join the mass exodus of their compatriots to seek asylum abroad.

As such, it was initially controversial in some parts of the agency headquarters in Geneva. Nevertheless, it succeeded in surviving the ongoing volatile crises in the war zone, won acceptance by both combatant parties, and gained an increasingly impressive array of support in the international community. And when in 1992 the new High Commissioner, Sadako Ogata, had had time to look into the matter, she ruled in its favour. It thus made significant contributions to the concepts and practice of international protection. Moreover, with the determination of the present High Commissioner, Antonio Guterres, to operationalize protection for internally displaced persons (IDPs), the Sri Lanka programme in the early 1990s is of topical relevance in recalling the institutional obstacles encountered by that pioneering initiative and in showing what can be done, and how.

Fieldworkers?
Most books on conflict are written by journalists and academics. Yet the position of a fieldworker is one of the most authoritative vantage points from which to observe and analyse a frontline situation.

Terrorism?
The manifestations of terrorism in Sri Lanka say much about the causes of this international phenomenon, the nature of movements which perpetrate it, and their continued practice of it even after ceasefires. These are matters of global resonance, most topically in Northern Ireland.

United Nations?
The story which this book tells is an object lesson in the impact which a United Nations agency can have in a sensitive situation where institutional bureaucratic weaknesses are heavily outweighed by the strength of the UN's legitimacy and moral position, and the committed professionalism of its staff.

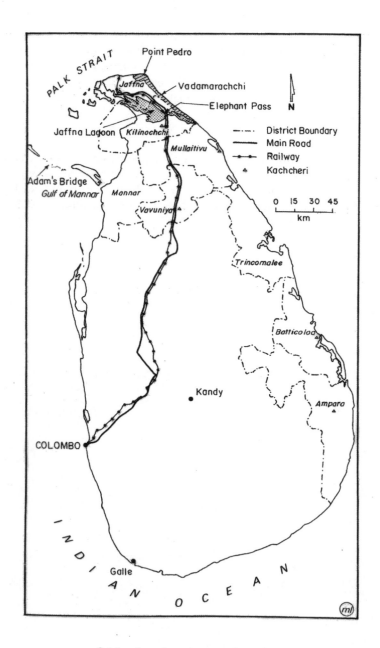

Sri Lanka, showing north and east

1. Refugees leaving for India

2. Madhu open relief centre with UNHCR staff

3. *Kachcheri* officials, clergy and UNHCR

4. IDPs moving into Madhu (I)

5. IDPs moving into Madhu (II)

6. Some farmers came with livestock

7. IDPs in Madhu

8. Getting lorries through the jungle

9. LTTE patrol on Mannar island

10. Bomb damage in Jaffna (I)

11. Bomb damage in Jaffna (II)

12. Muslims on Mannar island prior to expulsion

13. Muslims during expulsion from the north

14. Binod, Danilo, Aloysius Coonghe and Pipat

15. Pipat at Pesalai open relief centre

16. Cricket at Pesalai – an alternative to war games

17. IPKF memorial in Mannar

18. LTTE memorial in a Jaffna village

Part I
Introduction

1. UN crisis, dangers and opportunity

Protective neutral engagement – UN crisis – dangers and opportunity: civil/ethnic warfare, refugees and asylum seekers, terrorism – professional challenges

Protective neutral engagement

This book argues the case politically and professionally for a more active and effective United Nations role to protect civilians in intrastate conflicts, largely with reference to an innovative model devised in the midst of civil war – the protection-orientated relief programme of UNHCR, the refugee agency, in *Eelam War II* between the Liberation Tigers of Tamil Eelam (LTTE) and Government forces in northern Sri Lanka during the early 1990s.

The agency's programme in Sri Lanka at that time differed radically from its previous protection practice there and elsewhere in two key respects: first, in providing protection in a country of refugee origin at the source of an international exodus, rather than waiting until the fugitives had crossed the national frontier, entered a country of asylum and so acquired the status of refugees under international law; and second, in effectively extending international protection to *all* civilians in the operational area who were both endangered and potential international refugees (that is, not only the refugee returnees from South India who had been refugees before their repatriation and for whom the High Commissioner retained legitimate concern, but also other Tamil civilians in the locality who were displaced, and even more significantly, inhabitants at risk who had not yet fled their homes).

This was done within an operational strategy of what is best described as protective neutral engagement in the war zone, implemented with a range of pragmatically devised and integrated mechanisms – open relief centres, regular relief convoys across no-man's-land accompanied not by military escorts but by international civilian staff (significantly, there was no military involvement, even for technical or logistical back-up) and systematic modalities for protection monitoring and intervention – all of which were operated by an unusually small field team.[1]

[3]

UN crisis

Politically, the case for more and better protection of civilians in civil wars relates to the current complex UN crisis in which, while the world organization is undoubtedly in need of reform, it is being subjected to crude, unseemly bullying by the sole superpower, largely because of the principled position it took over the US-led invasion of Iraq. Although weakened thereby, the UN has emerged with its moral standing enhanced and its indispensability reaffirmed by its critical capacity to help clear up the resultant mess.

Even so, these are dog days for the United Nations, whose founding fathers at the end of the Second World War never envisaged the unipolar scenario of today, when it has to face an over-mighty member state with material power way beyond the reach of any potential rival. As a result, UN integrity continues to be impugned – short-sightedly, and with irresponsibility to the point of perversity – by concerted pressures from a Washington whose judgement has been so corrupted by its own hubris that it is incapable of perceiving not only the inevitably limited duration of its current tenure of sole superpower, but also the extent to which its international actions of late have been proving the very case which they were intended to demolish – namely the fundamental need for the principles, professionalism and integrity of the United Nations. To many elsewhere in the world, including a significant although as yet largely silent minority of Americans, such US attitudes appear as yet another tragic variation on the fundamental Actonian theme of the corruption of power,[2] in that although America's power is not absolute, it is exceptional; its cowboy attitude towards the rest of the world – especially for a country which in the past has contributed so generously to the formation of international ideals – is exceptional in its corruption of justly proud national values.

Indeed the UN came into existence at the end of the Second World War largely as a result of United States' idealism, in its early years enjoyed strong support from the US public and was served with outstanding distinction by many highly motivated American staff members.[3] While there was always the negative flip side, including Washington's readiness to exclude itself from norms of international behaviour which it nonetheless expected other member states to respect, its sometimes crude pressures and occasionally indifferent international manners, the UN continued to benefit from broad US support. But well before the end of the Cold War, the strongly positive attitude of the early years was already on the wane, while negative views of the world body were increasingly in the ascendant – a tendency which soared when the US attained sole superpower.

Thereafter, there were further manifestations of unilateralism and unwillingness to cooperate with multilateral initiatives and comply with international standards, as over the Kyoto Protocol on climate change, endeavours to oust the jurisdiction of the International Criminal Court through the conclusion of bilateral agreements, the denial of international standards of treatment for prisoners held in Guantanamo, and so-called "extraordinary rendition" – that euphemism for a deviously cruel practice in manifest contempt of universal values – to name some of the ways in which Washington has endeavoured to put itself above inter-national law and practice. Such a position is unacceptable to the greater part of the international community, the more so in coming from a country which continues to lecture the rest of the world on moral values. And in the run-up to the invasion of Iraq, flagrant disrespect for the United Nations rose to further heights of sole superpower hubris with the shabbily partisan treatment accorded to Hans Blix, the head of the UN weapons inspectors, and President Bush's hectoring that the UN would make itself "irrelevant" if the Security Council did not pass a resolution approving the US-led invasion of Iraq.

However, with profound irony, the refusal of the UN to approve such intervention in the event proved precisely the opposite: the centrality of United Nations' international authority, the universal-ity of its normative values and the indispensability of its agencies' applied professional skills. Moreover, as its unique legitimacy and moral authority in sensitive international affairs was reaffirmed and strengthened thereby, its significance as the appropriate framework within which the international community could take the measure of the sole superpower emerged with a clarity hitherto unknown. The extrication of the United States from the ugly situation that had been so very much of its own making was only feasible on the basis of the impartiality and professional expertise of the UN field-orientated agencies. Yet another development which has reinforced the author-ity of the UN has been that military intervention without due UN authorization has been widely discredited as too dangerously blunt an instrument with which to attempt to right global wrongs. The dangers of unilateral action have been clearly shown by the rise in tension in the Middle East following the Iraq invasion, the damage done to intercommunal relations in Europe and the reality that the world is now a much less stable and secure place than it was before.

Dangers and opportunity

In particular, more and better international protection in conflict relates constructively to a number of dangers which beset the international community today and are likely to intensify in the years ahead: civil/ethnic warfare, the rising numbers of refugees and asylum seekers who flee to other countries to escape its various manifestations and the seeds of terrorism which it sows, not to mention the vexed question of "humanitarian" intervention.

Civil/ethnic warfare

Over the last two decades, civil wars, usually with deep ethnic and historical roots, have become a global problem – while governments and institutions remain uncertain and diffident as to how best, if indeed at all, to respond within the framework of the international system. With its complex causes and deadly dynamics, the acute humanitarian needs of civilians living in frontline conditions and the extent of the terrorist dimension within which it has been fought – including the extreme difficulty of terminating such a national disaster once hostilities have commenced – the Sri Lankan conflict is a prime example of this widespread and intractable phenomenon.

In that respect, the UNHCR programme model devised and developed in northern Sri Lanka in the early days of *Eelam War II* was never intended to end the conflict. Nor was its aim to reconcile the bitterly opposed elements in both communities which sustained the fighting. It did, however, provide an operational framework for much-needed humanitarian action within which UNHCR was able to establish satisfactory working relations with both combatants on a back-to-back basis, as discussed in Chapter 16. This enabled its international staff to circulate freely and establish open relief centres on both sides of the line, organize and lead regular food convoys across no-man's-land to support them, and monitor military access to the centres in Government-controlled areas. The significance of such modalities went beyond the operational procedures they directly implemented to the humanitarian care and concern which they expressed and the modicum of dignity and trust they introduced into the intensely partisan atmosphere of the war zone. They also helped in a number of ways which, although small in themselves, when taken together were constructive in the overall situation.

One such was the flexible pragmatism which made possible the development of innovative mechanisms and methods across the range of needs and response, as indicated in subsequent chapters. And, most importantly, they encouraged the counsels of enlighten-ment – strengthening the hands of sensitively intelligent individuals on both sides of the line in their shrewd perception that it was in their respective best interests to avoid the worst excesses of civil war. However, as a programme model, protective neutral engagement was essentially the product of humanitarian pragmatism judiciously applied in response to the urgent needs of one highly complex ground situation. As each civil war situation is unique and there are often as many significant variations in conditions as there are fronts on which it is being fought, the process of adapting procedures and mechanisms which have worked well in one situation to another is problematic and not to be undertaken lightly.[4]

The dangers and difficulties of attempting to extrapolate the Sri Lankan model of protection in conflict were well illustrated in post-genocide Rwanda where an attempt was made by the then UN Department of Humanitarian Affairs[5] to establish what it inaccu-rately called "open relief centres" in the context of the forcible return to their villages of internally displaced persons following the closure by the government of the camps where they had hitherto been living under the protection of UN peacekeeping forces (UNAMIR II). In the event, the protection provided in these centres was negligible, largely because the rationale of the Sri Lankan programme was entirely inappropriate in the Rwandan context.[6]

Even in low-intensity wars, there are at least as many situations where a programme model such as Sri Lanka's could not have worked, as where it might have provided a valid protection option. Among these are the so-called "collapsed states", where the central organs of governance have been unable to maintain authority and security. Another is where, as in the Caucasus, one or other or both of the combatant forces in the several conflicts in the region is unable to suppress traditional practices of kidnapping for ransom in areas where they are operating.[7] Yet another is where the United Nations in general and universal humanitarian standards in particular are held in contempt by the government concerned. Both Somalia and Sierra Leone have fallen into the first hapless category at various times during the last decade. And as regards the third, Iraq under Saddam Hussein was one such country, and the former Yugoslavia under Slobodan Milosevic another. Nor indeed, short of a sea change in the attitude of the government in Khartoum and a sharp improvement in the security situation for international fieldworkers, could protective neutral engagement on the Sri Lankan – or any other model without decisive military support – provide a solution to the current problems of civilian protection in Darfur.

Once conflicts sink to such anarchic levels of contempt for human life and dignity, the scope for an international agency team to play an active protection role without some form of military back-up, if not altogether excluded, is drastically reduced to the point where its benefit is questionable. Put another way, an agency's role has to be closely and constructively engaged with the daily reality of humanitarian needs in a conflict in order to make a worthwhile difference: a mere passive observer role without engagement geared specifically to redress or other ameliorative action is of doubtful value – and not what this book is advocating.

Fortunately, however, Sri Lanka's was a civil war in which the United Nations was regarded by both combatant parties with a certain respect – even as part of the solution – and in consequence they were open to persuasion that there was enough common space between their respective interests for them to accept an active UN agency protection role in the war zone. The topical resonance of UNHCR's active protection role in Sri Lanka is thus not as a one-size-fits-all programme model for international protection in internal conflict – still less as a quick-fix for ethnic warfare. Rather it is presented as a professional method in which the bottom-up field process of closely observing and analysing population-displacement dynamics in a war zone is an indispensable prerequisite to determining the appropriate response mechanisms for a specific ground situation – a point which has particular resonance with regard to the UN debacle at Srebrenica (Chapter 18, p. 265).

Refugees and asylum seekers

Although asylum – the right of an individual fearing persecution in his or her own country to seek, but not necessarily to be admitted to, refuge in another country – is established in UN and regional human rights and refugee instruments, it is increasingly under threat from mass migratory flows towards industrialized countries which in recent years have risen to levels that are difficult for governments to manage. This is of course an immigration as well as a refugee problem and therefore one which is fuelled by and inter-connected with a wide range of non-asylum considerations. These include unprecedented prosperity in the industrialized countries and rising expectations which cannot be adequately satisfied in developing countries, the cheapness of air travel, and the proliferation of people-trafficking networks to the extent that it is often difficult in practice to distinguish an asylum seeker from an economic or social migrant. Nevertheless, the continuing flight of persons from states suffering endemic insecurity and civil warfare greatly increases the scale of international displacement. And in consequence, some countries have resorted to crudely restrictive measures, such as Australia's use of naval warships to intercept and divert boats carrying asylum seekers and the UK's proposals for an EU immigration policy which would in effect have had claimants to refugee status interned in camps outside the union,[8] that are unworthy of the international community in the twenty-first century, or unworkable – or both.

As related below (p. 143), the significance of the ground situation in northern Sri Lanka in the early 1990s was that there was a substantial group of endangered civilians who for a variety of personal, family, economic and work reasons did not want to flee abroad if there was a viable alternative available for them at home. At that time, there was concern and controversy within the refugee agency that any such programme might prejudice the right to seek asylum. But in Sri Lanka – save in the exceptional circumstances following the assassination of Rajiv Gandhi, when the Indian authorities considered the atrocity to have been planned and perpetrated by the LTTE and were understandably incensed – Tamil civilians who wanted to continue their flight to India were not prevented from doing so. And over the years, many thousands of civilians in the conflict-affected areas were able to use the open relief centres to stay temporarily, pending sufficient improvement in the conditions in their villages to enable them to return home.[9] At the same time, there was clear advantage for the international community in avoiding the political and social difficulties entailed in internationalizing a problem which could be dealt with more effectively and expeditiously – not to mention economically – within the country of conflict.

Although such programmes are not without the risk that officials in receiving countries might cite their existence to justify negative asylum policies, there is no evidence of this having happened in relation to Sri Lanka. With the maintenance of appropriately strict vigilance by the refugee agency, it can be reasonably hoped that such a potentially negative development could be prevented. Moreover, it needs to be more widely appreciated that programmes delivering an active protection role at the source of an armed conflict within major countries of refugee origin can help to reduce the strain of mass migratory movements on liberal asylum policies in receiving states.

Terrorism

Since 11 September 2001, the international community has been obsessed with the menace of international terrorism, yet nonetheless has signally failed to focus clearly and constructively on the politically problematic conditions that continue to generate it. Of course, the continuing threat from international terrorism calls for massive response by way of sophisticated and effectively vigilant security measures. But the heavily politicized hype with which the "war on terror" is presented, and what is as yet its evidently less than stellar success, might perhaps indicate the possibility that it is missing some of the finer points of what it's all about.

For the British, terrorism was a perennial imperial problem which manifested itself whenever there was a deeply humiliated and frustrated political group with a revolutionary agenda. The Irish Fenians in the nineteenth century and their twentieth-century successors, the Irish Republican Army (IRA) and its splinter groups, the Zionist Irgun in Palestine in the period leading up to the foundation of the Israeli state and the Greek Cypriot EOKA in the fight for the independence of colonial Cyprus were but a few of the groups which long kept imperial officialdom working on the political knife edge between terrorism on the one hand, in the form of violent subversion with spectacular outrages designed to draw attention to the perpetrators' particular cause, and on the other, the often rough but broadly legitimate freedom struggles which led ultimately to independence. With such a wealth of relevant experience, it is salutary to note a former director general of MI5, the British counter-intelligence service, Stella Rimington, warning that the "war on terror" cannot be won unless the causes of terrorism are eradicated by making the world free of grievances.[10] And Sir Richard Dearlove, former head of MI6, the secret intelligence service, considers that the West is doomed unless it regains the high moral ground in the war on terror.[11] Unfortunately, however, the reassurance of such wise counsels on national security is offset by the tendency of the present incumbents of Downing Street to listen to the White House rather than to Whitehall.

Be that as it may, at a time when, from Sri Lanka to Northern Ireland, the difficulties of eradicating the terrorist virus once it has incubated are evident, there is – in addition to the fundamental security response – a need for more prophylactic treatment of conditions which conduce terrorism in the first place. In that regard, an international protection role within a conflict of such extremes as Sri Lanka's of course cannot itself prevent the development of terrorism. By clearly upholding international standards of care and concern in the midst of the war, an active programme of humanitarian protection within it helps reduce the deep sense of ethnic injustice, despair and deprivation which feeds the growth of militancy and intensifies it from one generation to the next. It is thus a vital part of any intelligent course of treatment, without which a conflict can only sink to greater depths of intercommunal hatred that in themselves further aggravate the difficulties of eventual peacemaking while intensifying the suffering of all those directly affected and the consequent difficulties for the rest of the world.

Although the present embattled position of the UN is acutely uncomfortable for its leadership, it cannot conceivably give in to US bullying, even temporarily, without incurring a massive loss of credibility and imperilling the entire international system which, although undoubtedly in need of reform, still provides the only feasible framework within which to improve global peace, security and prosperity in the twenty-first century. At the same time, the UN's re-emergent moral authority provides a historic opportunity which the world community will ignore at its peril.

Rather than do less, the need is for the United Nations to do more, particularly in raising its game through the work of its field agencies, not only with better presentation of their existing work but also greater readiness to put together solution-orientated programmes focused on world problems in selected situations where the commitment and skilled pragmatism of professional fieldworkers can make a significant impact.

The importance of the UN providing international protection for civilians in war has long been recognized, but unfortunately with little effective response in terms of developing models and methodology for internal conflicts without military involvement.[12] The reason why there has been so little progress in that direction to date has been attributable at least in part to the parlous state of the UN in recent years, to the extent that proposals for the world organization to undertake new functions, however much needed, have been readily dismissed on the ground that even in its present form the UN was finding it difficult enough to survive. But this was ever an error of judgement, and is all the more so one now in the aftermath of the invasion of Iraq, when there is pressing need for authentic multilateral measures to reduce tension and restore global confidence.

In this context, the challenge for the UN is to develop an active protection role for civilians through its agency programmes in coordination with national governments and whenever possible without military involvement. In other words, it must act in accordance with the principles of protective neutral engagement, of which UNHCR's initiative in Sri Lanka was only one example, rather than through intervention with tendentiously humanitarian intentions. This needs to be seen as a necessary and feasible response from an international community that is more enlightened and confident of the values it wants to prevail in the twenty-first century, as well as a more appropriate form of expression for legitimate international concern.

Professional challenges

Professionally, this is the story of how a radically innovative model for UN protection of civilians in conflict addressed the humanitarian and security challenges of a highly volatile ground situation, and survived comparably hazardous pressures from an unfavourably disposed bureaucracy in Geneva. It is an experience which says much about two crucial aspects of the nature of international protection in conflict: first, what it is, what it is not, what it can reasonably expect to be; and second about its feasibility – how far it is achievable in the context of the institutional hang-ups and inter-agency rivalries in the UN system. It is thus notably topical in the context of UNHCR's recently found enthusiasm for extending protection to IDPs, the success of which unfortunately cannot be altogether taken for granted in view of its reluctant and largely deficient response to the challenge of broadening protection in line with twenty-first century needs.

2. International protection in a civil war

Incident in the Jungle – Mannar – an innovative protection role

Incident in the jungle

3 APRIL 1991

Two bombs were dropped shortly after daybreak. We heard the loud booms and faintly felt the distant blast on each occasion. The areas being targeted by the Air Force couldn't have been more than a few miles away, down the same jungle tracks we would shortly be passing over in order to get back to Vavuniya en route for Colombo. We were in Madhu, the Roman Catholic shrine in the midst of the jungle territory controlled by the Liberation Tigers of Tamil Eelam (the LTTE) in northern Sri Lanka, where UNHCR had set up an open relief centre for the benefit of refugees and displaced persons who were fleeing the fighting. I had been showing round two diplomats of a supportive western European country who had wanted to see for themselves how the UN refugee agency's small, but innovative programme for protective relief in Mannar district was working out on the ground.

Three days previously, we had arrived from Colombo, transiting Vavuniya, the last major town held by Government forces, which commanded the roads to the north. At Thandikulam, on the northern edge of the town, there was the last Army checkpoint before entering no-man's-land. On the far side – just in sight – was the LTTE checkpoint, on the fringe of the territory they controlled. Beyond, along frequently flooded and near-impassable jungle tracks, lay Madhu.

During their stay, the visitors had taken a thorough look around, talking to refugees and displaced persons and to the church dignitaries, the local Sri Lankan officials who were implementing the Mannar relief programme, as it was called, and the UNHCR staff who were outposted in the field office which formed an integral part of the centre. They had been fully briefed on the centre's rationale, which was to provide persons in flight along the jungle routes to the Mannar coast with essential relief

[13]

items such as temporary accommodation, food and a medical clinic, in a relatively secure location. That the centre was operating very visibly under UN insignia helped contribute to the sense of security provided by the remoteness of the shrine and its surrounding impenetrable jungle. But even in the relatively low-intensity conflict conditions of sporadic fighting between the LTTE and Government forces, mostly on the periphery of the jungle, there was no question of UNHCR or any other humanitarian organization being able to guarantee protection or security. It was for the individual to decide for him or herself – usually the latter – whether to remain in Madhu, to move on or, in the case of those living in the vicinity, eventually to move back home when the immediate danger from fighting had passed. By the time the visitors left Madhu, another 450 persons who had been fleeing the Army's offensive against local LTTE positions entered the open relief centre, increasing its population to over 20,000. Later that day, on the way back through the villages in the jungle, there was more dramatic evidence of the way in which it was providing protective relief for civilians caught in the midst of the conflict.

We did a radio check with the UNHCR office in Colombo, which in turn checked with the Joint Operations Command (JOC) of the Sri Lankan military. The latter said that a curfew had been imposed indefinitely, while Government forces were advancing into the jungle from Vavuniya, and that we should stay put in Madhu for the duration. All of us wanted to get back to Colombo for various reasons – one of the diplomats was a desk officer in his foreign ministry and had a tight schedule to get back there – so we decided to push on, cautiously. Reluctantly, JOC accepted this, instructing that we follow curfew procedure strictly by flying a sheet-sized white flag on the front of the vehicle and proceeding very slowly. This we did, taking with us a patient who Médecins Sans Frontières (MSF) said needed treatment that could only be provided at the base hospital in Vavuniya. We also took the opportunity to lead back a column of empty lorries which two days before had brought in the Government-provided food supplies on the Vavuniya–Madhu run.

It had rained heavily during the night. We surged slowly through large pools of brown water, fervently hoping they didn't cover deep potholes in which we would get stuck, until we began to leave the dense jungle forest behind and eventually reached a village in a clearing. We soon saw that this was where one of the early morning bombs had fallen, as we were waved down by a small group of villagers by the roadside, including one who was lying down, badly wounded. His companions said that two villagers had been killed and pointed to their corpses laid out nearby. Then another group of twelve men on bikes, with a maximum load of personal possessions strapped behind and most also with a family member poised on the crossbar, passed slowly by, back down the track to Madhu. All were silent, visibly numbed with shock and tension and preoccupied with distancing themselves from the danger that had suddenly shattered their lives.

We radioed to Madhu, calling for the ambulance in the open relief centre to pick up the wounded man and pushed on slowly down the track. At the next village, we came across a group of 300 to 400 people on the move, some walking, others on bikes and a fortunate few with ox carts piled high with basic household items and family members sitting on top – all heading back towards Madhu. There were some wounded among them and another two corpses were being carried by silent relatives. A grim scene by any standards. But what extraordinary good luck to have empty lorries with us. We loaded them up with the fugitive villagers and sent them back to Madhu, leaving the more seriously wounded to await arrival of the ambulance.

Pressing on, a good hour later we came up against an Army checkpoint, the furthest its armoured column had reached in the push that day. There we saw two young lieutenants, smoking and relaxing after the day's work. Once they had overcome their surprise at seeing the likes of us suddenly appearing from out of the dense jungle, they were friendly enough, but said that we would not be able to continue on our way to Colombo. We politely protested, arguing our need to get there that night. Then a stout major with a jovial manner appeared, saying that he had heard what we wanted and that there wasn't a problem. We could proceed. We got back into the Landcruiser and pushed on slowly, and the major shouted laughingly that we didn't need to go *that* slowly. At the other end of the village, we came up against a newly erected roadblock where some tree trunks and heavy furniture had been thrown together to make a barrier. There were no soldiers on duty to move back the barrier and let us through. We waited for a bit to see if anyone would come to let us out. Meanwhile, a chopper which we had noticed when we first arrived at the other end of the village, again appeared above us, circling a couple of times. I remarked to my companions that I was feeling a bit egotistical with all the attention it was paying us. But soon there was a rustling in the bushes beside the road, as three or four soldiers came out, rather sheepishly – evidently they had been dozing – and removed the barrier, sleepily waving us through.

We travelled down the road at moderate speed. Ahead, there were some soldiers in jungle-green Army fatigues. In accordance with normal practice, we got out of the vehicle and walked slowly towards them, so that they could see that we were unarmed. But when we had nearly reached them, the chopper suddenly reappeared above us and zoomed down, with its guns blazing. We all dived into the wood at the side of the road and took what cover we could – mostly no more than a tree trunk which we tried to keep between us and the chopper as it circled round firing, with the whip-cracking noise of bullets tearing into the trees (fortunately not the ones behind which we were taking cover). The chopper continued to circle round, firing for several minutes. When eventually it flew off, we all shouted to each other to foregather on the road. The "soldiers" towards whom we had been blithely walking, had in fact been LTTE cadres, who on this occasion had not been wearing their normal "tiger-stripe" fatigues, but Army jungle greens. It used to be said that even if the uniforms of both sides might on occasions be indistinguishable, the LTTE would be wearing rubber sandals, not boots. True – but not a difference easy to spot at a distance.

After conferring briefly, we got into the Landcruiser and headed slowly back towards the village held by the Army, whence we had come. But after three or four minutes, we all dashed for cover into the thicket at the roadside once more, as a small fixed-wing bomber (Sia-Marchetti) flew over us and started to drop bombs. The machine-gunning carried on, as the chopper circled round and round before finally flying off. Afterwards, one of my (much younger) companions told me that, greatly to their surprise, as soon as the bombs had started to drop, I had thrown myself flat on the ground – a 50-year throwback to the London blitz of 1940, when as a very small boy I was programmed to do just that in order to avoid bomb blast. (I hadn't even realized I was doing it.) The LTTE, whom we had left down the road, had by now caught up with us. I can't remember if they were speaking Tamil or English or even just gesticulating expressively – but whatever, there was no mistaking what they meant: "—— —- —- and keep going!" After quick discussion, we did just that, but kept the Landcruiser windows open, listening and watching the skies for anything untoward, particularly the return of the chopper or bomber. We pressed on faster and passed round my hip flask, the contents of which had seldom tasted better.

An hour or so later, we reached an LTTE checkpoint and passed through it into no-man's-land, which on this occasion was living up to its name – deserted and eerie.

We stopped at the barrier just in sight of the Army checkpoint on the far side. The soldiers there beckoned to us to approach. We walked forward with papers in hand. Once we got there, they were cordial, but said that we would have to wait, as their officer was sleeping and there was an order from "higher authority" that no one was to pass until the next day. A charming prospect to spend the night in the Landcruiser in no-man's-land from which the LTTE had launched an attack only the night before.

There was more discussion until an agreeable lieutenant whom I knew arrived and said that we could pass – but we had to leave with them the patient whom MSF had entrusted to us. We argued his need for treatment at Vavuniya hospital but the lieutenant was suspicious, saying: "These innocent-looking people are sometimes guilty." Eventually, we went off to see the major on duty. He turned out to be quite approachable, a volunteer, who in normal life worked in the People's Bank. He agreed that we could take the patient to the base hospital. That task completed, we all had cold drinks and decided to push on to Colombo that night.

Stopping on the way back for a meal at the Kurunegala rest house, we tried to hold a "post mortem". Clearly, the chopper had not been aiming at us, even if it had felt like that at the time. We had just got in the way, as the pilot moved in on his target. But we had also made a bad mistake in turning back to the Army-held village after the first rounds of firing from the chopper – by so doing, we had unknowingly given the LTTE the opportunity to use us for cover as they moved up towards the Army position. This the pilot would have seen from his vantage point on high – and it accounted for the second round of machine-gunning from the chopper and the eventual bombing from the Sia-Marchetti, which was trying to stop the LTTE advance.

Had it all been set up before we left the village? Probably not entirely so. There had been significant glances between the major and the two lieutenants when we were told that after all we could carry on to Colombo. Indeed the major's cheery encouragement to us to drive faster might possibly now be seen in a rather different light. Then there was the chopper that had appeared above us at the same time. We certainly hadn't been pushed into a trap: there was the evidence of the sleeping soldiers as we had exited the village. But perhaps the major had thought that it wouldn't do us any harm to be used to flush out the LTTE whom he knew to be around, so that the Air Force could then shoot them up.

We pressed on, very tired, but happy to be alive, reaching Colombo shortly before midnight. By this time, I had decided not to lodge a complaint with the JOC in the morning. In proceeding against their advice, we had taken a calculated risk and had managed to get through unscathed. The rest was not much more than one had to be prepared for when trying to play an active protection role in a civil war.

I never saw the desk officer diplomat again, but heard that when debriefing with the diplomatic corps before leaving Colombo, he had been strongly supportive of the role we were playing, commenting that he "didn't know the United Nations did that sort of work". He was right. Previously, it hadn't.

Mannar

Mannar is a remote district in the north west of Sri Lanka comprising a large expanse of dense jungle on the mainland, where the above incident took place. It is joined by a three kilometre causeway to a long, banana-shaped island of the same name with a coastline of extensive lagoons and white sandflats, from which a chain of barely submerged rocks and sandbanks reaches out into the Palk Strait and nearly meets the Indian subcontinental landmass.

Despite its economic impoverishment, Mannar is richly endowed with colourful legends of prehistory and stories of both ancient and modern history. Thus, the submerged sandbanks between India and Sri Lanka figure in both Hindu and Muslim traditions: according to the Hindu epic *Ramayana*, they were built as a bridge by the great and just king Rama in order to lead an army into Lanka to rescue his wife Sita after her abduction by Ravana, the demon king of the island, while the name "Adam's Bridge", by which it is now generally known, reflects the Muslim belief that the first man passed over it after his expulsion from paradise. Moreover, traditions and archeological remains suggest that the Indo-Aryans from the north and the Dravidians from the south of India – respectively the forebears of the present day Sinhalese and indigenous Tamils – both passed through the Gulf of Mannar before landing in Lanka.

From early historical times, it was inhabited by Tamil Hindus. During the period of their commercial predominance in the region in the eighth century, however, Arab traders established a settlement on the island, gave it its present name and laid the foundations for the prosperous Tamil-speaking Muslim communities which continued there until October 1990, when they were expelled by the LTTE. In the sixteenth century, with the missionary activity generated by St Francis Xavier on the south-west coast of India, Roman Catholicism arrived on the island and a large Catholic community was established, with fine churches in the fishing villages of the littoral. And later when the Portuguese set up a base there, they used it to control the much-coveted pearl fishery at Aripu, exploit the external trade in cinnamon and gems on the Lankan mainland and interfere in the internal affairs of its kingdoms.[1] Early in the subsequent Dutch colonial period, the persecution of Catholics led to the establishment of a Marian shrine at Madhu, deep in the mainland jungle, which in time came to be respected by all religions.

Mannar has long been a place of passage for travellers moving between Sri Lanka and the subcontinent, whether as pilgrims, traders, immigrant labourers or, most recently, as refugees. Its significance in the present story is indeed primarily as the principal route for persons seeking refuge in South India from the fighting and insecurity of the *Eelam Wars* in the north east of Sri Lanka. (The fishing villages on the northern coast of Mannar island provide the shortest, safest and cheapest crossing of the Palk Strait.) And when the refugees returned home, either of their own accord or under officially organized arrangements, they mostly passed through Mannar.

It was in these surroundings of unsurpassed natural serenity that the grimly dramatic events and troubled endeavours in this story of international protection during a critical period of the Sri Lankan civil war were acted out.

An innovative protection role

Protection had not turned out the way I had envisaged when I first arrived as UNHCR representative in mid 1988 to head the agency's monitoring and reintegration programme for Tamil refugees who were repatriating from South India under the "Indo-Sri Lanka Agreement to Promote Peace and Normalcy" (the 1987 Peace Accord). Although already highly problematic by that time, this early Sri Lankan peace initiative seemed to offer the refugee agency the opportunity to make a constructive contribution in promoting and monitoring voluntary repatriation with an extensive house-building programme and by making small inputs into the infra-structure of the communities into which the returning refugees were reintegrating (with projects for vocational training, fisheries, minor roads and the like).

Since then, however, the course of the conflict had developed dramatically – and for the civilians caught up in it, disastrously. First, the IPKF, which had been deployed in the north east to guar-antee and enforce the Peace Accord settlement, had been with-drawn, causing the immediate collapse of the regional administration it had supported. The second peace initiative under President Premadasa that followed had ushered in a hope-ful period during which there had been a ceasefire between Government forces and the LTTE together with high-level talks between the parties that focused on ways to bring the Tigers into the political mainstream; but this had aborted abruptly as a result of events in Batticaloa which, although in themselves intrinsically trivial, were nonetheless sufficient to spark the conflagration that spread like wildfire throughout the north east, and started *Eelam War II*. Thereafter, the war entered a period of hitherto unequalled intensity with the LTTE maintaining control of most of the north, including Jaffna city and the peninsula together with the extensive *Vanni* (jungle area), while in the east it dominated much of the countryside and carried on deadly guerrilla warfare in and around the towns.

Unsurprisingly, the renewed and intensified hostilities triggered massive displacement of Tamil civilians in the north east – includ-ing the group of refugee returnees whose reintegration into their home areas UNHCR had been monitoring during the previous two and a half years. Most of those in flight were now moving along the refugee route – the tracks through the *Vanni* down to the coast and across to the northern shore of Mannar island to the short and easy crossings of the Palk Strait to asylum in South India and beyond. In each of these three periods – under the IPKF dispensation during 1988–89, the contemplated aftermath of President Premadasa's peace initiative in mid 1990 and the early part of *Eelam War II* – the protection role of the refugee agency was (or in the case of the second scenario would have been if it had transpired) distinctly different. During the IPKF period – effectively a regional peace-making protectorate – UNHCR was monitoring Tamil refugees who had returned in conditions of insecurity and sporadic guerrilla warfare. As a protection role, this was essentially passive in that it relied primarily on the presence of international agency staff in some sensitive areas where they were in a position to witness – and to report on – abuses that affected the refugees whose reintegration they were monitoring. (At that stage, there was neither the legal basis nor practical leverage for it to have done anything more.)

In the briefly hopeful period between the start of the IPKF with-drawal from the north in December 1989 and the eruption of *Eelam War II* in June 1990, UNHCR was looking beyond the end of its rein-tegration programme to a quasi-permanent ceasefire-cum-peace settlement of sorts that, at least in the early days, would inevitably have been unstable. In such a situation, some Tamil refugees in the diaspora would wish to return home, while governments of the principal countries hosting large numbers of asylum seekers would also want to send them back. In those conditions, the UN High Commissioner for Refugees in Geneva would need to be advised authoritatively by the UNHCR representative in Sri Lanka as to whether it was safe for Tamil refugees and asylum seekers to return home; this function would need to be exercised in close coordina-tion with the non-governmental organizations principally involved in the welfare of Tamils in the host countries.

With the sudden eruption of *Eelam War II* in mid 1990, however, the refugee agency was again facing an entirely different scenario, in which there was an imperatively immediate need to protect the refugee returnees who were now either stranded in the midst of or fleeing from the civil warfare that had set the region ablaze. For UNHCR, the protection situation presented a range of complex problems.

One complication was the controversy over what, if indeed any, action the agency should appropriately take. The challenge in the north was most unusual, if not unique, in that Sri Lanka was not a country of asylum to which refugees had fled and where, according to the agency's traditional practice, it would have normally provided protection because of the international refugee status they had acquired by fleeing their own country. On the contrary, it was a country of refugee origin; the agency's legal responsibility for Tamil civilians caught up in the fighting was only in regard to the refugee returnees whose repatriation and reintegration it had been monitoring. These formed a comparatively small group in relation to the large majority of IDPs and endangered local residents in the conflict-affected areas; most of the uprooted people had no status in international law other than as nationals of and within their own country, Sri Lanka.

Moreover, the ground situation was that of a war zone in a fiercely fought conflict. Officials in the agency headquarters in Geneva who for various reasons were against its further involvement in Sri Lanka could thus claim that any programme in that zone would inevitably entail unacceptable levels of insecurity. It might endanger both the affected civilians, who might be dangerously deluded into relying on UNHCR's capacity to protect them, and the staff members involved. There was also no precedent in the agency's field practice, no previously proved mechanisms and methodology that could help shape the form of response. And finally, there were funding problems – at that time, there was an acute funding crisis and therefore some elements sounded the shrill alarm of financial stringency in order to excuse UNHCR from further responsibility for the Tamil refugee returnees now that hostilities had revived.[2]

But the small agency team in Sri Lanka felt differently. Naturally, in view of its close involvement with refugee returnees during the previous two and a half years, it was strongly motivated to do what it could for them now that they were caught in the maelstrom of disastrous events. It also knew the problem, the terrain and some of the key actors, and so was in a position to evaluate authoritatively what could and what could not be done on the ground. It therefore invoked the High Commissioner's legitimate concern for the returnees under the so-called "soft law" provisions of the relevant Conclusions of the UNHCR Executive Committee on International Protection, which it argued still obtained.[3] The team proposed the utilization of unspent funds from the reintegration programme, which by then was of course defunct, in order to launch a small protection-orientated relief operation for the remaining returnee caseload, together with other Tamil civilians among whom they were living in identical conditions of hardship and danger.

In the particular circumstances, many might perhaps consider this modest proposal as no more than equitably applied common sense. But initially, despite due approval by the High Commissioner, Thorvald Stoltenberg, for reasons indicated below (Chapter 10) it attracted controversy and encountered significant bureaucratic opposition in certain quarters in Geneva. Moreover, in early November 1990 Stoltenberg unexpectedly resigned and the programme's legitimacy under the UNHCR mandate was immediately challenged by opposed elements within the agency. But although the operation was subjected to unprecedented bureaucratic restrictions, it nonetheless proved itself on the ground, was supported by the Government, appreciated by the Tamils, accepted by both combatant forces and attracted a wide range of support in the diplomatic community. When eventually the new High Commissioner, Sadako Ogata, had fully taken charge of the agency, she found in its favour. Moreover, Washington – the only Government to maintain reservations throughout the critical first year – eventually moderated its negative attitude to the programme.

In consequence, the refugee agency stayed in Sri Lanka and developed an innovative protection role for the benefit of persons internally displaced and at risk in the war zone, in addition to refugees who had repatriated voluntarily. Since the start of the present peace process in January 2002, apart from its traditional function of assisting and monitoring refugees who repatriate voluntarily, it has facilitated the relocation and return to their homes of over 400,000 IDPs, while some 325,000 persons remain displaced.[4]

* * *

The complex background is outlined briefly in the following introductory chapters:

- Chapter 3, "Roots of militancy, seeds of terrorism" presents the situation not as the product of a supposedly ancient tradition of cultural animosity between Tamils and Sinhalese, but as the result of the still unresolved problems of political transition from a prosperous and relatively harmonious multicultural colony to a parliamentary democracy with a large Sinhalese majority, but without adequate constitutional safeguards for the important Tamil minority. The terrorist dimension is illustrated as a reaction to the long succession of anti-Tamil rioting and the increasing frustration and humiliation of able and determined Tamil youth.

• Chapter 4, "Ironies of a peacemaking protectorate" analyses the failure of the Indian peacemaking intervention under the 1987 Peace Accord in relation to the contradictory objectives of Indian policy, but concludes that the level of military abuse of the civilian population would have been significantly higher but for the Indian Army's tradition of professionalism in international peacekeeping. It also considers the role of the IPKF as peacekeepers and explains UNHCR's developing function in monitoring repatriation.

• Chapter 5, "UNRWA and UNHCR protective practice" briefly outlines the entirely separate evolution of UN protection practice pursuant to the respective mandates of the two refugee agencies, UNRWA (Relief and Works Agency for Palestine Refugees in the Near East) and UNHCR – the former pragmatic and "hands-on", and the latter based more on the strict obligations of international legal instruments. In such respects, the irony of UNHCR's experience in Sri Lanka was that in the absence of prior appropriate precedent for action – but not of obligation – the universal refugee agency found itself developing a role of protective neutral engagement which, unrealised by those involved at the time, resembled more in style that of its sister agency for Palestine refugees than its traditional practice.

3. Roots of militancy, seeds of terrorism

Jaffna Tamils – transitional conundrums pre-independence – colonial culpability? – unheeded storm signals post-independence – Radicalization of Tamil politics – seeds of terrorism – militant groups – caste and conflict – July 1983 – Eelam wars and peace initiatives

Jaffna Tamils

By tradition the Jaffna Tamils are a very conservative people with a strictly caste-structured society and a formidable reputation for distinguished achievement in the learned professions and civil service in their own and other countries. In the early twentieth century, their reputation in fields of professional endeavour had already spread outside Sri Lanka to other south Asian and south-east Asian countries, and with the diaspora in the latter half of the century, it was to spread to the industrial countries of the West.

How is it then that over the last 20 years a people so conventional, prudent, almost sedentary in their preferred field of activities, has taken to the rigours of militant guerrilla warfare and given birth to the world's most deadly liberation movement, with a readiness to use terrorist tactics when it sees fit? One part of the answer lies in the complex roots of the Sri Lankan civil war, another in the mettle of the people themselves, and yet another in the way in which the seeds of terrorism are sown. And all together, they make this relentlessly internecine conflict a cautionary tale of our time – particularly for a century whose initially high hopes for peace and progress turned sour so soon.

The roots of conflict lie in a long series of developments: the deterioration in Sinhalese–Tamil intercommunal relations in the latter years of British colonial rule; the constitutional and political impotence of the Tamils in the early years of independence; the blockage of traditional Tamil avenues for professional and educational advancement; their cultural humiliation and increasing personal insecurity culminating in the nationally cataclysmic events of 1983; the progression from militant political action to separatist warfare which occasionally morphed into acts of terrorism; even in the dynamics of the caste system during the conflict. All these suggest answers to the "why and how the Jaffna Tamils?" question and help bring into focus the complex interaction of the Sri Lankan conflict's constituent elements. And in so doing, they also help explain certain common aspects of past, present and no doubt future terrorist-tainted civil wars elsewhere in the world.

There are some positive aspects to this story: how eventually enlightened elements on both sides made a start – however slow, impeded and fragile it is proving to be – on the long and arduous road to peace; and at the micro level, how an international protection role in a war zone can help to reduce the suffering of civilians, strengthen the counsels of enlightenment on both sides, and indeed have some very small yet significant impact on the broader international plane. It is from the latter frontline and grass roots standpoint that this book is written.

* * *

The civil war between LTTE and the Sinhalese-dominated forces of the central Government in the north east of the island has often been presented as a quasi-determinist effect of ancient animosity that dates from the time when the Indo-Aryan ancestors of the Sinhalese landed from north India and the Dravidian forebears of the Tamils crossed over from South India. This view also considers the conflict to have been sustained by deep religious and cultural differences over more than two millennia of Lankan history, from the early Sinhalese and Tamil kingdoms to the latter centuries of Western colonialism, of which British rule was only the third and last period. There has been much coverage to that effect in the international media, often embroidered with some of the more richly colourful stories in the *Mahavamsa* – the most important of the Sinhalese chronicles that recount the early history of the island. One such was the duel in the second century BC between Elara, the Tamil king of Anuradhapura and Dutthagamani, the Sinhalese contender, in which both were mounted on elephants, resulting in the death of the former.

However, several Sri Lankan historians from both communities – most notably the Sinhalese academic C.R. de Silva and the Tamil administrator and scholar Devanesan Nesiah – have cast doubt on the *Mahavamsa*'s presentation of the Elara–Dutthagamani contest as essentially one between Sinhalese and Tamils.[1] In that regard Professor de Silva points inter alia to the evidence that on the one hand Elara had considerable support among the Sinhalese, and on the other that Buddhism in the north was not suffering under his rule. More recently, Dr Nesiah has argued persuasively that the vexed Sinhalese–Tamil controversy over who arrived first on the island and therefore has the better claim to be the "founding race" is in fact a "non-issue". He points out that neither the classics of Tamil literature of two millennia nor their folk tradition reflect a fundamental hostility between the two communities, between whom there was an almost uninterrupted friendly coexistence over the centuries. This leads him to the conclusion that the traditional intercommunal hostility reflected in the *Mahavamsa* was a political construct that was kept alive and used by the Sinhalese leadership for political purposes from time to time.[2] This view would seem to tally with C.R. de Silva's observation that the authors of this chronicle were writing several centuries after the event, at one of the few times when Sinhalese–Tamil tensions were high and thus they could well have reinterpreted such a historical event in the light of their own contemporaneous situation.[3]

Furthermore, Dr Nesiah emphasizes that the numerous wars throughout the millennia in which the rulers were respectively Sinhalese and Tamil were more often the product of local dynastic rivalry than ethnic animosity. Thus, owing to the absence of a royal caste (*kshatriya*) in the Sri Lankan tradition, many local kings chose to marry women of that caste from South India. In some such cases, the king was succeeded by a close relative of the queen, who would take on a Sinhalese Buddhist identity and establish a new dynasty with wide acceptance in the kingdom. Such was the case with the Nayakkars from Malabar, from whom Sri Wickrama Rajasinha, the last King of Kandy (who was deposed by the British in 1815), was descended.[4] And in the British colonial period of the early twentieth century, the significant social and political divisions related to caste and class rather than the largely ethnic-based issues of language and religion.[5]

For what they are worth, there are in addition the personal impressions of neutral outsiders such as I, whose humanitarian work gave us the opportunity to observe the two communities at close quarters, both in Colombo and in the war zone. On first arriving in the country, I was surprised to find that away from the conflict, Sinhalese and Tamils who were not immediately involved in it managed to maintain many of the formal courtesies and decencies of day-to-day contacts for which Sri Lankans are traditionally renowned. Whether or not such politeness was partially superficial and served to mask the depth of distrust and bitterness between the two communities, it spoke for the relatively low level of intercommunal hatred in comparison with similar conflicts elsewhere in the world. In Europe, for example, in both the Balkans and Northern Ireland there are still some on both sides who exploit opportunities to express centuries-old prejudices, and evidently obtain perverse satisfaction from communal confrontation.

Bradman Weerakoon, the shrewd advisor to President Premadasa who features prominently throughout this book, always insisted that apart from the conflict, the differences in outlook between the Sinhalese and the Tamils were in fact very slight. This was a point that I was able to confirm for myself when I was crossing and re-crossing no-man's-land in the early part of *Eelam War II* and forming positive impressions of the combatants as individuals on both sides of the line. It was not that they were better on one side than the other; quite the contrary: on the scale of human quality, many were much the same, and shared more of the common culture of their divided nation than they cared to admit. In its origins, the Sri Lankan civil war of the last 20 years is much more an unresolved problem of transition from a colonial regime to parliamentary democracy on the Westminster model than the relict of alleged ethnic animosity in antiquity.

The following overview briefly analyses the complex and problematic modern history of the conflict which provides the geopolitical background to this book.

Transitional conundrums pre-independence

Westernized elite and elected representative politics

The early years of the twentieth century saw the highwater mark of harmony and political solidarity between the Sinhalese and the Tamils of the Westernised elite, with their exclusive class outlook, yet also with sharp caste divisions within the respective communities. Thus, they united to press the colonial administration to introduce an elective element into the legislature. And when an "educated Ceylonese" constituency was established in 1911, it was won by a Tamil, Ponnambalam Ramanathan, against his principal Sinhalese opponent, Marcus Fernando, largely because votes from the latter's own community were split by rivalry between the high-caste *goigama* and the lower-caste *karawa* to which he belonged.

However, this timidly modest move by the colonial administration towards elected representative politics was soon to disrupt much of the traditional harmony, as the Sinhalese majority increasingly came to recognize the strength of their numbers, while the Tamil minority grew apprehensive for the future. Progressive measures of enfranchisement in the legislature ratcheted up rivalry and suspicion between the two communities. When the Ceylon National Congress was formed in 1919, it was largely an attempted compromise to preserve the existing ratio of Sinhalese and Tamil communal representation in the perspective of constitutional progress – but one that did not succeed. As early as 1926 the Governor, Sir Hugh Clifford, was reporting to the Colonial Office in London that the differences between the Sinhalese and the Tamils were being accentuated, with the latter suspecting the former of plans to dominate the political scene by sheer weight of numbers, while the Sinhalese resented the Tamils' reluctance to accept their position as a minority in a Ceylonese nation.

Donoughmore Constitution

When in the following year the Donoughmore commission was appointed to review the constitution, its most pressing problem was how to reduce intercommunal dissension and distrust over constitutional, and particularly electoral, development. On communal representation, the Tamil leadership was divided, with the idealistically all-island Jaffna Youth Congress strongly opposed to it and in favour of universal suffrage, while some of the old guard Tamil nationalists took the opposite position.

In the event, however, the constitutional commissioners categorically rejected communal representation as "a canker on the body politic, eating deeper and deeper into the vital energies of the people" and standing in the way of the necessary realization by the diverse population of their common kinship and obligations.[6] They therefore proposed radical changes in central government institutions and in the composition of the electorate, including a State Council with executive as well as legislative competence operating on committee-system lines, as in the League of Nations and London County Council of those days. Officially, the State Council was regarded as a halfway house on the road to fully responsible cabinet government on the Westminster model – but one that was widely condemned and deeply unpopular, particularly with the Tamils.

The Second World War and the Soulbury Constitution

During the Second World War, Ceylon was promised full responsible government under the Crown with the exception of defence and external relations. D.S. Senanayake, the (Sinhalese) Leader of the State Council, had a draft prepared with the technical assistance of Ivor Jennings, which incorporated his ideas of cabinet government on the Westminster model, together with some safeguards for minorities.[7]

In response, London sent out another constitutional commission to review the proposals, headed by Lord Soulbury.

Again, there were deep misgivings among the minorities, especially the Tamils. As the All-Ceylon Tamil Congress put it in its representation to the commissioners: "the near approach of the complete transference of power and authority from neutral hands to the people in this country is causing in the minds of the Tamil people, in common with other minorities, much misgiving and fear."[8]

The Congress's leader, G.G. Ponnambalam, had long been campaigning for the so-called "50–50" formula for balanced representation in the legislature, whereby no one community could on its own dominate the others. But the Soulbury commissioners rejected that plan on the ground that it would be reintroducing communal representation by the back door. They did, however, recognize the need for minority safeguards, and so recommended an enhanced package designed to facilitate the election of minority candidates, together with a clause (Section 29(2)) to protect minorities from legislative discrimination.

Colonial culpability?

To what extent can the 150 years of British rule in the island be held accountable for the woes of modern Sri Lanka? This is not so much a question for liberally minded Brits with an uneasy conscience over their imperial past as a measure of the significance of past imperialism, of whatever national provenance, as a cause of widespread ethnic conflict throughout the world of today. Any attempt at a balanced answer is of course inevitably both complex and controversial. But with surprising irony, the case against the British derives less from their record in achieving their ends as harsh imperialists, even in the early period of ruthless expansion, than from their role as constitutionalists during the last 40 years of colonialism, when they were painstakingly doing their best to find an equitable formula for transition from a multicultural colony in which one race had a large majority to parliamentary democracy on the Westminster model.

Of course, unreconstructed anti-imperialists can never accept that there was any case for taking Ceylon. Initially, British objectives in seizing the Dutch maritime colonies had been essentially strategic – to gain possession of the unrivalled anchorage of Trincomalee, or at least to keep it out of the hands of their principal rivals in maritime imperialism, the French.[9] They were the third such colonial power in line, ousting the Dutch, who had themselves previously driven out the Portuguese. If the fortunes of war had been otherwise and the French had succeeded in establishing themselves on the island, the eventual regime would have been very different – but not necessarily better for the inhabitants of the island during the last century and a half of colonial rule that was to follow.[10] That the annexation of the historic kingdom of Kandy was accompanied with much intrigue, rapacity and misrule in the early years is undeniable. But such behaviour was far from exceptional during that period and was by no means confined to the British.

Some might trace the roots of British responsibility for the current conflict back to the Colebrooke–Cameron reforms of 1833, as a result of which the maritime provinces were joined together with the kingdom of Kandy in one unified administration for the entire island. But the benefits of establishing centralized administrative control were to be seen in the peace and prosperity enjoyed in the later nineteenth century. And if the two parts of the island had been kept apart, precisely the opposite charge of divide-and-rule would surely have been made.

Some Sinhalese have attributed a significant part of their problem with the Tamils to the perception that the minority community was unduly favoured by the British as regards education and government jobs in reward for their loyalty. Certainly, Sri Lankan Tamils and Christians were better placed. But might not this have been more a result of the historical accident that Christian missionaries – American as well as British – had established excellent schools in Jaffna earlier than elsewhere in the island? It was this that gave the Tamils a head start in developing their capacity to educate

[31]

and professionalize themselves, which indeed remains one of the key elements in the modern diaspora.

Moreover, as regards the historic process of decolonization, whereby dependent territories of the former empire were transformed into independent nation states, one of the many charges levelled against the British was that they usually started preparing for independence too late – and then left too soon. In most colonies in Africa, democratic institutions did not have time to take root at the centre and decolonization of the civil service was delayed so long that the ominously named "crash programmes" of localization were all that was feasible. But this was far from being the case in Ceylon. Since early in the twentieth century, the colonial administration had followed a determined policy of recruiting and training national personnel for the Ceylon Civil Service, including the elite administrative grades. By 1937, expatriate entry had ceased and within two years the proportion of nationals had risen to 78 per cent.[11] Thus by independence in 1948, there was a competent professional civil service manned very largely by Ceylonese. And as regards political development, the big picture was of a colony that was a "model" – in its latter days, both peaceful and prosperous and with a well-educated population – progressing with political maturity along the road of responsible government to full independence within the Commonwealth. The Independence Constitution of 1948 could moreover be seen as the product of colonial evolution, having been preceded by seven previous constitutions that stretched back to the earliest days of Crown colony government in 1801. Indeed the first eight years of independence from 1948 to 1956 were, as Professor C.R. de Silva has put it, "by and large ... a period of continuity with the late colonial period in both policy and personnel".[12]

Less can be said for the British record as architects of the constitutions that were to take the country forward to independence. Although the 1931 Donoughmore constitution was intensely unpopular at the time, there were points in its favour, such as the executive committee system. This was administratively cumbersome but nonetheless provided valuable experience in governance for the political leadership of all communities and tended to encourage a spirit of compromise among them. Moreover, in the absence of well-organized political parties, the prominent role of backbenchers prevented any one group, communal or otherwise, from dominating the Council.[13] Much good work was also done to improve education and social services. However, the introduction of universal suffrage at one go under the Donoughmore constitution was a bold step that was only partially successful. It was intended to move political life on healthily from caste, communal and class allegiances towards a broader national identity, but it constitutionally entrenched the Sinhalese in a position of unassailable majority power by virtue of their superior numbers. And far from dissolving the island's pattern of communal politics as had been the intention, it stimulated and strengthened the divisions.

Did the British put the country on the wrong road by introducing universal suffrage at a time when party political life was still embryonic? At the time, the decision was taken with the very best of progressive intentions by the Labour government and its Fabian Colonial Secretary, Lord Passfield (a.k.a. Sydney Webb). But in Britain itself, which had benefited from a gradual widening of the franchise as a result of increasing popular pressure over most of the previous century, the introduction of universal suffrage had only been taken two years previously. In Ceylon, however, the last election had involved no more than 4 per cent of the population, and universal suffrage had hardly featured as an issue in the evidence given to the Commission.

It is easier to criticize than to see what else could have been done short of continuing with communal representation in some form, which the commissioners feared would have impeded progress towards responsible government. Were there no alternative models? The introduction of a federal constitution or a virtual partition of the island would have been regarded as unacceptably radical – and significantly neither was proposed. The stark reality was that there was no politically feasible solution that could have fixed the inter-communal fault line in 1931. For the British, who were committed to developing the country towards responsible government, the horns of the dilemma were indeed sharp.

Thirteen years later, as the time for the final transfer of power was fast approaching at the end of the Second World War, the Soulbury commissioners were wrestling with the same problem. By then there was even less room to manoeuvre. They went through some soul-searching as to whether British parliamentary democracy was an appropriate framework within which the deep divisions of a new unitary state could be peacefully resolved. But noting that this was what most politically active Ceylonese wanted, they recommended a constitution in line with British practice, which on the whole worked well. Yes ... it did – in their day. But today, how ironically much broader is the range of constitutional thinking in the United Kingdom, with devolution in place and working in Scotland and Wales, the possibility of federation not excluded as an eventual solution, and the incorporation of the provisions of the European Human Rights Convention into UK law by the Human Rights Act.

In three key respects, things did not work out in the way the Soulbury commissioners had envisaged. First, events were to prove that the prohibition of communally discriminatory legislation provided by section 29(2) of the constitution largely failed to achieve its purposes, since discrimination in everyday life occurred mostly through public administration rather than overt laws. Second, the constitution they recommended had envisaged that there would be a substantial period of self-government, prior to full Dominion status. But that was not to be; after the end of the Second World War, the tide of history in South Asia was running out fast and taking the British with it. India and Pakistan became independent in August 1947, and once early independence had been promised for Burma, Ceylon successfully pressed its objectively much stronger case.

Consequently, the period of self-government was drastically foreshortened and the country became independent on 4 February 1948. But the Tamils had been counting on such an interim period as a time when the much needed political compromises and adjustments could be made between the two communities. Even the Sri Lankan Tamil academic A. Jeyaratnam Wilson, a stern critic of the Soulbury commissioners' thinking, was of the opinion that an extended period of self-government might have provided substantial, although not total, protection within a constitutional framework headed by an impartial governor.[14] Third, although the Sinhalese have always proudly upheld their tradition as sportsmen on the playing field, their political leadership did not heed the commissioners' headmasterly exhortation to play the game straight and fair in the political arena after independence.[15] The British were proud of their excellent relationship with the political elite in Ceylon and its impact on the process of nation-building ("More Ceylons and fewer Burmas" appropriately became the Colonial Office watchword for decolonization throughout the remainder of the empire).[16] But as a result, the country was deprived of the compulsive pressure of a mass movement for independence, which in the struggle to get the British out might have helped forge a more robust national identity. Sri Lanka was not alone in having been a model colony which found itself facing the consequences of unresolved internal conflicts following independence.[17] But among the many political complexities that have contributed to the obduracy of its conflict, this is the most cruelly ironic.

Unheeded storm signals post-independence

Deprivation of Indian Tamils 1948–49

Signals of the coming storm began to appear shortly after independence and recurred with increasing urgency until it finally broke with the events of July 1983. In 1948/1949, the United National Party (UNP) administration passed legislation which effectively deprived nearly a million Tamil plantation workers of Indian origin of their citizenship and voting rights. Apart from its manifestly discriminatory nature, this measure upset the balance provided by minority weighting in the legislature that had been a key element in the compromise on which the Independence constitution had been accepted. Thereafter, it was much easier for a major Sinhalese party to ignore the wishes of the Tamil minority, yet obtain a majority in parliament.[18]

Tamil Federal Party

Shortly afterwards, the Tamil Federal Party was formed under the leadership of S.J.V. Chelvanayakam with the objectives of achieving a federal union of the two Tamil-speaking provinces, the termination of state-aided "colonization" by Sinhalese in the north east, the unity of all Tamil-speaking peoples in Ceylon and for both Sinhala and Tamil to be recognized as state languages.

Sinhalese populist pressures

Meanwhile, within the Sinhalese community, populist pressures on language and religion had been gaining strength, particularly among the discontented but influential constituency of those educated in Sinhala who felt themselves to be seriously disadvantaged by the use of English for official business and so opposed the agreement to grant Tamil equality with Sinhala as an official language. In this way, the "Sinhala only" movement had developed and, under the influence of the *Sangha* (Buddhist clergy), had become linked to the issue of state support for Buddhism. The political opportunities attracted the ambitious and frustrated S.W.R.D. Bandaranaike, who in 1951 broke away from the ruling UNP and founded the Sri Lanka Freedom Party (SLFP), which encompassed greater sympathy for Sinhalese cultural sensitivities while paying less attention to Tamil interests. Religious pressures continued, particularly with the celebrations in 1956 of the *Buddha Jayanti*, the 2500th anniversary of Buddha's attainment of nirvana. When "The Betrayal of Buddhism", a report prepared by the unofficial Buddhist Committee of Inquiry, appeared in February 1956, it bitterly lampooned the elite and governing UNP, calling them "Engalanka people" and saying that they neither knew Sinhala nor cared about Buddhism.

S.W.R.D. Bandaranaike and the "Sinhala only" Act of 1956

The effect on the Kotelawala UNP administration was devastating. Shortly afterwards, the SLFP formed an anti-UNP coalition which S.W.R.D. Bandaranaike led to a sweeping victory at the polls, whereupon he immediately introduced proposals for an Official Language [the so-called "Sinhala only"] Act, which declared that Sinhala was "the one official language" and made no reference to Tamil. In reaction, the Federal Party organized marches throughout the north east to converge on Trincomalee where it held a convention which adopted resolutions requesting parity of status for Tamil and Sinhala, the cessation of state aid for Sinhalese colonization in traditional Tamil homelands, regional autonomy for the Tamil-speaking provinces and the restoration of citizenship and franchise rights to the hill country Tamils.

Bandaranaike–Chelvanyakam Pact 1957

The Bandaranaike–Chelvanyakam ("BC") pact of 1957 reflected an effort on both sides to reduce intercommunal tension and to that end partially met Tamil concerns on language, colonization, autonomy and the status of the Indian Tamils in the hill country. But a deadly dynamic was already intensifying the conflict between the two communities, as on the one hand the Tamils were frustrated at the slowness of implementing the pact, and on the other there was mounting opposition to it among the Sinhalese. Now in opposition, the UNP exploited the situation, claiming that the BC pact was undermining the unity of the country and the status of Sinhala as its only official language. Its leader, J.R. Jayewardene, the future President, led a Buddhist march to Kandy, which inflamed the situation.

The most serious increase in communal tension came when the Ministry of Transport sent nationalized buses to Tamil areas with "Sri" in Sinhalese lettering on their number plates and the Federal Party responded by launching "anti-Sri" campaigns to tar over and replace the lettering with Tamil script. Bandaranaike soon ceded to strong pressure from a group of Buddhist monks who, together with a minister in his cabinet, Mrs Vimala Wijewardene, congregated on the lawn of his residence and refused to move until they had obtained abrogation of the pact in writing. Tension ratcheted up as the Federal Party resolved to launch a non-violent campaign of direct action, while Sinhalese extremists organized anti-Tamil rioting, on a much larger scale than in 1956, in which over a thousand people were killed and many more made homeless. From this critical moment, the Tamils realized that they could no longer rely on the state to protect them.

Assassination of S.W.R.D. Bandaranaike

In September 1959, there was a further dramatic deterioration in the situation, when S.W.R.D. Bandaranaike was assassinated by an extremist Buddhist monk. Previously, he had made a further attempt at reconciliation by putting on the statute book the Tamil Language Act, which provided for Tamil to be used for administrative purposes in the north east. In so doing, he had plotted a possible route out of the minefield of confrontational language politics into which he had led the country. Whether he would in fact have been sufficiently steadfast to have taken it if he had not been brutally removed from the scene can only be conjectured, as when his widow, Sirimavo Bandaranaike, led the SLFP to victory at the polls in July 1960, she not only ignored this Act, but pressed on with implementing the "Sinhala only" Act to the full. In response, the Federal Party launched yet another campaign of non-violent action in 1961, which included the organization of a parallel postal service, the persuasion of Tamils to conduct their business and correspondence with the mostly Sinhalese Government officials in Tamil and the massing of crowds to block entrances to Government offices in Trincomalee and Jaffna. These crowds were dispersed by the security forces with brutal force, resulting in many injuries.

Republican Constitution of 1972

After the second administration of Sirimavo Bandaranaike swept to power in 1970, Sinhalese–Tamil relations deteriorated still further. One of the new Government's first steps was to turn the lower house of parliament into a constituent assembly in order to adopt a new constitution that was strongly orientated in favour of Buddhism and the Sinhala language. The legislature became supreme, the courts lost their power to review legislation and even the puny safeguard of section 29(2) in the Independence Constitution was dropped.

Radicalization of Tamil politics

Tamil views of the state and their relation to it changed radically during the years 1970–74. Initially, the Federal Party had been at pains to emphasize that its objectives did not go beyond the achievement of a federal constitution within a single state. But the impact of the 1972 constitution was powerfully conducive to the closing of ranks among moderate Tamil groupings. In a meeting in Trincomalee in May 1972, the Tamil United Front (TUF) was formed to embrace the Federal Party, the All-Ceylon Tamil Congress and, although it was later to withdraw, the hill country Tamil Ceylon Workers' Congress of S. Thondaman. The TUF made six demands: for the parity of Tamil with Sinhala, guarantees of full citizenship for all Tamil-speaking peoples who had made Sri Lanka their home, a secular state with equal protection for all religions, guarantees of fundamental rights, provision for the abolition of caste and untouchability, and the acceptance of a decentralized structure of government as the basis for a participatory democracy.

When Chelvanayakam resigned his seat in parliament in protest at the imposition of the new constitution, he defined the choice for his people in the following historic words:

> In view of the events that have taken place, the Tamil people of Ceylon should have the right to determine their future,

whether they are to be a subject race in Ceylon or they are to be a free people.[19]

From its foundation in 1949 until the mid 1970s, the Federal Party under Chelvanayakam's leadership had tried to defend the Tamils against the ravages of resurgent Sinhalese nationalism with a combination of parliamentary tactics, whenever that was possible, and by non-violent protests and civil disobedience whenever it was not. Admirable though this policy was by universal liberal standards, it had manifestly failed to meet the needs of the Tamil community, particularly its youth. Separatist sentiment continued to harden, and in 1975 the Tamil United Front changed its name to the Tamil United Liberation Front (TULF). At its first national convention the following year, it adopted the Vaddukoddai Resolution, which accused the Prime Minister, Sirimavo Bandaranaike, of having ignored its last attempt to win recognition of the Tamil nation without jeopardizing the unity of the country. The resolution called on Tamils in general, and in particular their youth: " to come forward and throw themselves fully in the sacred fight for freedom and not to flinch until the goal of a sovereign state of Tamil Eelam is reached."[20] Chelvanayakam died in March 1977, still hoping that the separatist struggle for Eelam would be non-violent. But militant Tamil youth had already made the first irrevocable moves towards violent struggle against the Sinhalese-dominated state.

Seeds of terrorism

In a community so obsessed with its political impotence and insecurity, cultural humiliation and youthful frustration as the Sri Lankan Tamils, it was not difficult to discern the ways in which the seeds of terrorism were first sown with militancy, and germinated thereafter as the situation intensified. First, the communal balance in the legislature was upset by the effective disenfranchisement of Tamils of Indian origin shortly after independence (see above, p. 35); the adoption of the republican constitution in 1972 reduced minority safeguards and more firmly entrenched Sinhalese ascendancy (see above, p. 38) and when the debate on the "Sinhala only" bill began and the Tamil Federal Party staged a non-violent demonstration on Galle Face green opposite the parliament building, it was attacked by hoodlums, while the police stood by.[21] In the mob attacks on Tamils which followed in Colombo and in certain settlements elsewhere, more than 150 people, mostly Tamils, died in the first of a series of increasingly deadly inter-communal riots which followed those of 1958 and 1961, and were to recur in 1974, 1977, 1979 and 1981, and culminate in the nationally cataclysmic events of 1983.

Such dire political developments were reflected in the cultural field with the formal adoption of Sinhalese following the 1956 Act as the language of administration, even in Tamil areas, and establishment of the primacy of Buddhism under the 1972 constitution. These were compounded by acts of immense insensitivity by the police and security services. The police charged the crowd in Jaffna with batons and tear gas on the last night of the fourth International Conference on Tamil Research in 1974, resulting in a stampede in which there were many casualties. In May 1981, the Jaffna library, with its 97,000 books and unique manuscripts, was burned by the security services.[22] The impact of these pressures was felt most acutely by impressionable and able Tamil youth, who from 1956 found their preferred avenue of professional advancement blocked by language requirements, and their access to higher education reduced by communally discriminatory "standardisation" procedures and a district quota for university admissions introduced in 1972.

Among many others, the cases of Prabhakaran, the LTTE leader, and Kittu (Sathasivam Krishnakumar), one of its most distinguished commanders, illustrate how impressionable and able Tamil youths reacted to such a range of pressures on their community. In normal conditions, Prabhakaran would in all probability have followed the sober traditions of his family and the customary Tamil middle-class career pattern of studying for exams and entering the civil service or professions, rather than taking to the rigours of freedom fighting tainted with terrorism. Even if he had had an inclination towards a more adventurous life, one can perhaps surmise that in more normal conditions he would have been likely to content himself with the more enterprising activities of some of his fellow *Velupillai* caste members and neighbours in Velvettiturai, the fishing town on the northern coast of the Jaffna peninsula (generally known as "VVT"), as fishermen, seafarers and smugglers, who took advantage of the winding coastline of the Vaddamarachchi, its proximity to India and opening onto the sea lanes of the Bay of Bengal and beyond (see below, p. 44).

But conditions were not normal: there are accounts of Prabhakaran listening attentively to his father's discussions with friends and visitors at their house in VVT on the deteriorating conditions of Tamils in the south and being particularly affected by reports of atrocities committed in the succession of anti-Tamil riots. One such incident was of a Hindu brahmin in a southern town in the 1958 riots, who was caught by a mob, tied to a bed, doused with petrol and burnt alive.[23] Kittu had similarly formative experience when he witnessed the reception of injured and maimed Tamil children from Colombo after the 1977 riots.[24] The impression of such ethnic and cultural outrages helped germinate the seeds of militancy among Tamil youth and prepared the ground for their resort to acts of terrorism, of which indeed they were the mirror image.

Although there was little in the fields of professional endeavour to which Jaffna Tamils traditionally aspired that indicated an aptitude for the rigours and danger of guerrilla warfare, martial abilities emerged as part of the commitment to what their frustrated and humiliated youth passionately believed to be their just cause, and it developed with the increasing number of incidents in which they engaged the security forces in the north east. Thereafter, capacities for meticulous application, conscientious administration and planning, for which Jaffna Tamils were well known and had stood their forebears in good stead in more normal fields of activity, adapted well to their new role, as was to be seen in the able organization of combat units and smart operational tactics. Early on in the conflict, an Inspector General of Police ruefully admitted: "members of this [Tigers'] movement are not common criminals. They are educated, sophisticated youth, a factor which makes them all the more dangerous."[25]

Militant groups

Although by no means the earliest act of extreme political violence perpetrated by young Tamils, the killing of Alfred Durayappah, mayor of Jaffna, outside a temple on 27 July 1975 was nonetheless a landmark in that it was carried out by a small commando of the Tamil New Tigers (TNT) under Prabhakaran's leadership. The TNT had developed from the Tamil Students Movement which had acted as a nursery for future militant leaders. Shortly after this assassination, the TNT turned itself into the LTTE, which was destined to assert its ascendancy in the movement as the most powerfully motivated, disciplined and deadly of the militant groups. Thereafter, the young Prabhakaran's flair in leadership, tactical command and the selective use of terrorist action was portentous.

The extent to which militant groups were to proliferate in subsequent years was phenomenal. Rohan Gunaratna, the international authority on terrorism, lists a total of 37, each with its own colourful nom de guerre and acronym such as the Red Front of Tamil Eelamists (RFTE) and the Guerrilla Army of Tamil Eelam (GATE).[26] But Jeyaratnam Wilson observed that the multiplicity of these formations was not always altogether to the advantage of the Tamil cause, noting particularly the deplorable effect of their disunity in July 1983. He also had reservations about the role played by many of them in that although they were resistance groups fighting repression, they had "no properly formulated idea of national regeneration … essentially a nuisance to the Sinhalese state, but beyond this could not be counted as political forces."[27] In any event, by 1986, only the following five of the 37 groups were of operational and political significance:

Group	Leader
Liberation Tigers of Tamil Eelam (LTTE)	Velupillai Prabhakaran
People's Liberation Organization of Tamil Eelam (PLOTE)	Uma Maheswaran
Tamil Eelam Liberation Organization (TELO)	Sri Sabaratnam
Eelam People's Revolutionary Liberation Front (EPRLF)	K.S. Padmanabha
Eelam Revolutionary Organization of Students (EROS)	Velupillai Balakumar

In their embryonic stage, there was a certain fluidity in the composition of the various groups and on occasions some cooperation between them. Thus, Prabhakaran and Sri Sabaratnam – respectively the eventual leaders of the LTTE and TELO – both originally attended meetings of the same informal coterie in Point Pedro and, in early days, Prabhakaran was also associated with both the Tamil Students Movement and the Tamil Youth Front (the military wing of the TULF) and used to meet Amirthalingam and other TULF leaders on the quiet. Uma Maheswaran, the eventual founder and leader of PLOTE, having been at one and the same time chairman of the former youth movement and Colombo secretary of the latter. Another example of such relative cooperation in the early days was when EROS, the first group to send its cadres for guerrilla training with the Palestine Liberation Organization (PLO) in the Lebanon, decided to open up this facility to the LTTE.

But the early cooperation was soon to replaced by increasingly bitter and deadly rivalry. Thus, in 1979 Uma Maheswaran was in effect expelled from the LTTE by Prabhakaran and thereafter formed PLOTE. In 1980, Prabhakaran and his close supporters temporarily threw in their lot with TELO. In 1981, Padmanabha broke away from EROS and later launched the EPRLF. Then in January 1982, the LTTE attacked PLOTE in Jaffna and in May, there was a shoot-out between Uma Maheswaran and Prab-hakaran in Madras – both survived. In April 1986, the LTTE attacked and severely weakened TELO. In July 1989, Uma Maheswaran was gunned down in a Colombo street by an alleged renegade member. And so the infighting went on, with the LTTE steadily strengthening its position not only by its ruthlessness, discipline and tactical smartness and, but also by the greater clarity of its political vision.

Caste and conflict

Despite its strongly conservative influence in Jaffna society, the caste system in some ways indirectly favoured the emergence of militant groups. One was that as an essentially non-caste move-ment, youth militancy attracted young Tamils of both sexes who wished to escape the rigidities of caste disciplines – a factor which in particular helped recruitment by the LTTE, which despite its core leadership coming from the *karaiyars* (coastal peoples), had always had the widest mix of castes and religions in any group.[28] At least initially, each of the more significant groups had its own caste orientation: one example was PLOTE, which although originally claiming to be Marxist-Leninist in outlook and advocating a socialist revolution of workers and peasants, drew its members mostly from the highest-caste *vellalars* (farmers). Another was the LTTE; whose mostly *karaiyar* leaders were next down the hierarchy of dominance and, unlike the *vellalars*, who were dominant in Government service and the learned professions, were more enterprising in commerce and as seafarers. Traditionally, they were fishermen and pearl fishers who diversified into maritime trade with south-eastern India and Burma, particularly in transporting rice, tobacco and shells. The *karaiyars* were well represented in the Vaddamarachchi region and particularly VVT. Moreover, the *kadalodiekal*, their elite trading seafarers, engaged in large-scale contraband, making this small fishing port the "virtual smuggling capital of Ceylon".[29]

Unsurprisingly, the *karaiyars* have the reputation of being tough and enterprising, and have been described as standing somewhat apart from the Jaffna caste system, "not aspiring to compete with the *vellalars*, but not accepting their claim to domination either".[30] Nor indeed in the circumstances is it surprising that many LTTE leaders came either from the *karaiyar* caste and/or from VVT and the Vaddamarachchi (most notably, Velupillai Prabhakaran and several other leading LTTE members from VVT come from the *kadalodiekal* elite).

The extent to which the caste system may have been undermined by youth militancy in the conflict is as yet unclear, and indeed beyond the scope of this book. But in regard to the LTTE claim that they have succeeded in dissolving caste ties and endogamy, although Jeyaratnam Wilson concluded that they have been "eroded fairly extensively", he prudently observed that such a claim could not be tested until more normal conditions of peace had returned.[31]

July 1983

On 23 July 1983, the LTTE ambushed a 15-man Army patrol, codenamed "Four Four Bravo", close to Jaffna university, killing 13 soldiers. Although there had been attacks against the security services in previous years, this was their biggest loss and it is generally regarded as having started the civil war in the north east.

There had been increasingly deadly intercommunal riots over the years, but the scale of anti-Tamil violence which this incident triggered in Colombo and the south and east was without precedent. The official death count was some 400. But an impeccable source – Neelan Tiruchelvam – quoted an estimate of between 2000 and 3000 deaths. Within Colombo, almost 100,000 Tamils were displaced from their homes and an estimated 175,000 fled abroad as refugees.[32]

"Pogrom" is a highly emotive word – defined as "an organized massacre of a particular ethnic group".[33] There has been a long-standing and widely held belief that the LTTE ambush was the pretext for rather than the cause of what followed. There was evidence that some of the violence was organized and systematic, and what the Government said at the time – and indeed what it did not say – tended to bear out the view that there was a measure of complicity, probably at a very high level. On 23 July 2004, 21 years after the event, following the findings and recommendations of the Presidential Truth Commission, President Chandrika Kumaratunga made an unqualified national apology on behalf of the state to the victims of the July 1983 riots, some of whom received compensation.

At the time, however, its impact was cataclysmic. First, militancy was strengthened at the expense of constitutional and non-violent action – a development that was unwittingly assisted by the Government when it passed the Sixth Amendment to the constitution, requiring MPs to take an oath of allegiance to the unitary state. As a result, the TULF leadership refused to comply and decamped to Madras, leaving the Tamil constitutional constituency unrepresented in parliament. Second, young Tamils were now flocking to join the militant groups, which were soon to benefit from military training in India on a massive scale. Third, large numbers of well-educated and articulate refugees fled abroad and formed influential lobbies supporting the militant struggle, particularly through the LTTE. Fourth, the events of July 1983 helped to forge the complex ambivalence of the Tamils towards the LTTE, with many deploring the cruelty of its methods, particularly its acts of terrorism, yet implicitly accepting the need for a formidable movement to protect them. Fifth, the ensuing commencement of open warfare accelerated the decline in traditional moral values – especially the disregard for human life – which had started in the early days of militancy and which, in the current spree of fratricidal assassinations, is increasingly menacing the prospects for peace.

Eelam wars and peace initiatives

During the two decades years since the events of July 1983, there has been a series of *"Eelam wars"* in the north east, punctuated with a number of abortive peace initiatives:

- *Eelam War I* (July 1983 to July 1987)

- 1987 Peace Accord and Indian Peace Keeping Force (IPKF) deployment in the north east (August 1987 to March 1990)

- President Premadasa's initiative (May 1989 to June 1990)

- *Eelam War II* (June 1990 to November 1994)

- President Kumaratunga's initiative (November 1994 to April 1995)

- *Eelam War III* (April 1995 to December 2001)

- Prime Minister Ranil Wickremesinge's initiative of December 2001 and the ceasefire agreement of February 2002 during which some historic steps were taken on the road to an eventual peace settlement – although the talks were suspended by the LTTE's withdrawal on 21 April 2003 and implosive tendencies in both the north and the south have continued to undermine the basis of the peace process (see Chapter 15, pp. 221–2).

4. Ironies of a peacemaking protectorate

A flawed accord – IPKF as peacekeepers – UNHCR and repatriation monitoring

A flawed accord

> The IPKF is several things in Sri Lanka. It is an affirmation of our commitment to the unity and territorial integrity of a small country. It is an external projection of our influence to tell our neighbours that if, because of your compulsions or your aberrations, you pose a threat to us, we are capable of, or have a political will to project ourselves within your jurisdiction for the limited purpose of bringing you back.[1]

The unwritten rationale of the "Agreement to Establish Peace and Normalcy in Sri Lanka" (1987 Peace Accord), signed by the Indian and Sri Lankan governments on 29 July 1987, was that India would commit its might and muscle to underwrite conditions to bring a peaceful end to the conflict, while Sri Lanka would concede the substantial devolution package for the north east that it had so far withheld.

Thus, the peacekeeping provisions sought to bring about a complete cessation of hostilities within 48 hours of signature of the Accord. All arms held by militant groups were to be surrendered within 72 hours and thereafter the Sri Lankan Army and other security personnel were to be confined to barracks. If requested, India would provide military assistance to implement the provisions of the Accord and in an annex it was provided that an Indian peacekeeping force could be invited by the President of Sri Lanka "to guarantee and enforce the cessation of hostilities if so required" – the diplomatic formula for deployment of the Indian Peace Keeping Force (IPKF) throughout the north east that commenced on the day after signature of the Accord and terminated when its last contingents sailed from Trincomalee on 24 March 1990.

The northern and eastern provinces were to be joined administratively as an interim measure pending a referendum that would enable the people of the latter province, which included Muslims and Sinhalese as well as Tamils, to decide their future. There was to be an elected provincial council for the temporarily united province, with a chief minister and ministers controlling the provincial administration. Moreover, there was to be a general amnesty for prisoners held under the Prevention of Terrorism Act and for combatants, and special efforts to rehabilitate militant youth. Tamil was raised to equivalent status with Sinhala as an official language. Of particular importance for the present book – in that it brought UNHCR, the refugee agency, to Sri Lanka – was the provision that India would expedite the repatriation of Sri Lankan Tamil refugees. In an exchange of letters between the Indian Prime Minister and the Sri Lankan President, special provision was made to secure Indian strategic interests by precluding the military use of Trincomalee harbour and other Sri Lankan ports by any other country, and to restrict foreign broadcasting organizations with facilities in Sri Lanka.

Essentially, however, the Accord was an agreement between the two governments, deciding over the heads of the Sri Lankan Tamils, the shape of their political future.

* * *

Internationally the general reaction was to hail the Accord as an act of historically decisive statesmanship in resolving a complex problem that was causing widespread concern even outside the region. The Indian Prime Minister, Rajiv Gandhi, and the Sri Lankan President, J.R. Jayewardene, who had signed it in Colombo on 29 July 1987, were even nominated for the Nobel peace prize on the strength of it. But long before the last IPKF contingents had sailed back to India, the intervention that the Accord authorized had been severely criticized by certain authoritative Indian commentators, including A.P. Venkateswaran, a former Foreign Secretary.

The early international support was explicable in the context of concern at escalating tension between Delhi and Colombo over Jaffna since the beginning of the year. When the LTTE had declared that it was taking over responsibility for civil administration in the district, the Government in Colombo had imposed a food and fuel embargo. The Army began to move through the Vaddamarachchi region on the northern coast of the peninsula in order to cut the sea lanes that provided easy access for trained militants and *matériel* from Tamil Nadu. The campaign resumed at the end of May with the objective of dislodging the LTTE from Jaffna city, by which time the condition of the near 1 million civilian population in the peninsula was already giving cause for humanitarian concern, particularly in Tamil Nadu, where the state Government put pressure on Delhi to send relief supplies to Jaffna. After a tense four-hour stand-off, the Sri Lankan Navy turned back an Indian flotilla carrying humanitarian aid. The following day, a flight of Indian Air Force transport planes escorted by Mirage fighters violated Sri Lankan air space to drop relief supplies over Jaffna. Within a week, the advance along the northern coast was halted when the Sri Lankan Army was only twelve miles from Jaffna.

In such a context, the Accord looked to outsiders like the necessarily robust framework for resolving a major regional crisis with wide international ramifications. With the easy wisdom of hindsight however, such early international support seems relatively undiscerning – more an expression of relief than a considered evaluation of the merits of the plan in relation to the more sensitive points of the conflict.

Within Sri Lanka, however, the reaction could hardly have been more different. Among the majority Sinhalese, its signature immediately exacerbated the anti-Indian hostility which had flared up with the Indian Air Force's food drop on Jaffna. This affected Sinhalese at all levels of society: in the cabinet, there were powerful critics in Lalith Athulathmudali, the Minister of National Security and Ranasinghe Premadasa, the then Prime Minister and future President; Sirimavo Bandaranaike, leader of the main opposition party, the Sri Lanka Freedom Party, announced discussions with the *Sangha* (Buddhist clergy) to oppose the Accord; the Janatha Vimukti Peramuna (JVP) – the Sinhalese revolutionary nationalist party – put out posters and pamphlets calling for the assassination of President Jayewardene.

Meanwhile, on the streets of Colombo, there was widespread rioting on 27 July, and this continued to spread even after a curfew had been imposed. When Rajiv Gandhi landed in Colombo two days later for the official signing ceremonies, the situation was near to eruption. There was a noisy demonstration of some 10,000 Sinhalese at Katunayake airport, which included Buddhist monks. The Prime Minister absented himself from the official reception for his Indian counterpart. On 30 July, when the latter was reviewing the Sri Lankan Navy guard of honour, a naval rating hit him with his rifle butt. JVP extremist action continued thereafter in many parts of the south, with widespread destruction of Government property, in which buses in particular were targeted. And when the Accord was being discussed in the parliamentary complex on 18 August, there was a grenade attack from which the President escaped unhurt, but several ministers, including Lalith Athulathmudali, were seriously injured.

Within the Tamil minority, whose political future the Accord attempted to settle without significant consultation, unsurprisingly there was general resentment, albeit with variations in the scale of bitterness. The principal Tamil militant groups other than the LTTE – EPRLF, TELO, PLOTE and EROS – were no more than informed of the Accord shortly before it was due to be signed; they were brought or merely summoned to Delhi in order to comply by giving formal approval. However, a special effort was made to secure the LTTE's agreement, with strong carrot-and-stick pressure on its leader, Velupillai Prabhakaran. He had been sounded out in Jaffna by an Indian diplomat before he was flown by helicopter to Delhi. Quite what happened there is not altogether clear. Later, Prabhakaran was to claim that he was held virtually incommunicado. But although a substantial financial inducement was offered to secure his acquiescence, the LTTE leader continued to express serious reservations and eventually managed to communicate them to Rajiv Gandhi in person shortly before the latter left for Colombo for the formal signing ceremony.

* * *

In the very early days, some events went according to the plan envisaged in the Accord. Thus, the IPKF was deployed in the north east and was generally welcomed by the Tamils. The greater part of the Sri Lankan Army in the region was flown to the south, while the remaining units returned to barracks, where they were to remain until the IPKF withdrew two and a half years later. The procedural steps to establish the provisions of the Accord in Sri Lankan law were initiated with the Thirteenth Amendment to the Constitution and the Provincial Councils Bill. But tensions were already mounting on all sides: among the Tamils, between the LTTE and their rival militant groups EPRLF, ENDLF, PLOTE and TELO (although the smaller EROS group was usually disposed to support the LTTE);

and between the Tamils and the Government over the vexed question of further Sinhalese "colonization" within Tamil traditional homelands. Thus, there were several kidnappings and minor skirmishes between the LTTE and the groups opposed to it. These led to the treacherous massacre of 34 PLOTE leaders and cadres in Batticaloa on 13 September, and an engagement between the Tigers and the EPRLF on 24 September when the latter group suffered most of the 80 fatalities. The LTTE also killed some 200 Sinhalese settlers and chased away or destroyed the homes of 10,000 others in traditional Tamil areas.

By this time, the principal players on both sides of the Sri Lankan divide had already begun to act in ways which, if not in direct violation of the Accord, evidently indicated more of a wish to wreck it than make it work. Thus, by the time Prabhakaran returned to Jaffna on 4 August and addressed the welcoming crowd, he declared that the process "disarms us suddenly ... without working out a guarantee for our people's safety and protection". He went on to say in so many words that the Accord did not provide a permanent solution, that he was only going along with the handover of weapons to the IPKF because he wanted to avoid a clash with India, which he said he loved, and that he was determined to continue to fight for the ultimate achievement of Tamil Eelam. The following day, a start was made with the handover of arms when "Yogi" Yogaratnam, one of the LTTE leaders, made a symbolic transfer of some 600 (mostly obsolete) weapons to the IPKF. Thereafter, the transfer of arms continued, but in a desultory and unconvincing manner, which resulted in the IPKF extending the transfer deadline.

There was already much agitprop by the LTTE against the Accord, and tension ratcheted up with one disastrous event after another. On 15 September, Thileepan, the young political leader in Jaffna, started a hunger strike in support of several demands which the Accord had not met, including lack of progress in setting up the interim administrative authority. His death, eleven days later, electrified the political atmosphere in the north east.

Worse was to come on 3 October, when the Navy – which, unlike the Army had not been confined to barracks under the terms of the Accord – intercepted a boat carrying arms to Trincomalee, together with a group of armed LTTE cadres, including two regional leaders, Pulendran and Kumarappa, who were then detained in the Air Force base at Pallaly outside Jaffna. The incident immediately and dramatically intensified serious misunderstandings of the Accord among the different actors. The Government claimed that the group was in violation of the Accord in carrying arms after expiry of its limit for their surrender and that it wanted to question them in Colombo. The Minister for National Security, Lalith Athulathmudali – who had opposed the Accord – added that Pulendran was wanted in connection with a massacre of civilians, hinting that as it had not occurred within the north east, it might not be covered by the terms of the Accord. For their part, the LTTE maintained that their cadres were permitted to carry arms for their personal security and that the action of the Sri Lankan Navy had violated the Accord. Initially, the IPKF tried to block the transfer of the group to Colombo by surrounding the hangar at Pallaly air force base in Jaffna where they were being detained, but then withdrew the guard. D.N. Dixit, the Indian High Commissioner intervened in vain to try and prevent their transfer to Colombo.[2]

Then, on 5 October, just before they were to be emplaned, the group swallowed cyanide capsules, whereupon eight out of twelve died immediately. After having read the telex traffic at the height of the incident between Brigadier Jayaratne in Jaffna where the LTTE cadres were being held and his superiors in Colombo, Rohan Gunaratna concluded that in his heart of hearts the Sri Lankan officer had not wanted to airlift the LTTE to the capital because he understood the grim repercussions of such action in the north east, but had been compelled to take it by commanders who were ignorant of the highly charged situation there.[3] The following day, Prabhakaran repudiated the ceasefire and eight Sri Lankan Army soldiers who had been captured some months previously were executed, while violent communal attacks on Sinhalese civilians broke out in Trincomalee.

On 10 October 1987, the IPKF launched Operation Pawan with the objective of occupying Jaffna by force. It was intended as a swift strike – *pawan* is Urdu for wind – but the fierce opposition put up by the LTTE precluded any such rapid accomplishment and it was not until 26 October that the IPKF definitively gained the upper hand. According to the IPKF, its losses were 262 dead (including 15 officers, of whom two were colonels), and 927 wounded, and the LTTE was estimated to have lost between 700 and 800. For its part, the LTTE claimed that among the civilian population it had documented at least 900 deaths, 451 serious injuries and 141 cases of rape during the fighting. At the same time, it said that half of the population of the Jaffna peninsula had been made homeless. In such circumstances, the IPKF was an easy target for the LTTE's bitter lampoon of "Innocent People Killing Force". Within weeks of its arrival in Sri Lanka, the IPKF had found itself engaged as a belligerent party in an intensely bitter civil war. Even more tragically, in the course of the fighting, it had caused heavy civilian losses and extensive damage to property among the Tamil community – the very people whose protection provided the ostensible justification for its deployment in Sri Lanka.

It was the firm belief of Lieutenant General Depinder Singh, the overall IPKF commander, that the "hard option"– the decision to use force against the LTTE that resulted in Operation Pawan – might possibly have been avoided if India had played its "crucial card .... of moral and material sustenance the LTTE has drawn from Tamil Nadu".[4] If there was any such possibility of such influence being used to bring the LTTE to heel, it was undeniably unfortunate to have pushed ahead with Operation Pawan. Even so, the high level of agitprop which the LTTE was maintaining against the Peace Accord gave the impression that, come what may, they were not going to accept it, if only because it undermined their chosen role as sole protector of the Tamils. Thus, if there had not been a major clash as early as October 1987, sooner or later one would have been inevitable. Nonetheless, this fateful operation – a near disaster for any professional peacekeeping force – proved to be but the first of a number of profound ironies that were to arise from implementation of the Accord.

Quite apart from any operational failures, it is impossible to ignore the fundamental weaknesses in decisions and in the planning upon which the Accord was based. In what he describes as "critical introspection", Mr Dixit admits that there was a collective failure of the Indian establishment in relation to Sri Lankan policy. "In fact there were periods when the Indian defense establishment, the intelligence agencies and the Ministry of External Affairs were working at cross-purposes."[5] But there was also on the one hand, underestimation of the complex fibre of Sri Lankan politics in general and in particular of the strength and tenacity of the LTTE, and on the other an overestimation of Indian capacity to overcome them with "political will backed by military might".[6]

* * *

[53]

To what extent can the Peace Accord be said to have delivered peace? By the time Operation Pawan was launched, the disarmament provisions were a dead letter, superseded by events which had seen the IPKF take Jaffna from the LTTE, but with the latter withdrawing to its bases in the jungle. From there, they waged a guerrilla war of attrition on the IPKF's outposts, and in their engagements with it in the jungle, inflicted heavy losses.[7] Moreover, in the urban areas, particularly Jaffna, the Indian force was unable to prevent the killing of civilians caught in the internecine fratricidal struggle between the LTTE and the militias of the Tamil groups opposed to it, which continued to be supported and trained by the Indians (more by the intelligence agency, RAW,[8] than by the IPKF). The failure to curb the excesses of these groups contributed significantly to tainting the tone of the regional regime they were supporting and to turning many Tamils against it. Towards the end of the IPKF period, these militias formed the nucleus of the so-called "Tamil National Army" that was trained and heavily armed by the Indians with the objective of defending the regional Government after the IPKF withdrawal. But in the event, they were rapidly routed by the LTTE in Amparai and Batticaloa after the IPKF pulled out of those eastern districts, and most of their cadres left Sri Lanka before the final Indian withdrawal.

As regards devolution, the provisions for temporary unification of the northern and eastern provinces with a common council and chief minister was carried into law with the passing of the Thirteenth Amendment to the constitution and the Provincial Councils Act. Although boycotted by the LTTE and uncontested in the north, elections were held in the east, albeit under strict security conditions, including curfews. Unsurprisingly, they were won by the Indian-supported EPRLF, leading to the appointment of Varatharaja Perumal as chief minister. But the authority of the regional Government depended heavily on Indian support and its credibility began to crumble when President Premadasa pressed for withdrawal of the IPKF and even entered into direct talks with the LTTE with a view to finding ways to bring the Tigers into the political mainstream. As the Colombo correspondent of the *Hindu* put it at the time, "the real agenda of the talks appears to be to find ways of getting Indian forces out."[9]

This was the second major irony in implementing the Accord: that eventually the two Sri Lankan combatants were making common cause with one another in order to secure the departure of the Indian force that had been inducted into the north east to guarantee the ceasefire between them. Thereafter, the regional Government's authority diminished progressively the nearer the time came for the IPKF to depart, while increasing numbers of its cadres and their families left in boatloads to seek refuge in India.[10] One of the provisions of the Accord had been to accelerate the repatriation of Sri Lankan Tamil refugees who had fled to India after the events of July 1983. But in the event, there was a third irony, namely that the Accord itself triggered yet another wave of refugees to India.

IPKF as peacekeepers

> We came in Peace
> We came for Peace
> We sacrificed for Peace[11]

My experience of the IPKF started in July 1988, when I arrived as the first UNHCR representative in Colombo to head the programme for reintegration of Sri Lankan Tamil refugees returning from South India. This involved interacting with the IPKF on the ground in the north east to the extent that refugee programme interests required. Following their withdrawal, I was asked by several diplomats in Colombo what were my personal impressions of the IPKF as professional peacekeepers, politics apart. My qualifications to comment were unimpressive, as I had arrived after the (disastrous) events of the early months, had no professional experience of peacekeeping and could only claim to have had occasional and geographically limited experience of the IPKF. Thus, I did not mention Operation Pawan. Nor did I dwell on the Velvettiturai massacre, which had so justly outraged the international community (I had no direct knowledge of it and felt that most of my interlocutors were likely to be at least as well briefed as I on what the international media had called "India's My Lai").

My comments thus related not so much to peacekeeping functions in the generally accepted sense as to the degree to which the IPKF had succeeded professionally in maintaining order in the north east and discipline among its own troops, together with the various anti-LTTE Tamil militant groups, who were armed and provided with some basic training by Indian agencies. The illustrations I gave were from the limited area where I had the most direct experience: sparsely populated rural Mannar, where the ordinary individual usually had a better chance of avoiding the conflict than had the inhabitants of urban areas such as Jaffna and Trincomalee. In particular, I recalled a very tense situation in August 1989, around the main hospital in Mannar town. It had been a typical LTTE operation – an intricately planned and ruthlessly executed ambush, when a night patrol of the Bihar Regiment was returning to its camp near the hospital. Some LTTE cadres fired on it in a feint attack and then ran away in the direction of the hospital with the patrol in hot pursuit, fleeing into the main courtyard of the hospital where their comrades had taken up positions on the second floor gallery. The latter then opened up with machine guns and rocket-propelled grenades (RPGs) and lobbed grenades onto the soldiers who had been lured into the trap below. As a result, 25 Biharis were killed and several others wounded. Keeping the tight discipline that the situation demanded if the Biharis were to be prevented from going on the rampage in another potential Velvettiturai massacre was very difficult for the officers concerned (primarily, the brigadier in overall command and the colonel immediately in charge of the troops). Yet it was accomplished – to the immense relief of the surrounding civilian population.

Another specific situation in Mannar which showed the IPKF to be professionally humane in the midst of provocative conditions concerned the bombardment of villages on the edge of the jungle, known to be LTTE stongholds, from which attacks on IPKF outposts had been launched. The IPKF had responded with heavy artillery barrages, as a result of which the inhabitants had fled to what they considered to be the comparative safety of the neighbouring temples and churches. I then informed the IPKF that, together with the Government Agent (GA), UNHCR would be moving into the area to evaluate. Firstly, the GA assessed the emergency needs of those villagers who had evacuated to temporary places of refuge, which UNHCR arranged to visit together with MSF and the Save the Children Fund (SCF), the two principal non-governmental organizations on the ground. Second, we went on to the most heavily bombarded village, where we were all relieved to see that it had sustained remarkably little damage, as most of the shells had fallen in the immense natural reservoir nearby, known as the Giant's Tank. On the way back, I called on the brigadier to discuss the situation and remind him of UNHCR's legitimate concern for the safety of refugee returnees, some of whom were living in the area which the

IPKF was bombarding. He assured me that he was doing his utmost to avoid hitting civilian targets, and that it was indeed this consideration rather than poor marksmanship that was causing so many shells to explode harmlessly in the reservoir.

As a disciplined professional officer, the brigadier was a rather aloof figure and our relations had never been more than cordial – on some difficult occasions, rather less. Nonetheless, I rightly sang his praises. With a commander who had been less professionally able to maintain discipline, things would certainly have been a good deal worse for the people of Mannar. Perhaps if UNHCR had not been present on the ground and able to report to the outside world any possible repetition there of an incident like the Velvettiturai massacre that had taken place in the Jaffna peninsula only three weeks previously, the outcome might possibly have been different. But that should not detract from the fact that, at least in Mannar at that time, a high standard of discipline was maintained, even to the extent of curbing some of the excesses of the Indian-supported Tamil militias.

What was the impact of the IPKF after Operation Pawan? From one perspective, at least until they began to withdraw in October 1989, they managed to maintain a rough framework of order against the background of guerrilla warfare and occasional heavy engagements in the jungle. But from another, the situation was of an unceasing low-intensity conflict, albeit one that was more or less contained and confined to certain areas. Whatever the spin, however, the grim reality for Tamil civilians in the north east was the same. The IPKF were performing a function somewhere on a scale that has at one end a neutral force acting in accordance with professional international peacekeeping practice, and at the other an army of occupation deployed in support of a client regime. The most appropriate description is a "peacemaking protectorate".

* * *

Some years later, I had the experience of working within the broad framework of a United Nations Peace Keeping mission – "UNAMIR II" in Rwanda – which enabled me to appreciate better the nature of such operations and of the value of the Indian Army's contribution to them. From such a standpoint, the significance of the IPKF function in north east Sri Lanka seemed a good deal clearer. They were there as a professional peacekeeping force – legally, as the invitee of the President of Sri Lanka to guarantee the cessation of hostilities[12] – a task for which they were well qualified in view of the Indian Army's proud UN peacekeeping record. But they were also the principal arm of India in underwriting, guaranteeing and implementing its own geopolitical objectives.

Rather than their unprecedentedly high level of casualties, it was this tension between the professional and the political aspects of their function that explained the evident unease of some officers at what was in effect their "mission impossible" in a dirty war. The expression of dignified professional dismay on the Gurkha regimental memorial in the wilds of Mannar quoted above was poignant indeed. Nonetheless, even taking into account the atrocities that occurred from time to time, the IPKF deployment was far from being a debacle on the scale of the subsequent US-led UN peacekeeping operation in Somalia. And the negative impact on the civilian population in the north east of having an alien military force in their midst would probably have been much greater if it had come from an army that was less disciplined and proud of its professional tradition in peacekeeping.

UNHCR and repatriation monitoring

Large-scale voluntary repatriation of refugees to their own countries is usually either "spontaneous" – the trade term for when they make their own arrangements – or "organized", when the countries of both asylum and origin cooperate, and UNHCR endeavours to ensure that movement is authentically voluntary and provides material assistance to facilitate reintegration. In Sri Lanka, however – prior to the 1987 Accord – there had already been a hybrid version of voluntary repatriation: the so-called "permission boats", whereby usually fairly small boats were authorized to take on board Sri Lankan Tamil refugees who had sought refuge in South India and to transport them across the Palk Strait to Mannar island.

The Accord *inter alia* provided that the Government of India would expedite the repatriation of Sri Lankan Tamil refugees from Tamil Nadu. UNHCR and other UN agencies had also been enjoined by UNHCR Executive Committee Conclusion No. 40 (XXXVI) to have funds available to assist returnees in the various stages of their integration and rehabilitation in their countries of origin. Consequently, on 31 August 1987, the Government of Sri Lanka and the refugee agency signed a memorandum of understanding under which the High Commissioner made an initial application from his emergency fund and the Government agreed to the establishment of the agency's presence in Sri Lanka, including the outposting of international field staff for the purposes of monitoring a programme of material assistance in the principal areas to which the refugees would be returning. In the initial reception period, assistance included emergency relief packages for each family, transit accommodation and transport to their home areas, and thereafter provided allowances for settling-in and repairing or rebuilding housing; this corresponded to the Government's "unified assistance package" for internally displaced persons, who were also beginning to return home during the same period. Important inputs were also provided to improve the essential socio-economic support structure in the communities to which the refugees were returning. The first of the organized movements from South India took place in late December 1987.

In any large-scale repatriation operation, there are essentially two phases of protection monitoring for returning refugees: the first, which usually takes place in the country of asylum before the movement commences, consists of professional verification that the refugees know what they will be doing and genuinely want to do it; the second is carried out after return to the country of origin and comprises UNHCR field staff maintaining contact with the returnees during reintegration in order to see that they are treated as far as possible in accordance with international standards. In both respects, the monitoring of Sri Lankan Tamil repatriants during 1987–89 was significantly different from normal practice.

During the first phase of monitoring, prior to commencement of repatriation, even the strongest supporters of the Sri Lanka programme had to admit that the procedures adopted were unorthodox. This was primarily because the Indian authorities would not permit UNHCR international staff access to carry out the standard voluntary repatriation interviews on Indian soil. Two staff members – normally Indian nationals – were permitted to board the boat that ferried the returnees across the Palk Strait. But it was only after the refugees had landed at the ports of entry in Sri Lanka that international staff were able to commence substantive interviewing to establish the voluntary nature of their repatriation. In the large majority of cases, the decision was positive. In cases where refugees expressed misgivings about returning home, UNHCR staff examined the facts to see if the motivation was validly referable to international criteria for refugee status. There were in fact only two such cases and their return to India was duly arranged with the competent authorities.

Such arrangements were undeniably less than ideal.[13] But with the prospect of a refugee agency programme to facilitate reintegration in their home areas, and particularly the presence of agency staff outposted there for monitoring purposes as some assurance that international standards would be observed, most of the refugees probably did want to come back. Moreover, in the subsequent reintegration phase, conditions were conducive to a relatively effective UNHCR monitoring role. Within the framework of close coordination with the competent national authorities, such monitoring enabled field staff to maintain the requisite "direct and unhindered access to returnees" and so made the High Commissioner's legitimate concern for the consequences of their return a reality on the ground. The bases for such impact were, first, the outposting of international field staff and their involvement in project management with the local authorities, especially in the housing sector, and second, the working relations established with the civil administration in the *kachcheris* – the GA and senior staff who belonged to the Sri Lankan Administrative Service (SLAS).

The housing project jointly administered by UNHCR and the competent local authorities was ideal for establishing close contact with the returnees. Field staff were brought into daily contact with them while ensuring that the necessary materials to meet the housing targets were procured during what was for much of the time a chronically unstable situation. But although UNHCR monitoring was fairly effective in periods of relative normality, from the protection standpoint it was weak during more difficult times. The legal basis for intervention was slender, and was greatly complicated by the political reality of security on the ground, with the IPKF maintaining order overall in the north east insofar as that was possible in a situation where the militias of the Indian-supported regional Government and the LTTE were involved in a ferociously fratricidal struggle. Thus, conditions were often such that interventions could be made on no more than a *pro forma* basis, or indeed not at all.

Nonetheless, as one of the earliest programmes to be directed within UNHCR Executive Committee guidelines for voluntary repatriation – most notably Conclusion No. 40(XXXVI) – this first operation in Sri Lanka for returning refugees broke new ground in protection monitoring within a country of origin. It showed the cardinal importance both of project functions that brought outposted field staff into direct and frequent contact with their charges and of professional interaction with the local authorities. It also however demonstrated the weakness in a highly unstable situation of what was essentially a passive role.

* * *

The repatriation operation in Sri Lanka skates on a glassy pond and the pirouettes and arabesques that we go through bear no resemblance to those in any other UNHCR programme.[14]

It was in such colourful terms that a senior analyst described the difficulties of mounting this operation in early 1989. But with the abrupt outbreak of *Eelam War II* in June 1990, the ice broke and the hard-won achievements of the previous two and a half years sank without trace, as the houses built were destroyed or abandoned, most of the utility vehicles donated to the local authorities were commandeered by the LTTE and, in the final irony of the Accord, many more refugees fled the north east during the first three months of the renewed hostilities than had been repatriated during the previous three years.

5. UNRWA and UNHCR protective practice

UNRWA: RAO programme in first intifada; *UNHCR: statutory and extra-statutory competence – evolution of voluntary repatriation monitoring – international protection in special operations – Executive Committee Conclusions on International Protection*

This book argues the need for the United Nations to protect civilians within internal and mostly ethnically-driven armed conflicts, wherever feasible without military support or logistical or technical interface with even UN peacekeeping forces. The present chapter focuses on the relevant programmes of the two UN refugee agencies: UNRWA (the United Nations Relief and Works Agency for Palestinian Refugees in the Near East), which began its operations in 1950; and UNHCR (the Office of the United Nations High Commissioner for Refugees), which was established in 1951 with competence for refugees throughout the world as defined by UN instruments, with the exclusion of Palestinian refugees within its sister agency's area of operations (the Israeli-occupied territories of the West Bank and Gaza and Jordan, Lebanon and Syria)

Both these subsidiary organs of the United Nations General Assembly were created in response to diverse geopolitical situations. UNRWA was set up to meet the needs of the many thousands of Palestinian refugees who had fled into neighbouring Arab countries as a result of the birth of the state of Israel and the first Arab-Israeli war. UNHCR was the ultimate heir to the older tradition of international solidarity which had originated after the end of the First World War, when the interest of governments and international humanitarian concern combined to tackle the problem of refugees stranded outside their legal countries of origin as a result of the war, the collapse of empires and the convulsions that followed.

Over the first half century of their existence, the ways in which the protection responsibilities of these two agencies have been defined, developed and applied have often been very different.

UNRWA

At its inception in 1949, UNRWA was not formally endowed with an explicit protection mandate, largely owing to the complex political tensions of the time, but also in view of existing institutional arrangements within the UN system whereby the United Nations Conciliation Commission for Palestine (UNCCP) was considered to have inherited protection-related functions. These included the use of its good offices with the local and community authorities to arrange for the operation of common services necessary for the safety and well-being of the population of Palestine.

In reality, however, there were gaps in United Nations protection for Palestinian refugees. as although the UNHCR mandate was interpreted as applying prima facie to those who were residing *outside* UNRWA's area of operations, those *within* it were excluded. Moreover, as the UNCCP in effect failed to provide for their protection to any practically significant effect, UNRWA began to address the problem itself with informal "hands-on" pragmatism. Thus, although described as "assistance", many of the services that it provided in fact helped to support the basic rights of Palestinian refugees, notably by way of registration and its health, education and relief programmes. And on occasions, it was able to extend a significant degree of protection through emergency crisis operations.

Nonetheless, Palestinian refugees were still in a particularly vulnerable position in their day-to-day lives. They complained of a very wide range of human rights violations through rough methods of riot control, prolonged curfews, administrative detention, harsh interrogation techniques, land confiscation for Israeli settlements, deportations and other violations of individual rights, including the prevention of family reunions, the closure of schools, the demolition and/or sealing of houses of individuals suspected by the security services, and shortcomings and disadvantages in recourse to the judicial system.

Following the Israeli incursions into Lebanon at the end of 1982, the UN General Assembly considered the needs of Palestinian refugees for protection and the means by which they might be satisfied, calling on the Secretary General in consultation with UNRWA to undertake effective measures to guarantee the safety, security and legal and human rights of Palestinians in the occupied territories. In response, UNRWA monitored the situation of Palestinian refugees in south Lebanon before the Israeli withdrawal and voiced its concerns in public statements. The Secretary General also followed up the General Assembly recommendation that UNRWA should issue identification cards to all refugees, regardless of whether or not they were in receipt of agency services, together with those who had been prevented from returning to their homes as a result of the 1967 hostilities – and in both cases to their descendants.

However, the first *intifada*, which started at the end of 1987, posed a more direct challenge to UNRWA's responsibility to protect. This was the first time that Palestinian refugees were actively and openly defying the Israeli occupying forces – and in doing so, they were getting hurt. In effect, this was a two-way challenge to the agency's mandate: at one and the same time to interpret it as requiring a more active protection role, yet also one which was appropriately flexible in the pragmatism with which it addressed specific new problems. As Georgio Giacomelli, its Commissioner General at the time, put it: "I believe that UNRWA's mandate is flexible, not explicit. We provide the refugees with the help they need, when they need it."[1] An example of such flexible pragmatism was how the agency turned its public health clinics into casualty reception centres for the treatment of Palestinians who had suffered beatings, been hit by rubber bullets, shot with live ammunition or exposed to various types of gas. An illustration of the more active protection role now adopted was the Commissioner General's initiative in temporarily assigning additional international staff members from posts elsewhere for protection duties in the West Bank and Gaza on the outbreak of the *intifada*.

Meanwhile, the Security Council passed resolution 605 in which it requested the Secretary General to examine the situation and report on ways and means of ensuring the safety and protection of Palestinian refugees under Israeli occupation. His report was based on the findings of the mission of Marrack Goulding, the Under Secretary for Special Operations, and in consultation with the Commissioner General.[2] In it, he incisively analysed the relevance of four different concepts of protection, of which the most immediately relevant in the Palestinian context was what he discreetly described as:

> protection in a less well-defined form ... "general assistance", in which an outside agency intervened with the authorities of the occupying Power to help individuals or groups resist violations to their rights (e.g. land confiscations) and to cope

with the day-to-day difficulties of life under occupation, such as security restrictions, curfews, harassment, bureaucratic difficulties and so on.

It was in relation to this category of protection as "general assistance" that the Secretary General envisaged an additional role for the Palestinian refugee agency and accordingly requested the Commissioner General of UNRWA to look into the recruitment of additional international staff for deployment in the occupied territories.

Although this was largely an endorsement and strengthening of the initiative which the head of UNRWA had already taken, it resulted in the creation of 21 new posts with the discreet designation of "Refugee Affairs Officers" (RAOs) for deployment on active protection duty in the occupied territories (nine for Gaza and twelve for the West Bank).

Various accounts describe the RAOs' duties as being to maintain an international presence in the refugee camps and villages, to tour intensively in their assigned areas of responsibility, showing the UN flag and keeping a look out for incidents and, to the extent that it was feasible, defusing such incidents and, to the extent that it was not, duly reporting them for follow-up and helping to evacuate the wounded, together with facilitating continuation of the agency's more normal assistance functions. One RAO said that he couldn't be too precise about what they did, commenting significantly that "Each situation in a confrontation has its own character. Each area is different. Each Israeli soldier is unique. We devise our plans as we go along."[3] In other words, the RAOs faced the unpredictable element in conflict the world over, to which flexible humanitarian pragmatism as practised by UNRWA is the logical response.

Most accounts emphasise the deterrent effect of the RAO presence, particularly in confrontations. As one authoritative source put it:

> it is not to say that the beatings have stopped, or that people have not been intoxicated by gas or that there have been no miscarriages of justice. But there has been quite clear evidence that where a Refugee Affairs Officer has been present it has had an inhibiting effect on the behaviour of those with power to harm.[4]

Given the nature of conflict itself, the success of civilian fieldworker engagement was relative. It was a palliative, not a cure – but one which in the particular ground situation of the first Palestinian *intifada* significantly reduced many of the worst excesses of open conflict. Among the many elements that made such a positive impact possible, the humanitarian neutrality of the RAOs engagement was the most critical. Particular attention was paid to establishing the professional objectivity and impartiality of their role, which Commissioner General Giorgio Giacomelli underlined when he said: "If we are to do our work, we must remain on speaking terms with everyone concerned with the refugees, including both Israel and the PLO."[5]

Accordingly, RAOs were enjoined not to be emotional, to avoid superior or didactic attitudes and in particular not to be partisan in their presentation.[6] And it was in this way that credibility in their working relations was built up with both sides.

The pragmatic flexibility which had been an important part of UNRWA's operational practice from the beginning also helped in dealing with the day-to-day volatility of events on the ground. Of particular importance was the acceptance by some few enlightened elements in the Israeli authorities that despite their many and difficult problems with the RAOs, the existence of such an active international humanitarian programme was broadly in their interest.

Such morals and lessons were of particular importance in the future when UNRWA's sister refugee agency, UNHCR, had to face the challenge of interpreting its own mandate to protect refugee returnees and other civilians who had been sucked into the vortex of civil wars elsewhere. One was Sri Lanka in mid 1990, at the outset of *Eelam War II*. But this was a challenge which was soon to be magnified operationally in the context of the historically cataclysmic events of the early 1990s, such as the aftermath of the Gulf War in Iraq in 1991, the break-up of the Yugoslav Federation later in the same year and the dissolution of the Soviet Union at the end of it.

For the United Nations, UNRWA's response to the protection challenge of the first *intifada* was a notable achievement in two important respects: first, as a constructively innovative initiative and, second, as a distinguished demonstration of what could be achieved by small but strongly committed teams of civilian professionals playing an active protection role in the midst of a conflict, especially when they had full support in the bureaucratic hierarchy and political backing in the Security Council that enabled them to get on with the job.[7]

UNHCR

UNHCR, however, had never taken overmuch professional interest in the field practice of its sister agency for Palestinians. UNRWA's experience with its active deployment of RAOs was a collection of lessons in protection practice that institutionally was largely, if not entirely ignored. When *Eelam War II* broke out in north east Sri Lanka in June 1990, the refugee agency was both morally and legally obliged to do what it could to protect the Tamil refugee returnees whose repatriation and reintegration it had been monitoring over the previous two and a half years, and UNHCR Colombo at least was searching for operational models with which to respond appropriately to this unusual if not unprecedented challenge. Yet UNRWA's RAO programme, from which there was so much to learn, was unfortunately never considered – simply because it was unknown. It was thus a significant irony that in the event the small UNHCR programme of protection-orientated relief that was devised pragmatically and implemented in the war zone of northern Sri Lanka in 1990 nonetheless resembled in certain respects the model developed by the agency for the Palestinians during the first *intifada*.

Of course the two ground situations were very different – in the occupied territories, there was a civil insurrection involving mostly young Palestinians taking on the Israeli Defense Force, while in the war zone of northern Sri Lanka, Tamil civilians were in flight and or danger from the fierce fighting between the Sri Lankan Army and the LTTE. But the way in which the two agencies went about trying to protect civilians in the conflict areas had a certain similarity, most notably in (a) deploying small teams of international staff who addressed pragmatically the immediate humanitarian needs of the affected civilian populations, and (b) their humanitarian neutrality, entirely without any form of military support or back-up, even of a technical or logistical nature.

* * *

Why was UNHCR, which had so often responded with skilful resourcefulness to the many changing challenges of forced displacement during its first 40 years, initially so reluctant to face the challenge of protecting in Sri Lanka in the midst of a conflict a group of refugee returnees whose repatriation and reintegration it had been monitoring over the previous two and a half years? In so far as the causes were authentically internal rather than externally prompted, the answer lies in the legally, geopolitically and bureaucratically complex – if not convoluted ways – in which the agency's competence had developed since it opened for business in 1951. This contrasted with the straightforwardly pragmatic way in which UNRWA had developed its protective mandate.

The following paragraphs endeavour to present in bare outline the intricacies of the evolving UNHCR mandate over that period.

Separate evolution of statutory and extra-statutory competence

By the end of the 1940s, solutions for the bulk of the caseload of the millions of persons displaced by the Second World War had been found – mostly through repatriation or resettlement by the United Nations Relief and Rehabilitation Administration (UNRRA) or its successor the International Refugee Organization (IRO). It was at this stage that the General Assembly resolved to establish the UNHCR to deal with the relatively small residual caseload in western Europe. In 1951, the agency was set up as a temporary programme for a period of three years with statutory competence for refugees who had fled their country of origin or remained outside it because of a well-founded fear of persecution.

But in the following years the problems of international displacement were not that simple, as here and there and from time to time there were groups of persons displaced outside their own countries who did not satisfy the well-founded fear of persecution definition in the UNHCR statute. Consequently, the agency's competence began to evolve in two main streams, one substantively under its own statute and the other authorized outside it.[8] As regards the former, the scope of the refugee definition became more widely applicable as a result of progressive instrumental and institutional developments. Thus, the original dateline in and most of the optional geographical limitations made by certain states to the 1951 Convention relating to the Status of Refugees were removed respectively by the 1967 Protocol and due notification of the extension of its obligations by the contracting state, largely as a result of the representations made by the agency to the governments concerned.

Regional instruments such as the Organization of African Unity Refugee Convention of 1969 broadened the refugee definition in

Africa, and the Cartagena Declaration of 1984 further expanded it in Central America.[9]

The later extra-statutory stream of competence, developed either by resolution of the General Assembly or the Economic and Social Council or at the request of the Secretary General, gave various new responsibilities to UNHCR. On a number of occasions, the agency was authorized, on an ad hoc situation-by-situation basis, to use its good offices and expertise to undertake special humanitarian tasks on behalf of persons whom the international community deemed it important to help, even though they did not satisfy the "well-founded fear of persecution" definition.

The often massive operational scale, the functional scope and the wide geopolitical range of the special operations were indicative of the effective humanitarian relief role that UNHCR was playing in relation to many of the world's most sensitive trouble spots, where its work came to be widely seen as part of their solution.[10] In Africa, the agency assisted groups who became refugees as a result of both decolonization and post-colonial instability – groups from Algeria in Morocco and Tunisia prior to the French withdrawal, from the Portuguese territories of Angola, Mozambique and Guinea before they gained independence, and from the civil war in the southern Sudan, together with the Rwandan Tutsis during the massacres before and after independence and Zaireans in flight from warring and instability in their key central African country. Then, when the liberation struggles had been won, and some of the civil wars ended, the agency played a leading role in organizing the repatriation of refugee groups, particularly to ensure that the terms of the amnesties under which they were returning were observed.

In Asia, there were Chinese refugees in Hong Kong, the mass influx of East Pakistanis into India during the war which led to the birth of Bangladesh, their subsequent repatriation and the UNHCR-led airlift between Bangladesh and Pakistan to relocate groups of refugees stranded on the subcontinent. Wars in South-east Asia produced large numbers of internally displaced persons within Cambodia, Laos and Viet Nam, and the agency had programmes of assistance for many of them, while those who fled into neighbouring countries were protected and mostly resettled by UNHCR in third countries. And in the Near East, UNHCR also had special programmes to assist internally displaced persons following the Turkish invasion of Cyprus in 1974.

Evolution of monitoring in voluntary repatriation operations

By the 1970s, the hitherto mostly separate development of the statutory mandate on the one hand, and of responsibility for special humanitarian tasks – which also sometimes included persons displaced within their own countries – on the other, were already beginning to intermingle. This occurred largely as a result of the mass voluntary repatriation operations that followed the end of internal conflicts in several African countries, when UNHCR tried to ensure that the terms of the amnesties were duly observed by the authorities when the refugees returned home. In this regard the nomination by the Secretary General of High Commissioner Sadruddin Aga Khan as coordinator of UN immediate relief assistance in the Southern Sudan in 1972 was a notable landmark.[11] It meant that, within the same special operational framework,[12] the High Commissioner was both carrying out his responsibility under the UNHCR statute to provide international protection by assisting governmental and private efforts to promote voluntary repatriation, and at the same time extending the benefit of rehabilitation and some socio-economic assistance to persons who had been displaced internally during the 17 years of conflict.[13] Another notable special operation in Africa which further developed UNHCR's monitoring role was the mass repatriation of Zairean refugees from neighbouring countries – especially Angola – following the presidential amnesty of 1978. There, the agency was accorded a supervisory function to ensure that the provisions of the amnesty were duly observed. A UNHCR sub-office was opened in Lubumbashi which was closely involved with the repatriation of the 155,000 Zairean refugees who returned from Angola. And concern for protection, which on occasions included interventions with the local military and civil authorities, necessitated the reinforcement of the sub-office with additional international field staff.

International protection in special operations

To what, if any, extent did UNHCR provide international protection for IDPs within the framework of its special operations? Formally, as late as 1981, the received institutional wisdom was that international protection was to be defined under the statute strictly in relation to refugees who were outside their own countries on account of a well-founded fear of persecution and therefore unable to avail themselves of the diplomatic or consular protection which governments normally provide their nationals. By virtue of the statutory cessation clause, protection was deemed to stop at the frontiers of the country of origin when the refugees returned home and thereby re-availed themselves of national protection. Within that perspective, any action that the agency might take for the benefit not only of IDPs but also of returnees was considered as something other than protection.[14]

However, such a restrictive view was increasingly under challenge from the reality of conditions on the ground in large-scale repatriation operations and the evolution of UNHCR's monitoring practice in response to them. As the formal view differentiated international protection from protective action appropriately taken on the ground by an international agency, it seemed near-paradoxical, particularly to fieldworkers. And in the event, as indicated below, it had to yield to the broader perception of the mandate reflected in the deliberations of the UNHCR Executive Committee.

Informally, on the other hand, where there were UNHCR staff outposted on the ground monitoring the repatriation of refugees pursuant to its statute, there was on occasion and in varying degrees a protection "rub-off" effect that benefited IDPs, even if they did not have the same strict entitlement as the repatriants. This however was essentially the by-product of a voluntary repatriation monitoring role, which in itself was relatively passive, consisting primarily of the presence of international humanitarian staff in key locations rather than active interventions and the operation of protective and protection-supportive mechanisms.

As regards material assistance programmes alone without the presence of monitoring staff, their beneficial impact in the midst of the volatile and unstable conditions that usually follow the end of conflicts is not to be underestimated. But rather than protection, such programmes were more appropriately considered as preparatory confidence-building measures, intended to promote conditions conducive to voluntary repatriation, as in the special operation in Laos.

UNHCR Executive Committee Conclusions

By the end of the 1970s, the UNHCR Executive Committee was already taking an interest in the agency's repatriation monitoring role, which was to produce two formal Conclusions on International Protection on voluntary repatriation, No. 18(XXXXI) in 1980 and No. 40(XXXVI) in 1985. Taken together, these reflected a broader view of the High Commissioner's evolving role in relation to the statutory responsibility to promote voluntary repatriation. Conclusion No.18 emphasized in particular the voluntary character of repatriation and diplomatically confirmed the High Commissioner's monitoring role in relation to guarantees given by the governments of the countries of origin. Five years later, the Executive Committee went a good deal further in encouraging the High Commissioner to take initiatives to promote voluntary repatriation and in endorsing his/her mandatory position in relation to such action.[15] This referred in particular to (a) legitimate concern over the consequences of returns he/she had assisted and (b) access, which the Committee considered should be direct and unhindered, in order to be able to monitor fulfilment by the authorities of the amnesties they had proclaimed. Conclusion No. 40 also drew attention to the importance of assistance for the reintegration of returnees as a factor in promoting repatriation, and stressed that from the outset of a refugee situation the High Commissioner should keep the possibility of voluntary repatriation under active review.[16] In effect, Conclusions nos 18 and 40 together codified in some detail the statutory responsibility which the Executive Committee authoritatively declared to be inherent in the High Commissioner's mandate.

What was the impact of these two instruments both as regards the refugee returnees – and indirectly some IDPs – and the High Commissioner's representatives on the ground? Some tended to downplay their significance as "soft law", the provisions of which were of normative but not binding effect on governments. However, first, in declaring that the High Commissioner's empowerment as regards the monitoring of repatriation was inherent in his/her mandate, they formally established this role in countries of origin. And, second, they strengthened the hands of UNHCR representatives in the field in (a) their dealings with the competent national authorities by stating international norms in an instrument that was formal and clear, and (b) in their relations with the agency headquarters in Geneva. The Conclusions gave authoritative guidance on the scope of the High Commissioner's mandate, which enabled field representatives better to advise him/her on appropriate courses of action when repatriation situations ran into difficulties on the ground.

Within two years of the adoption of Conclusion No. 40 in October 1985, UNHCR was involved in Sri Lanka with the repatriation of Tamil refugees from South India, and the provisions of these instruments were influential in establishing the scope of monitoring during the IPKF period. Moreover, they subsequently strengthened the legal and moral case for the High Commissioner's continuing concern for the refugee returnees who were caught in the war zone after the outbreak of *Eelam War II* in June 1990. However, the ground situation in the midst of the latter conflict demanded the development of an operationally more active and pragmatically engaged protection model than was then known to the agency's field practice.

A major theme in this book is thus the need and scope for constructive innovation with protective models at the source of refugee outflows. In this regard, legal authority is, of course, the fundamental basis for appropriate action. But in a context where there are usually important variables in the situation – particularly, the levels of intensity of fighting in the war zone, and the extent to which the staff deployed there are protection-minded and able to establish working relations with the combatants at all levels from checkpoints and patrols upwards – it cannot be the whole story. The following analytical narrative of experience during a critical period in the Sri Lankan conflict explains why.

Part II

Between war and peace

December 1989 to June 1990

6. Hopes for peace, fears of war

December 1989 to June 1990

"Liberated Mannar" – bush warfare in UN Vehicles –
cross-currents in Colombo – National Day – travelling hopefully
in the north – countdown in Trinco

By December 1989, the IPKF had already completed its programme of de-induction (phased withdrawal) in Amparai and Batticaloa districts in the east and it was the turn of Mannar in the north west – a situation of concern for UNHCR because it was the district with the highest concentration of refugee returnees from South India whose reintegration the agency had been monitoring during the previous two and a half years. Moreover, a high level of tension was reported on Mannar island owing the presence of a small but heavily armed detachment of the Tamil National Army (TNA) – the defence force originally formed by the Indian-supported regional administration, most of whose cadres had either disbanded or left for India. The residual TNA detachment was now dug in at Talaimannar pier on the tip of the island which commanded the crossing of the Palk Strait to India, where its evident state of nervous indecision gave cause for concern.

"Liberated Mannar"

First impressions in Mannar were good. Before going up to the *kachcheri*, I stopped in the dusty town centre, where the checkpoint signs and barriers of the now-departed IPKF had yet to be removed. A small crowd had gathered and many people were smiling, with some even giving the "Welcome to liberated Mannar!" greeting. They were not exuberant, but obviously happy, with the most optimistic among them cautiously hopeful that, just possibly, the worst might be over. Now, for the first time in several years, they could stay out as late as 10.30 at night and the feeling of relief and relaxation, albeit relative, was palpable.

At the Government Agent's residency – a dilapidated but spacious and cool Dutch colonial building – I was warmly received by Messrs Ganesh and Croos, two senior officers of the SLAS (Chapter 14, p. 205) in the district, both of whom typified the service's committed professionalism during the conflict. The situation was still too tense and uncertain for them to relax and, unsurprisingly, they were not as cheerful as the people in the streets outside. But they were reflective and just slightly hopeful: "We've had a terrible time in recent years trying to keep civil administration going – but now there is just a chance that a peaceful settlement might possibly be attainable," Mr Croos said in his slow and outwardly unemotional way of speaking. But after all he had been through since the conflict started in 1983, I knew what the thought of even the dimmest of lights at the end of the tunnel must mean to him. When I first met him two years before, he had described the daunting daily life of *kachcheri* officials in struggling to keep essential services going at a time when military control of the district was passing backwards and forwards between the Tamil militant groups and the central government forces. Whenever there was crisis and danger, he said that it was only constant prayer that kept him going. Born in a Roman Catholic village in the district, as an adult he had converted to an evangelical sect and in all my many dealings with him, he always came across as someone of deep religious conviction. Of the many fine SLAS officers I had the privilege to work alongside as an international fieldworker, he was the most remarkable.

Later, Colonel Angamana – a level-headed and diplomatic Army officer – crossed the three-kilometre causeway from his camp at Talladi on the mainland to join in the discussions at the *kachcheri*. He seemed fairly confident that the "no problems" arrangement which had been the subject of high-level agreement between the Government and the LTTE would hold. Some of his patrols had encountered LTTE cadres, who, for their part, had also confirmed the understanding. He said that the LTTE had not entered Mannar town other than to check for booby traps in the installations vacated by the EPRLF cadres – when their small detachment had been met by rejoicing inhabitants. For the time being, he was not sending armed patrols into the town. The security situation was complex and tense. But ironically the tension derived not so much from relations between Government forces and the LTTE as from the uncertain intentions of the TNA detachment at Talaimannar. As yet, there had been no fighting; but with the presence of small Army and Navy detachments in the immediate vicinity, the situation was potentially highly explosive. The colonel expressed the hope we all shared that the TNA force would soon quietly get on boats for India.

At "Sunny Village" – the compound outside Mannar town originally built for a Soviet oil exploration team but now used by international aid agencies – morale was high, with no question of having to pull out now that there was some chance of stability.

In the event, the TNA detachment did indeed leave Talaimannar – but not before it had tried to surround the small Army camp and killed three soldiers. And it withdrew only when the Navy attacked it from the sea. It slipped away quietly for India during the night – only three days after the IPKF withdrawal – to the immense relief of every one else in Mannar. And in the following weeks the district continued to bask in the same cautious optimism, with the LTTE guarding the coasts against possible TNA infiltrators from India and maintaining an office in Mannar town, while their top political leaders remained in the villages. For its part, the Sri Lankan Army was also keeping a low profile, staying mostly in Talladi camp on the mainland and usually only crossing the causeway onto Mannar island to contact *kachcheri* officials and to replenish their drinking water supplies. As was so often the case, the evident equilibrium owed much to the qualities of the principal actors: Colonel Angamana, the Army commander at Talladi, and Suresh, the young LTTE political leader, while the civil administration in the *kachcheri* – particularly in the person of Mr Croos – was performing an ongoing intermediary role to settle the inevitable small frictions which would have otherwise escalated dangerously in such a highly charged situation.

Bush warfare in UN vehicles

Meanwhile, in the power vacuum created by the IPKF withdrawal, the LTTE and the TNA and its allied groups were fighting it out in a number of fierce engagements. As these often depended on sudden surprise attacks for their success, mobility was of the essence and so both groups were grabbing whatever vehicles they could lay their hands on. Thanks to the UNHCR refugee reintegration programme, large numbers of 4 x 4 vehicles suitable for the rough roads and tracks of the north east had been donated to the relevant local services for housing, health, agriculture, fisheries etc.

Of particular combat value were the pickup trucks on which RPGs could be easily mounted and rapidly deployed. But any four-wheel drive vehicle was valuable military *matériel* in that type of fast-moving bush warfare.

In one such engagement, with the rival militant group, PLOTE, the LTTE had "borrowed" some such vehicles and there had been a potentially uglier incident in Vavuniya, when one of their cadres had pulled out a grenade to support his demand for a tractor; the situation had been defused by the coolness of the UNHCR field officers involved, when they calmly refused the request – and got away with it.[1] Of course, in such conditions commandeering by the militant groups could not be avoided, but UNHCR credibility required that it did what it could to see that the expropriated items were returned to the local authorities. What could be done? As regards the LTTE in the north, paradoxically, the contacts were made in Colombo via Bradman Weerakoon, the Presidential Advisor on International Affairs, whom President Premadasa had recently appointed to this position of exceptional influence outside the structure of line ministries in central government. From Sri Lankan friends, I heard that he had had a distinguished career working his way up in the Sri Lanka Administrative Service tradition (he had been Government Agent in a couple of districts) and that successive prime ministers – whatever their party – had found that they could not dispense with his professional counsels. Although he was personally modest and approachable, I knew that getting access to him would be problematic in that I would be competing for his time with ministers and ambassadors, not to mention the President himself, and that it would be difficult to see him at short notice, as the immediate situation demanded.

Nonetheless, after several days I got an appointment on my assurance that the matter was urgent and would take no more than 15 minutes. On that basis I could only pass the brief message that the LTTE had to lay off us, return the vehicles and let us get on with implementing our programme – or else we would have to pack up and go. He patiently heard me out, said that our programme had his support and that he would inform the President immediately, recommending that General Attygalle, head of the Government contact team in the then ongoing Government/ LTTE talks, speak to "Yogi" Yogaratnam, his LTTE opposite number, and so let the message filter down from on high to the leaders in the districts. By the time I got up to leave, I had taken just 13 minutes.

The next day, I drove to Vavuniya and went straight to the *kachcheri* where the Government Agent asked me to wait, as "Dinesh", the LTTE district commander, was in the next office addressing a meeting of *grama sevaka* (village headmen). A few minutes later, I bumped into a bearded man of rather slight build in camouflage fatigues. After we had introduced ourselves and over-come our mutual shyness, we moved the chairs to make a small circle. With the GA acting as interpreter, I started off on a rather long and, to my interlocutors, doubtless tedious speech about UNHCR's problems of credibility and funding if the LTTE took the vehicles we had donated to the local authorities; they had to be returned.

Dinesh responded immediately to the effect that the LTTE had supported the UNHCR programme during the past year; what had happened to the vehicles was exceptional and had been brought about by logistical imperatives during the heat of a local engagement. Of the commandeered vehicles, he said that some would be returned immediately and the rest shortly. Some had been repaired and would indeed be returned in better condition than when they had been borrowed. Such a situation would not recur. I concluded by emphasizing the impartiality of our function during the conflict, which he seemed to accept, and we parted on good terms.

The day after, I drove on to neighbouring Mannar, where there was an identical meeting with Suresh, the district leader, with iden-tical results. The informal procedure set up by Bradman Weerakoon, whereby messages were passed to the top LTTE leadership through the ongoing Government/LTTE talks, had worked – like a dream. But of much greater importance was that mutual relations of trust, with immediate access in emergencies or times of particular diffi-culty, had been established, and were to provide the critical support for the agency through many crises over the next two years.

In the east, however, getting back the UNHCR-donated vehicles commandeered by the TNA et al. was not so easy, although para-doxically the LTTE was the separatist group and the TNA supported the still legally competent North East Provincial Council.

Constitutionally, the position was complex. In providing that the Northern and Eastern provinces should be temporarily merged pending a referendum on their political future, the 1987 Peace Accord had stipulated that they should have a single Governor, as well as an elected joint Provincial Council and a Board of Ministers. The Thirteenth Amendment to the Constitution and the Provincial Councils Act had translated these provisions into Sri Lankan law and the President had appointed General Nalin Seneviratne, a widely respected former Armed Services Chief, to this constitutionally key post. A physically large, Sandhurst-trained officer, he had always been ready with shrewd and helpful advice throughout the two years since my arrival and so I sought his support on that occasion, requesting that he prevail upon Chief Minister Varatharaja Perumal, whose provincial administration was the competent authority for law and order and – less formally and much more importantly in the present context – the godfather of the relevant militant groups. The Governor agreed to take up the matter with Mr Thambirajah, the most influential EPRLF politician in the absence of the Chief Minister. But a few days later, a radio news flash announced that he had been killed in an LTTE ambush at Nilaveli on the eastern coastal road.

Cross-currents in Colombo

In so far as the work of a UNHCR representative in a country where there is a major programme is ever "normal", the quasi-diplomatic functions in the capital are principally to maintain relations with key officials in the government and liaise with the diplomatic community, particularly with the representatives of supportive governments. But in Colombo, as a result of the civil war in the north east there were particular complexities. Thus, as regards the government, interlocutors were broadly divided between those who supported the UNHCR presence and programme in the country and those who were against it, with the result that relations varied significantly from ministry to ministry.

This was only too apparent from the calls and contacts I made one busy day in early February. First, I went to the chambers of the Attorney-General, Sunil de Silva, in the imposing courts complex at Hultsdorf, where the atmosphere and style was the same as is to be found in state counsel offices throughout much of the Commonwealth.

Sunil, an impressive, broadly-built figure with a dry sense of humour, was a strong supporter of the UNHCR presence, doubtless largely because it helped ease some of the pressure on him at the annual session of the UN Human Rights Commission, where he regularly led the Sri Lankan delegation. Indeed the reason why he had asked me to call was that he would soon be leaving for Geneva and needed briefing on the situation in the north east and what UNHCR was doing there.

I then drove through the congested traffic of central Colombo and down the Galle road to the Ministry for Rehabilitation and Reconstruction. Because of the situation, there was no reconstruction and it was concentrating almost entirely on rehabilitation, where UNHCR had the largest and most active programme for which this ministry was the designated government counterpart. Among our many friends there, I saw Tilak Chandrasekera, the Secretary and Sunil Abeyratna, the (political) Coordinating Secretary. But there was quite an atmosphere; obviously, changes were anticipated.

At the end of the afternoon, Dr Devanesan Nesiah dropped in at the UNHCR office. A distinguished senior SLAS officer who had been Government Agent in Jaffna during the 1983 troubles, he had spent the last six years at Harvard, where he had just completed his doctorate on positive affirmation. Unsurprisingly, he had always strongly supported the UNHCR presence. We talked of current politics in the north east and social customs in Jaffna. It seemed that most people were resigned to the LTTE getting undisputed power and hoped that they would get it fairly quickly, so that there would be fewer reprisals. Resolution of the very complicated constitutional position of the North East Provincial Council was slowing progress towards dissolution and new elections – which, in the current absence of the TULF, the LTTE would of course win.

A day later, there was a meeting at the Foreign Ministry which was very different in atmosphere and style from those of the previous day. Bernard Tilekaratne, the Foreign Secretary, a portly, dignified man who talked well (almost held forth), was also a leading exponent of the negative attitude towards the UNHCR presence. I had requested the meeting to protest – very diplomatically, of course – at UNHCR not being included on the diplomatic list in the way that other UN agencies were. This was not a mere technicality, as without inclusion easy circulation and contacts within the diplomatic community – a necessary part of a UNHCR representative's work – became problematic. This was an old issue, which predated my arrival as the first representative in mid 1988. But every year, some different (and weak) excuse had been given for UNHCR being left off the list. In fact, the Foreign Ministry didn't want UNHCR in the country because it maintained that Tamils seeking asylum outside Sri Lanka were economic migrants rather than refugees – and the presence of UNHCR was strong evidence to the contrary. The meeting with the Foreign Secretary was very diplomatic, with both of us alluding to the problem as though it was no more than a minor technicality, while each knew full well that for the other it was nothing of the sort. In the end there was a procedural compromise.

But the underlying problem was likely to remain.

However, I had one good friend in the Foreign Ministry in the person of "Bala" Balasubramanian, a Jaffna Tamil who held one of the two Director General posts.

When I had first arrived knowing nothing about the country, he had kindly taken it upon himself to put me wise to some of the less obvious ins-and-outs of Colombo diplomatic life. Once when we were discussing the unpopularity of the UNHCR presence in his ministry, he had burst out laughing, saying "It's like having to call the AIDS doctor to the house!" Historically, we had been accepted because of active support from some powerful ministers, in particular Lalith Athulathmudali, at that time the key Minister of National Security.

Outside the circle of governance, and refreshingly different, was Neelan Tiruchelvam, the internationally renowned human rights lawyer and founder of the International Centre for Ethnic Studies (ICES) in Colombo. He had been a member of TULF, although by the time I got to know him, he had long since ceased to play an active part in politics. Nevertheless, on the fringe of political life, he was a highly influential figure. We often met after my field trips in the north east, when we would have wide-ranging discussions and in this way he became a true guide, philosopher and friend.

His particular support for UNHCR's presence and work clearly related to his very diplomatically phrased view that the "organs of state are not always impartial".

* * *

Much of my time in Colombo before returning to the field was spent in diplomatic contacts, particularly with the embassies of European countries, Canada and Australia, which had large numbers of Tamil asylum seekers. All were very interested, as the large majority of diplomats never got up to the north east, and conditions there were likely to determine their governments' policies on asylum seekers.

Most had been sceptical at the generally fairly upbeat reporting I had given of the situations in Mannar and Vavuniya and in particular the *modus vivendi* of the authorities and the LTTE there. There had still been some residual suspicion that the Indians might try to maintain a small force, probably in Trincomalee, after the 31 March deadline for withdrawal, and that some of the anti-LTTE militant groups might take to the jungle. I summarily dismissed both points: the Indians now realized that they had burnt their fingers badly in Sri Lanka, and for the militant groups they supported to talk of taking to the jungle was mere bravado – they had made themselves very unpopular with their frequent excesses and the forcible conscription of young boys into the TNA. And most importantly, they did not have the mettle of the LTTE, either in motivation, discipline or tenacity.

My view at that time that there was a distinct possibility of an LTTE-dominated order coming about in the north east by mid year was regarded as far too optimistic by the majority of diplomats, although naturally all were interested in the possibilities of such a scenario. "Possibly OK for the north," they would say. "But what about the east, with the Sinhalese and especially the Muslims?" To which my usual response was: "Where there is strong political will and ruthlessness, such as Premadasa seems to have, some measure of partition of sensitive areas might possibly be negotiated." In any event, donor interest was showing signs of life as the Brits, the Americans and others were keen to see if the areas predominantly under LTTE control, such as Mannar and Vavuniya, were as calm as I said, so that they could get on with implementing their long-delayed aid projects.

National Day

4 FEBRUARY 1990

During the two minutes silence in the morning ceremony at Independence Square for "those patriots who died for Sri Lankan independence", I doubted if I was alone in thinking not only of those who had died in the mostly historically distant rebellions against British colonial rule, but also of the suffering and heroism of the much greater numbers of Sri Lankans on all sides in recent years, whether in the north or the south, who were fighting each other to defend conflicting perceptions of the appropriate structure of state.

In the afternoon, there was a cultural pageant at Sugathadasa stadium – a lively show with coordinated mass gymnastics, aerobics and, of course, the traditional drummer dancers from Kandy, with their red and white headbands, bare torsos, white drawers and long drums slung horizontally across their shoulders, as they marched forward and swayed rhythmically from side to side. Altogether, it was a fine, confident performance in line with the traditional Sri Lankan flair for pageantry, and meant much in the context of national recovery after the situation during the earlier part of last year. Then there had been near-insurrection in the south, with the most brutal and callous killings on both sides, not to mention the Tamil question in the north east and the burning issue of the continued presence of the IPKF.

The situation is more peaceful and promising now than it has been for many years. In his speech, the President spoke of the need for a "a fairer and more tranquil future". Like everyone else present, I found myself sending up a prayer that this might indeed be granted and reflecting that no people on earth deserved the horrors which Sri Lankans had suffered in recent years. Objectively, Sri Lanka has so much going for it; few countries flow with such milk and honey. And, apart from the conflict, the Sri Lankans themselves are decent, good-hearted people, with a predominantly liberally democratic outlook. When, before the Second World War, Nehru visited Ceylon, he had marvelled at its serenity and relative absence of problems compared with the turmoil of India then in the throes of the independence struggle – in the light of the subsequent events in both countries, a comment of profound historical irony.

Travelling hopefully in the north

As ever in the north east, security varied very significantly from one district to another. Further to the north, in Jaffna, the IPKF de-induction programme was proceeding day by day, with its units pulling back in progressive stages from the outer reaches of the peninsula towards Jaffna town, while the LTTE, which mostly had its camps on the periphery, advanced on their heels. The stage had been reached where the IPKF had withdrawn to the port at Kankesanthurai and the airport at Pallaly – the planned points for final departure – from which they continued to patrol the approach roads. Thus the LTTE was now in control of most of the town, including the suburb of Nallur, where the UNHCR field office was accommodated in a villa near the extensive Kandaswamy temple.

Although tense, the situation was fairly stable, with both the IPKF and the LTTE taking professional care to avoid clashes.

Just how dramatically the scene was changing as the IPKF withdrew was apparent during a field trip we made at the end of February, driving south from Jaffna along the western coastal road where the dense *Vanni* jungle of the interior met the desolate salt flats bordering the Gulf of Mannar. Unsurprisingly, the LTTE had long been active in such terrain and at times of particular tension, there had been some 30 IPKF checkpoints. Now they had all gone and had not been replaced by the LTTE; indeed throughout the three-hour trip, I saw only three LTTE cadres – teenage lads, proudly wearing their tiger-striped camouflage fatigues – who had been relaxing outside a house on the outskirts of Jaffna.

The exit from the town was along raised roads through low-lying paddy fields, which were still being harvested. Further on, raised causeways, originating from before the Napoleonic wars when the British replaced the Dutch as the colonial power, struck out into the shimmering waters of the lagoon. At the end of one such causeway, a good half hour out from Jaffna, we reached a small two-car ferry which chugged across the channel to Thirunaggar on the far shore. As a small town in a strategic position, it had seen much fighting. The old Dutch fort with brick walls several feet thick was virtually in ruins and the road in the immediate vicinity was full of unfilled potholes – or rather bomb craters. The countryside was desolate, yet attractive: flat, sandy scrubland not far back from the sea, although mostly out of sight of it, with tall palmyrahs with their spiky leaves standing like sentinels guarding the landscape. Eventually, after only two and a half hours of bumpy riding, we made it to the stretch of coastal road that runs past the Army camp at Talladi, commanding access to the three-kilometre causeway leading to Mannar island.

In the IPKF days, a 1700-hrs curfew had been strictly enforced and I recalled several dashes to get to the causeway before it was closed for the night. How the atmosphere had changed – it was now possible to drive slowly across it, enjoying the superbly serene seascape of the sheltered lagoon with the island in the distance. Now the guns were silent, man was no longer trying to kill man, and for once aggression was confined to the animal kingdom, where we saw a brown, broad-winged fish eagle swooping on its prey in the Jaffna lagoon. It had been several years since a journey could be made in such conditions of timeless tranquillity.

On the road back from Mannar to Vavuniya, all the old IPKF checkpoints that had also made this route so frustratingly slow for most of the last two years had gone and we were now driving through villages flying red and gold LTTE flags, although except for an occasional cadre, the Tigers themselves were not much in evidence.

Everyone was wary about the future, but there was some hope that the worst was past and the atmosphere was much more relaxed than it had been for several years.

In the north, it was a time for travelling hopefully.

Countdown in Trinco

It was not so good in the east, however. In Batticaloa, there had been a build-up of a 3000-strong force comprising TNA and EPRLF cadres supporting the regional administration, which the LTTE had attacked after the IPKF departure. Two days of fierce street fighting resulted in a resounding victory for the LTTE force. (The police put the body count at over 100, while the LTTE claimed nearer 500.)

Thereafter, the power equation between the LTTE and the central Government forces – which had been present but had not taken part in the fighting – remained unresolved.

The local police commander, now supported by the Sri Lankan Army contingents which had moved into the district after the IPKF withdrawal, told the LTTE that ultimately law and order should be the responsibility of the police. The LTTE opened an office in the town and a spokesman, Nirmal, said that of course the LTTE would be willing to cooperate with Sri Lankan security forces – "but our political aspirations must be achieved." In reality, the situation remained uneasy, unstable and potentially explosive.

Meanwhile, in adjacent Trincomalee district, anxiety was increasing as the date for the final departure of Indian forces approached. Even at the best of times, "Trinco" had always been tense. Its historic harbour with its unrivalled anchorage was still of international strategic importance. And there was a grisly record of communal instability among the Sinhalese, Tamils and Muslims, who made up its population in approximately equal proportions. For the previous two years, it had been the seat of the controversial Indian-supported North-East Provincial Council headed by Chief Minister Varatharaja Perumal; now it was the designated location from which the last IPKF contingents would be withdrawing. It was also host to the build-up of remnants of the TNA and its allied militant groups, which had fled there following their rout by the LTTE in Batticaloa. All these elements combined into a situation that was potentially volcanic.

By late February, tension was already escalating palpably day by day in the countdown to the IPKF departure. On the last day of the month, Varatharaja Perumal moved a resolution in the Provincial Council that henceforth it would function as "the National State Assembly of the Free and Sovereign Democratic Republic of Eelam". But this "Unilateral Declaration of Independence" (UDI) was retractable – to be reconsidered if the central Government accepted within one year the 19 demands made by the EPRLF (Perumal's party). It looked like the death throes of a doomed regional regime – not much fun for the unfortunate people in Trinco, but taken almost as comic relief in Colombo, where the press had a field day: "ridiculous", "an EPRLF ploy", "too early for April Fools Day", "hilariously funny" and other jibes. The LTTE issued a statement calling the declaration "insane", and the Indian High Commission announced that it did "not approve of *Eelam* in any form".

Then, in early March, there was Sri Lanka's most ironical refugee exodus, as several boatloads of EPRLF cadres and their families were ferried to India. The press mentioned a group of 3000 persons, the first boatloads of which were refused permission to land in Tamil Nadu and in consequence were diverted further up the Bay of Bengal to Orissa state, where it was reported that they were in danger from "tribals".

By 18 March, the IPKF had pulled out of the centre of Trinco town, withdrawing to Fort Clappenberg and China Bay – fortified military bases built by the Dutch and British in their respective colonial days. With memorable views of the vast anchorage, they were highly appropriate places for another historic departure. Meanwhile, the LTTE was moving cadres into the town, where the Army and Navy were already well installed in their bases. And on 24 March, the last contingents of the IPKF sailed away from China Bay in Trinco harbour, with Sri Lankan guards of honour and to the strains of military bands playing "Auld Lang Syne".

So ended a remarkable chapter in Indo-Sri Lankan relations, and more broadly South Asian history. In the 1987 Peace Accord, India had both underestimated the complex obduracy of the Sri Lankan Tamil problem and overestimated its own capacity to bring the parties into compliance with its perceptions of a settlement. Some distinguished Indians, including the former Foreign Secretary A.P. Venkateswaran, condemned the intervention. Many claimed, and at least some Sri Lankans accepted, that (occasional atrocities apart) it had brought the LTTE to the negotiating table with the Government. Perhaps – but not in the way intended.

7. Flux in Geneva, forebodings on the ground

Short honeymoon – UNHCR: to go or to stay? – forebodings–flashpoint – failure of a promising peace initiative

Short honeymoon

Following the IPKF departure, armed LTTE cadres were moving around in central Trincomalee, while Government forces were in high profile in an as yet unresolved power equation. I needed to see for myself if it was now safe to reopen our field office, which had been closed since the beginning of the year.

The Governor, General Seneviratne, greeted me warmly at his office on Orr's Hill which was now humming with activity. After a few minutes of talk about the changes, an alert figure in smart military fatigues put his head around the door and was shown in. I nearly did a double take on the introduction – it was "Reuben", the LTTE political leader in Trinco: a man whose recent actions and statements had been extensively reported in the Colombo press. He clearly understood English, but preferred to speak through the Governor's Secretary as interpreter. He was friendly enough and listened patiently when I spoke briefly about the UNHCR programme in Trinco and how we wanted to get on with it again. The LTTE leader then went into a huddle with the Governor at the other end of his desk – asking permission, which was readily given, for his cadres to search the ex-Chief Minister's house, now under heavy Sri Lankan Police guard.

They were also preparing for a second LTTE meeting with the Sinhalese IDPs in the fort. This was a highly sensitive matter, as the LTTE wanted them to return to their homes, but at the same time did not want them to go back to those villages which were considered – at least by the LTTE – to be Tamil. So the vexed and volatile issue of "colonization" in the east was already threatening to raise again its far from beautiful head.

Obviously, the meeting had been set up with a view to my seeing how well the situation was working out, with the Government in control, but in coordination with the LTTE. As intended, I was impressed.

However, at that stage, the constitutional situation was a lot more problematic than relations between the two sides on the ground. Although the central Government had in effect taken over the running of the Provincial Council, the position was uncertain: it was not "President's rule", nor from the strictly legal standpoint was it "Governor's rule", as the Provincial Council was still in being, albeit with most of its (EPRLF) members now refugees in India. The President had therefore issued a decree in which he dismissed the Chief Minister, Ministers and Secretaries of the Provincial Council on grounds of their absence from duty, while at the same time empowering the Governor to appoint Secretaries to get the provincial ministries working again.

Accordingly, General Seneviratne had promptly appointed his own Secretary as Chief Secretary of the North East Provincial Administration. Anything more than this essentially provisional arrangement would have required formal dissolution of the legally still-extant Provincial Council, which would have taken a good deal more time than was politically available. And in any event, there would have to be new elections, the organization of which would take even more time. Indeed the failure of the constitutional process to keep up with the pace of political events in the north east was to prove a major element in the subsequent early disaster.

Meanwhile, the President's speech in Parliament was decidedly up-beat: significant achievements were noted against subversion ("insistent clamour for terror to be removed at any cost and by any means available" – it certainly had been that), the IPKF had gone and the wounds in the north east were being healed with the establishment of relations with the LTTE. There were bullish comments all round on the economy, "peopleization", tourism etc.

* * *

Nilaveli, 28–30 April 1990

Briefly transiting Trinco town, we took the coastal road to reach Nilaveli several miles to the north. There had been several luxury hotels on the coast, but many had been blown up during the conflict. The Nilaveli Beach Hotel was one of the few that had been left unharmed – a luxurious complex, virtually abandoned in recent years, except for the small skeleton staff who maintained it. It was in a couple of bungalows there that the UNHCR field office in Trincomalee district had been accommodated from September 1988 to December 1989, when we were advised by Sri Lankan security to clear out – there was too high a risk of fighting between the LTTE and the TNA, who by that time had set up several camps there to train Tamil boys conscripted even from the school room to defend the doomed Provincial Council after the IPKF withdrawal. Nilaveli had always been a bit of a no-man's-land: very occasionally, the IPKF would turn up in force; on others, it was known that the LTTE were around (although they were seldom seen).

The difference now was dramatic. No longer was UNHCR the sole occupant. The hotel was full of holidaymakers: some foreign tourists, but mostly Sinhalese and other Sri Lankans from Colombo. Above all, the atmosphere had changed – to that of a good beach hotel anywhere in the world. The large swimming pool was full, mostly with kids splashing around and making a noise. The beach – that beautiful long stretch of white sand backed by drooping palm trees – now had the usual, but in recent years absent, multicoloured beach chairs and parasols.

For the first time since I'd arrived in Sri Lanka nearly two years before, I felt I could relax a bit, enjoy the scene and think of things other than work and the tensions and dangers of the ground situation.

UNHCR: time to go or need to stay?

Whether in foreign services, the military, international agencies, multinationals, non-governmental organizations or any other variation on institutions with a central bureaucratic headquarters on one side of the world and its local representation in the field on the other, there is ever, in varying degrees, a certain measure of tension and disagreement. In the present case, the differences between the field team in Colombo and the agency headquarters in Geneva focused on their respective responses to the key question of what – if any – useful role UNHCR could play in Sri Lanka once the current reintegration programme had been phased out.

In Geneva, some powerful elements responded negatively for a range of reasons. One of the main objections was the status of the reintegration project as a special operation of limited duration outside the agency's regular programme; it was being undertaken in a refugee country of origin and incidentally concerned with internally displaced persons, and was thus altogether perceived to be on the fringe of or even outside the High Commissioner's statutory mandate. The programme's was also incurring high per capita costs compared with most programmes elsewhere in the world, particularly in Africa.

Seen from Colombo, however, the perspective was quite different. The operation had had a significantly beneficial impact in north east Sri Lanka both as regards material assistance – where it had made important inputs in the reintegration process – and protection, where the presence of international staff on the ground and their monitoring role had been undeniably positive in effect. In bureaucratic jargon, the programme was already "phasing out", with a progressive reduction of staff, most of whom had either already left or were to leave shortly on reassignment to posts elsewhere in the world. Meanwhile, a small residual group of core staff based in Colombo was arranging for the transfer of activities to the competent local authorities, especially in the housing sector. As for the future, the answer depended essentially on the degree of progress that could be achieved in the ongoing Government–LTTE talks on removing the obstacles to the Tigers' entering the political mainstream. There was a chance of a rough settlement of sorts in the north east later in the year, and in such a scenario there would be need for the agency to play a small but significant protection role thereafter, with two field offices in Jaffna and Trincomalee. The field staff would be in a position to advise the High Commissioner on when conditions might be appropriate for the voluntary repatriation of Sri Lankan Tamil refugees, particularly from western European countries and Canada. Within such a UNHCR framework, it was envisaged that a counselling project could be established which would make it possible for non-governmental organizations concerned with Tamil welfare in countries of asylum to participate actively.

There was also the internal UNHCR question: the indifferent state of health of a great but visibly ailing international institution. Since the unexpected resignation of the previous High Commissioner, Jean-Pierre Hocke, in late October 1989, the UN refugee agency had been in a state of flux. Although Thorvald Stoltenberg had been elected by the General Assembly as the new High Commissioner and had taken over in the new year, there was a severe financial crisis that was putting strong pressure on him to scale down operations worldwide. And Sri Lanka was high on the list of those countries from which UNHCR's withdrawal was proposed. As a result, the new administration in Geneva had already reduced the normal bureaucratic timescale for phasing out the programme and in effect dictated swingeing staff reductions.

Strict financial controls were only to be expected in difficult circumstances. But they were being applied in a way that was ominous for Sri Lanka – and for the present programme or any successor that might be proposed – as staffing levels were to be pegged proportionately to programme costs. As we were already facing a funding shortfall, we would not therefore be able to justify more than a very drastically reduced staffing complement. What hope was there of more funding coming in from interested donors? That possibility had been neatly wrapped up in a bureaucratic "Catch 22": headquarters would not be seeking funds for Sri Lanka, nor would it be prepared to accept any that might be offered. In that way, we would be programmed to sink quietly over the next few months – unless I could get access to High Commissioner Stoltenberg and persuade him of the need for UNHCR to remain in Sri Lanka, two difficult tasks for which there was no immediate opportunity.

Such an occasion came in May when the new High Commissioner summoned to Geneva all his 83 "representatives", however designated, in order to brief them on the new order. He strongly emphasized that this was no normal financial crisis: UNHCR was really up against it with the donors, who were not going to give us sufficient funds to meet our programme needs, hence the programme and staff cuts. There was an itemized agenda over which he presided for the principal topics, to which representatives were invited to raise matters of particular concern in their areas. As his representative in Sri Lanka, I was interested in the international protection item and asked to speak on the High Commissioner's monitoring role in voluntary repatriation operations. Accordingly, I started off by pointing out that the note on his mandate circulated to fellow participants prior to the meeting had not included his responsibilities in relation to refugee returnee operations, which had been spelt out specifically by the UNHCR Executive Committee and formalized in its Conclusion No. 40. To myself, I wondered if the omission had been the result of professional oversight or, much more seriously, of an endeavour to present the High Commissioner's empowerment under his mandate as being less than in fact it was.

What I actually said, however, was incontrovertible – although evidently unfashionable, and no doubt impolitic, as Stoltenberg did not comment and none of my 82 colleagues from the field who were present uttered a single word on the matter. I had not so much been saying that the emperor was unclothed, as regretting that the keepers of the imperial wardrobe hadn't told him that he had some useful working clothes, should he wish to wear them. I also mentioned the need to address root and more proximate causes of refugee problems – which similarly failed to stimulate any expression of interest.

I had done what I could to save the UNHCR presence in Sri Lanka. Its future role would now depend on progress in the ongoing Government/LTTE talks to try to find a political solution to the conflict.

Forebodings

Unfortunately, by the time I got back to Colombo two weeks later, rising tension and increasingly widespread anxiety were the facts of daily life. In addition to talking to the LTTE, the Government was now also in contact with the LTTE-opposed Tamil groups – particularly the EPRLF – and this had clearly incensed the Tigers, reawakening many of the deep suspicions of the past. There were even rumours of the Army training EPRLF cadres at Negombo outside Colombo – an unlikely story, but one that well illustrated the LTTE mistrust of Government intentions. On the other hand, the LTTE seemed to be taking up the cudgels on the highly sensitive, but hitherto separate, issue of the up-country Tamils of Indian origin in the tea-growing areas. After the mutual discretion on both sides during the last year of coexistence on the basis of a ceasefire and ongoing talks, each side now seemed to want to openly embarrass the other.

By far the ugliest portent had been the assassination of Sam Tambimuttu, the MP for Batticaloa, who, together with his wife, was shot dead in broad daylight on 7 May on leaving the Canadian High Commission in central Colombo. I used to run into Sam from time to time on the diplomatic reception circuit when I was in Colombo and he had helped me to understand some of the intensely convoluted politics both in and relating to the north east. In particular he had taught me much about his own party, the EPRLF, which he had joined after the effective demise of TULF, but about which he made no attempt to hide his reservations: "controlled by a very few men, mostly outside Sri Lanka".

He was a kindly man, who had been nauseated by the way in which the EPRLF-controlled North East Provincial Council had been forcibly conscripting Tamil youths into its puppet TNA during the previous summer. Evidently, the LTTE had taken very seriously the Government's recent contacts with the remnants of the EPRLF – and as a consequence, Sam had been eliminated by a relentless killer squad, as had the old TULF leadership (Amirthalingam, Yogeswaran and their colleagues), who had been treacherously murdered in the house in which they were staying in Colombo the year before.

The changing military situation in the north east, particularly in Jaffna, was another sign of rising tension. The LTTE were now digging in, preparing fortifications, trenches and bunkers in strategic places (around the fort, in the city and at the edge of the runway at the Pallaly military airport). Road blocks, the absence of which had been such a welcome feature of the landscape since the IPKF withdrawal, had now started to re-emerge – the only apparent difference being that they were now manned by young LTTE cadres instead of seasoned Indian *jawans*. All vehicles were now being checked and listed by the LTTE, including those donated by UNHCR to local authorities for the implementation of its projects. It was clear that they would be rapidly commandeered at the commencement – or, more likely in anticipation of – hostilities. As yet our own vehicles, those we used ourselves, had not been touched, but it would have been naive to expect that they would remain so, should the balloon go up.

The most notable change was the disenchantment among the people. The LTTE were by now much less popular than immediately after the IPKF withdrawal, a brief period when they had mostly behaved very well and kept a relatively low profile. Primarily, the problem was "taxation" – described by many who were subjected to it as "extortion".

How to interpret all that was going on? To describe relations between the Government and the LTTE over the past year as a "honeymoon" was a bit of a strain on language. But nonetheless it had been a period during which a ceasefire held and there were ongoing high-level talks between the two sides with a view to working out solutions to their differences. Was this relatively happy period now over? Evidently – and succeeded by bloody-minded brinkmanship on both sides. Not necessarily a prelude to fighting, but highly dangerous.

At the German embassy reception on 23 May, everyone was apprehensive about the turn of events. One Sri Lankan interlocutor to whom I was explaining my respect for Premadasa's political acumen wouldn't have any of it. "Astrology," he retorted, almost angrily. And when I countered that the President had what I called "political horse sense", he conceded grudgingly, "He just gets by." Two days later, reviewing developments over the previous three weeks with my International Committee of the Red Cross (ICRC) opposite number, I kept on trying to avoid the word "deterioration" – but without success. Undeniably, the positive trend towards normalization apparent since the IPKF withdrawal in March had been halted.

This could just be the brinksmanship in tough top-level negotiations that often precedes a final settlement. But the many pessimists around considered an outbreak of fighting inevitable. At the current peace talks in Jaffna, shown on TV, the Tigers seemed mostly sweet and reasonable, although, of course, sticking to their demands for repeal of the Sixth Amendment and dissolution of the North-East Provincial Council. Hamid, the Minister of Justice, who was chairing the Peace Committee, looked tired. Mahattaya (Prabhakaran's no. 2), seemed to do most of the talking, at least while the cameras were on.

On 30 May, everyone was full of the improvement in attitude of the LTTE, hoping that there wouldn't be hostilities. I agreed, believing that the current tensions between the LTTE and Government – with deployment of LTTE cadres in hostile manoeuvres and the corresponding macho remarks of some Army generals – might be not much more than the last minute brinkmanship to be expected on both sides, as each reconciled itself to the reality of having to give up something in order in order to get a settlement.

The next two weeks, however, were widely expected to be critical for the future of the north east. On 31 May, I met General Seneviratne, the Governor, during a visit to Colombo, briefed him on the UNHCR position and heard what he thought of prospects in his region. As to the latter, he was none too optimistic. Constitutionally, he said, it was a mess, with uncertainty as to what the precise legal position was regarding the politically all-important question of dissolution of the Provincial Council in order to clear the way for elections. It would require the enactment of legislation to resolve these difficulties and that would inevitably take time. Then, in any event it would be two months from dissolution before elections could be held. My hope for a stable administration to be established by mid year looked unlikely, which pushed further back the earliest date for any significant return of asylum-seekers. Moreover, there was the LTTE demand for repeal of the Sixth Amendment, which the Governor considered unlikely to come about. He agreed with my basic optimism to the extent that it was in the interest of the President that there should be a settlement – but nonetheless remained doubtful about the future. As for the possibility that UNHCR might pull out, he seemed depressed, saying that whatever group gained power in the north east, they would want UNHCR to stay and help (especially if it should be the LTTE, as seemed likely).

In early June, watching events in the north east from Colombo was an increasingly anxious business, as the following notes indicate:

1 June: Quite a day for colleagues from the field – a succession of both UNHCR staff and *kachcheri* officials. From Jaffna, Asad – our Bangladeshi colleague who was the last international staff member in the field office there – came back full of the news of the LTTE's high military profile and vigorous activities such as building strategic fortifications – tunnels and trenches around Army positions in the fort and on the fringes of Pallaly airport, and a new jetty at Velvettiturai on the northern coast – and the frequency of its road convoys, with lorries now painted green. He seemed convinced that there would not be war and that what was going on was just a demonstration of LTTE military might and preparedness, in case the Army might get, as he put it, "funny ideas". Asad was now alone in Jaffna, living in the field office at Nallur, near the temple. Recently, he had prudently decided not to go out unless there was a programme matter requiring his specific attention.

Later in the afternoon, Danilo Bautista arrived by road from Trincomalee, where the situation was reported calmer than in the previous week. Even so, there was plenty of tension, with the LTTE now maintaining a very high profile both militarily and politically; Tamil displaced persons were being settled along the coast road to Nilaveli and Tamil "colonization" was being pushed at Milepost 90, a key area along the Trinco–Colombo road. The Army now remained mostly in barracks – the result of the President's "no confrontation" instruction, which in effect seemed to be leaving the LTTE carte blanche to do what they liked.

Then Mr Croos came in from Mannar, as usual well

informed and balanced in his analysis: "The situation in Mannar? ... Calm compared with other areas in the north east – as good as can be expected in the current unsettled conditions of political vacuum when there are heavily armed forces around." The prospect now seemed to be of a constitutional stalemate, with the LTTE increasingly doing their own thing. If so, the momentum for peace and stability couldn't be anything like what I had been hoping for. In such a scenario, UNHCR would be unlikely to be involved in the foreseeable future in facilitating the return of Sri Lankan Tamils, let alone their reintegration, so perhaps we should be thinking of pulling out by the year end. In any event, we had to leave things prepared locally as best we could with what resources remained. In the latter respect, there was a meeting with colleagues Aziz, Binod and Mahmoud to prepare for the housing project meeting in Vavuniya the following week, when we would be setting out arrangements to transfer progressively all implementation of remaining housing targets to the competent local authority and selected local non-governmental organizations (NGOs) with a view to completing a total of 7000 units before the end of the year.

8 June: Today brought bad news: a shoot-out outside Vavuniya between an Army convoy and the LTTE at a roadblock when a corporal was killed and several wounded on both sides. Some Army officers blamed the major in charge of the convoy for not having observed the agreed procedure for consultation prior to sending out military convoys.

One particularly worrying aspect was that the Army rank and file were reportedly getting nervous and it was rumoured that officers were having problems in maintaining discipline – if it should break, even in only a few incidents, the escalation could be disastrous. With the constraint of the "no confrontation" order from on high, the Army felt it was being sorely tried by LTTE actions.

9 June: Raja – our Tamil driver who passed as Sinhalese – said that the people in the bus in which he travelled to work were hotly criticizing the President for being too favourable to the LTTE. Unsurprisingly, they had been quite excited about the Vavuniya incident.

10 June: "The inevitability of another war between the LTTE and the Sri Lankan forces is very much in the southern psyche. ... But at no time in the history of the conflict have we come as close to some kind of durable political solution as we do now". Such was the prophetic comment of Rita Sebastian, a columnist in the *Colombo Sunday Times*, underlining the cruel irony of the situation.

Flashpoint

11 June: "Batti very bad, Bill!" someone blurted out, accentuating the tension of the moment with unconscious alliteration. The story was that the LTTE had attacked an Army convoy on a routine trip to collect rations from Batticaloa town, killing 14 men. Also, Police posts in the area had been occupied by LTTE cadres and some 200 policemen taken prisoner. Later the news improved to the extent that the situation was being contained. There had been several serious security problems in Batticaloa over the previous two years, but they usually had not spread outside the district. The Army casualties would be a political bombshell in the south, where the President was trying to drum up enough parliamentary support to repeal the Sixth Amendment to the Constitution, an LTTE precondition to participation in elections for the new North East Provincial Council.

12 June: I got up early to prepare to go the critical meeting on transferring housing construction under the UNHCR programme to the local authorities. It was to be held in Vavuniya, where the latest news was that it was quiet. All of us thought that the way events were developing, if we didn't hold the meeting now, we never would, and so decided to go ahead. Then came news that the situation was deteriorating in Batticaloa, where the Army casualty toll had risen to 40. And the trouble was beginning to spread to ... Vavuniya. So bang went our housing meeting. Thinking of the impossibility of holding it or anything like it in the foreseeable future, I realized just how much had been lost by the present outbreak of fighting.

Jaffna was reported quiet, but with LTTE preparations afoot around the fort and on the approaches to Pallaly airport. I rang round to Caroline Elms at the UK High Commission, Robert England at UN Development Programme (UNDP) and Dag Larsson at North American Aerospace Defense Command (NORAD) (none of whom had yet been informed). Later, Caroline phoned back to say that the Air Force was in action up the coast at Kalkudath – the war zone was expanding. Later we heard that 70 Sinhalese families had been flown out of Batticaloa.

Spoke to Asad in Jaffna on the landline and told him to get the next plane out, and then got out three long telexes to Geneva on security staffing and funding. In the evening at the Philippines National Day reception, everyone was talking animatedly about the situation and rumours were flying around: good ones, such as the negotiation of a ceasefire to start the following day (which proved to be correct) and nightmarish ones, such as that the 200 policemen taken prisoner had been shot by the LTTE.

13 June: The arrangement of a ceasefire from 12 noon was announced on the radio; meanwhile fighting continued in Batticaloa, with official, though unpublished, casualties rising to 60.

Asad got out of Jaffna on an Air Force plane at the end of the morning – one of the last foreigners to leave. Reports of life in Jaffna in recent days were much as expected: tense and uneasy, waiting for trouble which now seemed inevitable, but which most people had not expected to come so soon. Offices were open and children going to school. But there were fewer people on the streets and traffic on the roads was thinning out. There had been some firing by the LTTE near Pallaly airport, but the commanders on both sides had managed to defuse the incident – quite the best news around, although unfortunately exceptional. Preparations were being made by Government forces at Pallaly Air Force base to have reinforcements and armaments flown in.

In the evening at the NORAD reception, talk was naturally gloomy. One or two of the negative old hands were saying "told you so". Others – especially Sinhalese guests – were indignant, with much justification in view of the rumours of the police taken prisoner being shot in their hundreds. For those of us who had been working in the north east, it was a very sad occasion. The circumstances in which the fighting had broken out were tragi-comic in their intrinsic triviality. And why hadn't the incident been defused, as had similar ones before it? Why had the LTTE been so precipitate? They already had the substance of much that they wanted, or would soon have got it with only a minute modicum of patience. Now that fighting had started again, even if there was a ceasefire that held, the way back towards normality would be much more problematic. At the very minimum three or four months would have been lost, probably much longer – and, of course, the longer hostilities continued, the more difficult a recovery would be. Remembering '83, Tamils in Colombo were feeling uncomfortable.

14 June: First thing in the office, the news was that the fighting in Batticaloa had intensified overnight. The Mannar *kachcheri* came on line to ask about payments to beneficiaries under the housing project, but also enquiring about the press report of Tamil youths being rounded up in Colombo. I reassured them that as far as I knew it was only for identity checks and in one part of the city. The Mannar situation was reportedly quiet, as indeed it always has been during the last two years, save when there had been open fighting. The Police headquarters – in the old Dutch fort strategically placed at the end of the long causeway from the mainland – was now in LTTE hands. But there was no fighting between the LTTE and the Army, which was remaining in Talladi camp at the mainland end of the causeway, and only coming out for essentials, such as rations and water. I thought of Colonel Angamana, the Army commander, Suresh, the LTTE District leader and the SLAS team in the *kachcheri* – all of whom had been doing their utmost to avoid conflict. What must they be feeling now?

In the afternoon I called at the UK High Commission and saw David Gladstone, the High Commissioner, who had driven to Jaffna over the weekend and thought the situation likely to work out peacefully. The sudden outburst of fighting in Batticaloa was attributable largely to headstrong elements; but nevertheless, they were clearly being backed up by the top LTTE leadership. We agreed that if the rumours about the police prisoners being shot turned out to be even only partially true, the LTTE would have lost irretrievably the battle for international sympathy.

* * *

But the rumours proved to be largely true, the ceasefire didn't hold and *Eelam War II* had started.

Failure of a promising peace initiative

After such an unexpectedly calm and even promising few weeks in March and April 1990 immediately following the IPKF withdrawal, what had gone wrong? Unsurprisingly, there are many theories, of which one of the most thought-provoking, and worthy of particular attention because of its author's strong admiration for Premadasa, is Dayan Jayatilleka's view that essentially "Premadasa's behaviour was depriving the LTTE of an enemy, while the war weariness of the Tamil people may have congealed into an irreversible peace sentiment."[1] It was thus to escape from the corner into which he was being pushed by Premadasa's peace initiative that Prabhakaran took his decision "to go back to war", "to strike". Stimulating though this analysis is, it is based largely on assumptions: such as that a decision had already been taken by Prabhakaran by the time of the fateful incident in Batticaloa on 11 June 1990, and that "the best outcome that could have been realistically striven for at that time would have been a long-term, almost permanent armed truce" and that no one in the Government, not even Premadasa, understood this.

As to Prabhakaran's "premeditated bad faith", there was certainly deep frustration on the LTTE side at the failure of the Government to make progress in repealing the Sixth Amendment to the Constitution and dissolving the North East Provincial Council. But the LTTE's resentment was very understandable, as the Sixth Amendment applied to members of local authorities as well as to MPs. It thus stood squarely in the way of LTTE cadres contesting elections both to the Provincial Council and to the Parliament, without which the movement could not enter the political mainstream, which was largely what the Government/LTTE talks were meant to be about. In such circumstances, the LTTE's insistence on its demands being met – *vide* the forthright warning to the Government issued by Anton Balasingham, its principal negotiator, during a public address in Jaffna as late as 20 May 1990: "This is the last chance we give you. If you fail, we are prepared to wage war" – spoke more for intense frustration which precipitated hasty over-reaction, rather than for deception and bad faith. Progress on the repeal was blocked because President Premadasa could not obtain the necessary two-thirds parliamentary majority that was required constitutionally. The problem with dissolution of the Provincial Council was primarily one of slow legislative procedures, although there was also less than the urgency which the LTTE expected.

The view that realistically the best outcome would have been a long-term, almost permanent, armed truce was widely accepted in the north at that time as the shape of things to come, whatever constitutional forms might be negotiated in the talks at the centre. But as to the conclusion that "no wing of the regime and no leading personality understood" it, the facts might possibly be read differently in relation to the respective positions of both the "hardliners" (Ranjan Wijeratne and supporters) and the "softliners" (led by Premadasa and represented in the talks by A.C.S. Hameed).

The hardliner position is criticized as having shown "a complete misunderstanding of the nature of their enemy, the LTTE", with specific reference to the demand that the Tigers surrender their arms and disband and be reformed within the national forces.

The former demand is termed "laughable" and the latter unrealistic. Such criticism was entirely justified as regards the impact of the demands on progress in the peace talks. But was that really what the hardliners wanted? Might they not have very well understood that the "long-term, almost permanent armed truce" was indeed the way things were going on the ground – and decided that if the Government could not get a better deal than that, it was as well to abort the talks by making demands that they knew the LTTE would not accept? As for the "softliners", is it credible that as shrewd and resourceful a politician as Premadasa would not have understood that, constitutional trimmings notwithstanding, the reality of a negotiated peace at that stage would have been pretty much an "armed truce"? Even so, why did he not do more to make progress in meeting the LTTE demands which would have cleared the way for its entry into the political mainstream? The answer lies perhaps in the state of political play at a time when Premadasa had lost possession of the ball to Ranjan Wijeratne, his State Minister for Defence, who was running hard with it, capitalizing on the frustration of the Army at being virtually confined to barracks as a result of the Presidential "no confrontations" order.

Eventually, the Government did deliver on dissolution of the Provincial Council by getting the necessary legislative amendment through Parliament – but tragically only after the fateful events of 11 June 1990 had pre-empted further progress towards a negotiated settlement.

The evidence of the weeks prior to 11 June 1990 supports neither the charge that Prabhakaran took a premeditated decision to go to war nor that Premadasa showed political incompetence. *Eelam War II* started because of an incident which was adventitious and in itself utterly trivial, yet nonetheless sufficient to spark a conflagration in the highly combustible conditions of Batticaloa. Prabhakaran's initial reaction to events there, according to a highly respected intelligence source, was to order that restraint should be exercised, but that fire should be returned.[2] The largely spontaneous combustion of events on the ground thereafter is a matter of historical record – although we may hope that one day more will be known from both sides as to precisely why the ceasefire, arranged with the LTTE by A.C.S. Hameed on his missions to Jaffna, failed. I still see the events of mid-June 1990 in the way I wrote in my personal journal at the time:

> I don't accept the current mood of condemning Prabhakaran for bad faith and Premadasa for naivety and incompetence, but see the problem more in the light of the LTTE being a highly effective but paranoid war machine on the one hand and the Government's professionally war-minded armed services, led by the Army, on the other, with the political leadership on both sides being unable to control the bellicose reflexes of their own hardline elements once the shooting had started.

But for the implosion of events on 11 June 1990, dissolution of the Provincial Council would have opened the way for elections in which the LTTE would have participated and, with the abstention of the TULF, won overwhelmingly. Such a historic move by the LTTE in the direction of the national political mainstream would not in itself have brought peace, but would have established the conditions in which peace could have been realistically negotiated.

Of course there are many lessons which should have been learned from these tragic annals of lost opportunity, which are well recorded elsewhere.[3] One that might be added was the need for an incident-defusing mechanism, however informal, to be set up at the district level in which the professional skill and experience of the civil administration was utilized to the full. In Batticaloa, there was no such mechanism and over 600 Police personnel lost their lives at the outset, not directly in the fighting, but through getting caught up in uncontrollable events. In Mannar, on the other hand, there were channels to communicate and defuse incidents, and largely as a result, not only was there significantly less tension there than elsewhere, but as hostilities were breaking out the Government Agent was able to arrange for the safe exit of some 100 policemen, leading them out to the safety of the Sinhalese areas in neighbouring Anuradhapura district. If such a mechanism had been in place and functioning in Batticaloa in June 1990, the fate of many police officers, if not the course of the conflict, might have been different.

Part III

Eelam War II erupts

June to October 1990

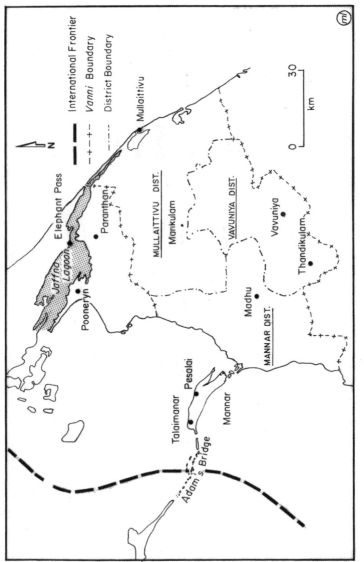

The *Vanni*

8. National implosion, international indifference

*Fighting spreads, Tamils flee – relief efforts – Geneva opts out –
damage in Trinco*

Fighting spreads, Tamils flee

The first two weeks of *Eelam War II* were a time of intensely frustrating inactivity for UNHCR and other international relief agencies. With the high volatility of the situation and the intensity of the engagements between the combatants in the north east, we were immobilized in Colombo until such time as the situation might improve sufficiently to enable us to get security clearance to move up there. Meanwhile, we had lost contact with the only group which was within UNHCR's strict statutory competence: the relatively small number of refugee returnees who had repatriated from South India under the 1987 Peace Accord, whose reintegration the agency had been monitoring during the previous two and a half years. They had been caught up in the mass of internally displaced Tamil civilians then trying to distance themselves from fighting in the war zone.

However, UNHCR was fortunate in having an unusually wide range of sources of information as to what was going on. Receptions on the diplomatic corps calendar were now unusually animated with the exchange of news and views, together with rumours that were alarming if not alarmist, but nonetheless an essential part of the picture; and from aid agencies, we got news of specific incidents. In addition, we had a liaison with the JOC in the person of Nihal de Zoyza, a former senior Air Force officer and now national officer with UNHCR, who kept us abreast of major military moves. In particular, we were managing to keep in touch with the *kachcheris* in LTTE-held Jaffna and Mannar. This was via landlines in the very early days before they were cut. Thereafter, we used the still-functioning two-way radios in our otherwise closed field offices, which soon became a vital communications link not only for UNHCR but, of much greater consequence in the overall emergency context, for the Government relief services.

In this way, while waiting for the situation in the war zone to stabilize sufficiently, we were able to follow from afar the grim events of the deepening conflict as they unfolded.

* * *

15 June: The newspapers have been full of the spreading conflict in Trincomalee, where the LTTE are attacking and taking over some police stations (notably at Uppavelli, near the UNHCR cluster housing project at Thirukadalur). But as yet the Tigers haven't launched a general offensive in the district – and probably are unlikely to do so, as Government forces there are too powerful. Clearly, the Army is building up for a counter-offensive – there are reports of helicopter gunships in action and heavy troop movements towards the east.

The news in from Mannar by radio is that it is hotting up there. The small Army post at Talaimannar is under attack, with retaliation by helicopter gunships and artillery fire from the nearby Navy detachment at the pier. In Mannar town, the situation is reported tense, but unclear. A few hours ago, there was a report that the Army camp at Talladi, commanding the mainland end of the long causeway to Mannar island, is surrounded by LTTE cadres who have taken possession of the town and the old Dutch fort at the island end of the causeway. Then came another report that Army troops at Talaimannar had withdrawn to the Navy compound at the pier – with 14 men missing.

From Trinco, the news was even worse, with 60 policemen at Kenniya station, which the LTTE has taken over, reported killed.

Back at home around 2100 hrs, Mr Croos phoned from the Mannar *kachcheri*. The situation there is not good – in capturing the Army post at Talaimannar, the LTTE has killed 25 soldiers and taken one prisoner, while the rest have been fortunate enough to have made it to the small Navy base at the pier. Many local inhabitants have moved out from Talaimannar down the coast towards Pesalai, the fishing village where they have taken refuge in the church and school buildings of the Roman Catholic mission and the *kachcheri* is organizing cooked meals.

Mannar town is now virtually empty, the population having decamped to various villages outside since a few shells, fired from the Army camp at Talladi on the mainland, landed near the old Dutch fort at the island end of the causeway (now occupied by the LTTE). One of the more macabre functions of the *kachcheris* over the years of conflict has been to arrange the exchange of corpses between the combatant parties (in Mannar, this is usually done at night in the middle of the causeway). On this occasion, the LTTE are having the corpses embalmed and coffins made – the fact that they are evidently trying to maintain some respect for the dead is one small positive detail in an immensely negative situation (in the east, they have reportedly been burning the corpses of the slain Police and Army personnel). Mr Croos himself is engaged in acting as go-between for return of the corpses and the one Army prisoner taken by the Tigers. In the process, he hopes it might be possible to bring about an ad hoc cease-fire. Col. Angamana at Talladi and Suresh, the LTTE district leader are well experienced in dealing with one another to defuse minor incidents of friction – but on nothing like the present scale of violence.

Mr Croos suddenly broke off, saying: "The 'boys' are here – I'll call back later." I waited with some misgiving, trying to imagine what was going on at the other end of the line. But after a few minutes he did indeed call back. The "boys" – the popular name for the Tigers in the north east – had come to talk about arrangements for handing over corpses. The number of inhabitants who have fled Mannar town to take refuge in outlying villages is currently estimated at 20,000.

16 June: Later, Nihal came round from the JOC with the latest information that it was prepared to share with the likes of us: that fighting in Batticaloa had subsided somewhat and Trinco was tense, but mostly under the control of Government forces. In Jaffna, there was some firing as the plane of Justice Minister Hameed – there to try to negotiate a ceasefire – had been taking off, but it hadn't come to much. But there were engagements around Mankulam, on the strategic road to the north, south of Elephant Pass. At the end of the day, the Sri Lankan Red Cross phoned to pass a radio message through us to their Jaffna branch regarding supplies.

17 June: The BBC and Colombo papers are full of the truce negotiated with the LTTE in Jaffna by Justice Minister Hameed as of 1800 hrs last night. But there are also many accounts of fighting and casualties. Generally, the view in the south is that the President had been leaning over backwards to try to accommodate the LTTE, while they had been negotiating in bad faith. Then there was a rumour, which proved to be true, that the truce wasn't holding, as fighting had started up again in Batticaloa. In Jaffna, there are small arms attacks on the Air Force base at Pallaly and heavy fighting around Mankulam on the strategic road south of the peninsula. Now that the truce seems to have failed, presumably Government forces will go on the offensive. There are the same sad stories in the press: of policemen being taken prisoner in large numbers, some of whom are said to have been shot by LTTE cadres; Army posts under attack; heavy casualties etc.

In the evening, I attended the Sri Lanka–UK Society dinner as one of a party of guests of a prominent Colombo businessman, Ananda Chittambalam – mostly diplomats, journalists and prominent Sri Lankans from all communities. Ranjan Wijeratne, Minister of State for Defence, was the guest of honour and made a good short speech.

David Gladstone, the UK High Commissioner, spoke of the Government occupying the "high moral ground" and being likely to continue to do so, if it kept good discipline among its forces. Of course, from one angle or another, the rest of us were talking about the north east and what most consider to have been the LTTE treachery in carrying on the negotiations in bad faith. Some Sri Lankans were also blaming the Government for being so slow to understand the game the LTTE had been playing.

But, personally, I doubt if the situation has been anything like so simple and clear-cut as that.

18 June: No one now talks of the ceasefire any more. And the papers just describe the many incidents of fighting, so far mainly in the east.

19 June: More Government forces are moving to the east and slowly winning back police stations and other strategic points taken by the LTTE.

Shirley Allan of SCF had the good idea to set up an informal information-sharing mechanism together with other agencies which are operational in relief work in the north east – principally, the League of Red Cross Societies, MSF and a number of smaller agencies. But with so many NGOs participating, most of whom want to speak even if they haven't got any information to contribute – too large and unstructured to be effective for more than information-sharing and solidarity; certainly not for action in a sensitive and fast-moving situation such as this.

20 June: The newspapers are full of the advance of Government forces, which are reported to have regained control of Batticaloa and other areas taken over by the LTTE in the past week. Attempts by the LTTE to force an entry into the Government-held fort at Jaffna are mentioned and there is also a report of the Army trying to clear the area around the Air Force base at Pallaly.

But by far the most dramatic news is the assassination in Madras of the EPRLF top leadership: Padmanabha, the Secretary-General, the former Finance Minister in the now defunct North-East Provincial Administration and several other officials – 13 persons all told who were shot down in the flats where they were staying. Two carloads of heavily-armed men had driven into the neighbourhood, asked where the group was staying and when they had found them, opened up with automatic weapons, killing them all before making their getaway. True to form, the LTTE hasn't claimed responsibility – a formality perhaps hardly required in the circumstances.

21 June: The diplomatic reception circuit in the evenings is now more than ever a valuable information exchange. Tonight, Gamini Weerakoon, editor of *The Island*, was voicing fears that the LTTE would resume their previous practice of massacring isolated Sinhalese villagers. With Caroline Elms of the UK High Commission, I discussed the relatively well-disciplined behaviour of the Army in Mannar – at this point an "old hand" bystander, who was here in '83 interjected: "But news of atrocities takes time to come through."

23 June: Refreshingly different has been the opening of this year's *Gam Udawa* ("village awakening"), held today at Pallekalle, a few miles outside Kandy. A magnificent pageant: elephants, floats, dancers – all that could be imagined for such an occasion, laid on with traditional Sri Lankan flair. After the pageant, the President spoke – as usual, a powerful orator. He spoke of *Gam Udawa* being in its twelfth year – his initiative, a plank in his programme, as was *Janasaviya* – the poverty reduction programme. (He has some very good ideas.) On the LTTE, he spoke in a statesmanlike manner: he had readily listened to them and tried to negotiate. But they had betrayed his trust by starting the fighting. He strongly emphasised that this was not a struggle against the Tamil people, but with the LTTE, and made it clear that the door was always open for negotiations.

Relief efforts

In an act of enlightened policy, the Government had accepted its responsibility to feed the mass of Tamil civilians in the LTTE-held north who had been displaced or made destitute by the resumption of hostilities. By the end of June 1990, it had resuscitated the emergency structure to maintain essential services and get humanitarian relief to the north east – originally set up during the 1983 troubles – with the appointment of Charita Ratwatte, the Secretary for Rehabilitation, as Commissioner General for Essential Services (CGES) and Dr Devane-san Nesiah, the former Government Agent in Jaffna, as Additional Commissioner General for the North.

Thereafter, day by day, either one or the other would be using the radio links between the UNHCR office in Colombo and its vestigial field offices in Mannar and especially Jaffna in order to assess humanitarian needs with the Government Agents and coordinate the delivery of supplies to the LTTE-held districts.

Early on 25 June, Charita Ratwatte arrived in the office and spoke to the GA in Mannar, where the story was much as had been expected: up to 48,000 persons displaced in some 20 improvised camps on Mannar island for whom food supplies were urgently needed. Charita proposed sending them by sea through the small Navy post on the tip of the island, from where the GA confirmed that he would be able to collect and distribute on the island.

But delivery by sea for mainland Mannar, where there was the largest concentration of IDPs, was excluded for a number of reasons. The only alternative – trucking food overland from the south – could be dangerous. As Dr Nesiah put it, recalling his previous experience in the 1983 troubles, crossing the line by road was always a chancy business ("when you are in no-man's-land, the driver quite often gets shot") and politically sensitive in that the LTTE would not accept the coming and going of Government-led and organized convoys in the territory it controlled.

Ideally, this would have been a function for the ICRC, but it already had its hands full with delivering food to Jaffna by sea. And although various non-governmental organizations might have been willing to undertake it, and were indeed soon to take occasional relief convoys through to Madhu, the Roman Catholic shrine in the jungle where there was the largest group of IDPs, the Government was not prepared to entrust them with such a large and sensitive project on a regular basis.

Thus, although the need to deliver food supplies was increasingly urgent, the shape of a satisfactory logistical solution was not immediately apparent.

Next day, the bridge in the middle of the three-kilometre causeway connecting Mannar island to the mainland was blown up, and consequently the two MSF nurses at the hospital on the island would have to be brought out by boat. When the nurses got back to Colombo, they painted a sad picture of large groups of IDPs on the island, most of whom had taken refuge in the villages surrounding the town.

By the end of the month, there seemed to be a lull in the fighting, with not much more than skirmishing in the east as the LTTE pulled back to the jungle and the Army moved on slowly into Batticaloa town, prudently mindful of mines and booby traps in its path. I thought of "Yoga", the SLAS stalwart who had recently been appointed Government Agent in Batticaloa, who would be holed up in the *kachcheri* inside the Dutch fort – safe, but beleaguered. The professionalism and commitment of the civil administration, which managed to stay in place and keep essential services going whatever forces might have the upper hand (whether the Army, the IPKF or the LTTE), was one of the few redeeming features of governance during the conflict.

In the north, it was more of the same, with the garrison in the fort surrounded and the area just beyond the ramparts being strafed by the Air Force, which then attempted to drop food within the fortified perimeter. But Mannar appeared to be relatively quiet, with the island now an LTTE stronghold, save for the Navy post at Talaimannar pier. Such was the LTTE confidence there that they were now moving about without arms. Both sides were recruiting on a large scale. On Galle Face in Colombo, there was a two-kilometre line of youths queuing to join the Army, most of whom had been waiting overnight. And in the north, the LTTE were reported to be calling for volunteers from all persons, female as well as male, between 12 and 50 to report to the temples and churches – relentless preparations that boded ill for an early settlement.

Meanwhile, UNHCR radio traffic to Jaffna and Mannar was increasing by the day as Essential Services personnel liaised with the Government Agents concerning emergency food and medical supplies, the salaries of officials, the ICRC (which had yet to establish its own radio in Jaffna) and NGOs with projects in the north. Somehow, rudimentary civil administration as well as public transport services and the banks continued to function in Jaffna – owing in no small measure to the two-way radio link between the UNHCR office and the *kachcheris* in the north.

But while the Government was getting its humanitarian relief act together through the Commissioner General for Essential Services, the international community was already distancing itself from Sri Lanka. At a Dutch embassy reception, their visiting development aid team said that they would not be maintaining their previously pledged contributions. Several other donors said they were doing likewise. In the circumstances, this was understandable enough as regards development aid. But although there was much wringing of hands in the embassies, there was not much coming through in the way of humanitarian relief.

Geneva opts out

"You must be so busy with all these refugees!" The unintentional irony of that sympathetic remark by a Sri Lankan lady in Colombo served to underline the complex irony of the situation within UNHCR at this time. On the one hand, the mass of internally displaced Tamil civilians then on the move to escape from the fighting in the war zone were not "refugees" within the competence of the UNHCR statute but IDPs and, as such, nationals legally under Sri Lankan protection. This was because refugee status in international law requires that someone has fled or is otherwise outside his/her own country for fear of persecution. Its strict application in the context of north east Sri Lanka at this time meant that UNHCR could not concern itself with the IDPs who were fleeing by every available means of transport towards Mannar island, where there were the shortest, safest and cheapest crossings of the Palk Strait.

For those fugitives who made the crossing, the act of traversing the Sri Lankan-Indian frontier transformed their legal status to that of refugees in accordance with relevant international instruments. But UNHCR could only have acted substantively on behalf of IDPs before they fled Sri Lanka if it had been specifically requested to do so by the UN Secretary General. Usually, that authorization was no more than a formality that was readily forthcoming, if UNHCR had requested it. But in its mandatory restrictive mood at that time, the agency was most unlikely to do so. Indeed, as the hard-won achievements of the now defunct reintegration programme had been effectively wiped out by the fighting and the mass internal displacement and international exodus of refugees it had triggered, the reluctance in Geneva to do anything further in Sri Lanka had gained more ground. In particular, there was now fear that UNHCR might be drawn into responsibility for the mass of IDPs and a desire to avoid any such involvement, even at the cost of having to abandon the refugee returnees from South India whose reintegration we had been monitoring during the previous two and a half years.

In Colombo, however, we had a certain confidence in our professional position that UNHCR was bound to do its best for the refugee returnees who remained in the country, notwithstanding the relatively small size of this group.[1] But the extent to which some elements were prepared to go to prevent UNHCR Colombo playing even such a minor part in relief efforts in the north east soon became apparent when the competent review committee in Geneva abruptly abolished the posts of the two local staff members who were manning the radios in Jaffna and Mannar. The effect of this decision was not only to pre-empt any agency role in the conflict, but even more seriously to cut the vital communications link that were vital for the Government's admirable efforts to get humanitarian relief supplies to the displaced and destitute in the north. At first, I was stunned that a humanitarian organization could act in that way in a crisis where many peoples' lives were at risk. But soon I got over my indignation sufficiently to begin to devise ways of getting round this decision.

In an organization as bureaucratically centralized as UNHCR, even at the best of times, it would have been problematic for a far-flung field office such as Colombo to attempt to obtain the reversal of a decision taken by a competent committee in Geneva. And on this occasion, the time when the decision would be formally endorsed by the Deputy High Commissioner and thereafter set in procedural stone was only a few days away and included a week-end, when key officials would be difficult to contact. I discussed the problem with the Governor of the North East, General Nalin Seneviratne, who was particularly well placed to know what the loss of the radio links between Colombo and the north would mean for relief and essential services at that stage. At first, he didn't think I was being serious when I said that UNHCR would be closing down its radio at the end of the month. Then when he realized that I was, he was dumbfounded and said that I should do my utmost to prevent any such development, which would most certainly be very badly taken by the Government. This I very well knew, but had wanted to hear it said by someone in his position so that I could quote it in my dealings with Geneva. And as for the international community, I had no doubt that condemnation of such a move would be similarly harsh.

To cut short a long and unedifying story that said little for the bureaucratic ethics of a great humanitarian institution, the radio links were eventually given a last-minute reprieve in the form of a telex at the end of the month, temporarily extending the duration of the posts in question. This was the first of a number of initiatives taken in Geneva that impeded an effective UNHCR role in the conflict in the north east. But although Colombo had successfully resisted this attempt to write it out of the plot – save for an early and dishonourable exit from Sri Lanka – there was little or no precedent in institutional field practice for an appropriate role in such a conflict. What this might be would now therefore depend largely on the conditions and challenges we would find in the war zone when we could get there, together with the respective attitudes towards us of the combatants: the Sri Lankan Army on the one hand and its adversaries, the LTTE, on the other.

Damage in Trinco

By early July 1990, Trincomalee was reported to be sufficiently stable for a field visit to take stock of the situation in areas where refugee returnees from South India had been concentrated and UNHCR had previously been active with housing and fisheries projects.

With its views over the unequalled anchorage, Orr's Hill in Trinco town is as fair a residential area as can be found anywhere in the world, reminiscent of some Sydney suburbs, but with greater natural beauty. Anywhere else, this would be a very upmarket real estate area with luxurious villas and the like. Here there were few such buildings, and even those were mostly dilapidated: the best – now occupied by an NGO – had been the house of a lawyer killed in the '83 troubles.

Otherwise, housing was mostly of the semi-permanent local village variety. Someone at the bread shop was bemoaning the situation, saying that the Tamils had been through the same sort of troubles in the past (mostly in 1983), when two-thirds of their housing had been destroyed. Now the remaining third had gone. He was exaggerating, but obviously they had suffered a great deal. Later, the owner of a security guard company spoke of 500 civilian casualties and much burning.

Apparently what had happened was that the Army had come searching Tamil houses for LTTE (or their sympathizers). If a door was locked, they would knock it down. If they found signs of LTTE adherence inside (e.g. pictures of Prabhakaran, LTTE flags, posters), they would burn the house. Later, we drove round the town and saw extensive areas of burnt housing. Where were the inhabitants? The general consensus was that most (up to 75 per cent) were staying with relatives or friends and the rest in "refugee camps" – places with space and some perceived security, such as schools and churches or other places of worship.

First call was on the (Tamil) Deputy Inspector-General of Police Anandarajah near the Naval dockyard, who was doing his best to keep the police functioning on an impartial professional basis. But with communal conflicts about to explode and the intense and well-justified grievance against the LTTE for having shot so many of the Sinhalese and Muslim policemen they had taken prisoner, this was a formidably daunting task. Next, I saw the new Army coordinating officer, Brigadier Lucky Wijeratne – a burly and forceful professional soldier. His briefing was frank: he didn't want camps to be dispersed, preferring to put those who couldn't get back to their homes into Clappenberg camp at China Bay. He said that camps harboured terrorists and so it was better to have them in one place where safety could be provided. From the security angle, what he said was undeniable. But Clappenberg was in the midst of the Sinhalese area and Tamil IDPs would be unlikely to feel safe there, least of all in the present conditions.

* * *

In Trincomalee, UNHCR had had three NGO implementing partners for its returnee reintegration programme: the local Rotary Club, Eastern Human Economic Development (EHED) and the Trincomalee District Development Foundation (TDDF).

After leaving the Army commander, Danilo and I therefore sought out the president of the local Rotary Club, which had a house construction project at Uppavelli, just outside Trinco town. Thirukadalur ("village by the sea") was the name of a small cluster of returnee houses in a street running down to the shore, altogether comprising some 40 homes, either already built or in the process of construction under the UNHCR programme. It was an area where much property had been destroyed during the '83 troubles, so that when the returnees came back in 1987 and were assisted under the UNHCR programme, there was a lot of work to be done. Several damaged houses had to be repaired extensively and new houses built in place of those destroyed. As the implementing partner for this project, Rotary had achieved much and Thirukadalur had become something of a show place to which visitors were invited to see the benefits of the UNHCR programme. At the bottom of the street, just above the beach, there was a community centre, which was also used for the storage of building materials and to house several fishing boats donated by UNHCR to the fisheries cooperative. Altogether, it had had the rather hopeful and happy air of a small community that was regenerating.

The Rotary president willingly accompanied us on our visit to Thirukadalur. No one from the Rotary Club had been there since the recent troubles had started, and conditions were still not sufficiently stable to have made such a visit without us. We drove very slowly down the now desolate street. The old houses that had been repaired under the UNHCR programme were either burnt or in ruins: piles of rubble with charred beams. The newly constructed units were still

[122]

standing, but devoid of inhabitants and contents. At the cooperative store, the doors and windows were wide open, the stock of several hundred bags of cement had been looted, and the plaster crest of a fish and a boat which used to stand proudly over the entrance now lay smashed to pieces on the ground. Someone was walking in the ruins: "looking for loot," according to my companions.

On the coastal road to Nilaveli, there were two refugee camps: the Methodist church, with 100 or so families, and the Roman Catholic church with about 800 families. Father Leo, the chief of EHED, looked tired and invited us into his room, saying there were "too many flies out there". MSF had already mentioned the beginning of dysentery in this camp. "No one is starving here," Father Leo said, "but there is not enough food."

Further up the road, we arrived at the Nilaveli Beach Hotel, where the atmosphere couldn't have been more different from the happy holidaying mood I had found there in April. It was silent, sad and deserted save for the hotel staff. The barman, whom I had got to know over the last two years, was in tears with his small daughter in his arms. "I have lost another daughter and my wife is very ill in Colombo," he said. I soon learned from his colleagues that his situation was worse than he knew – his wife had died in the jungle some days back, when she had been trying to get away. Nobody had yet had the heart to tell him.

Then we saw Guy, the headmaster who ran TDDF, our third NGO implementing partner, who said much the same as the Rotarians: everyone had left home and was scared to come back. He welcomed my idea to start a pilot "return-home" scheme in a small number of housing clusters, with dry rations and emergency packs, but said it was too early.

Back in Colombo, I debriefed with Dr Nesiah, who was now coordinating relief services in the north, when he came in to use the radio in the office. He strongly supported my idea for a pilot project, but urged me to speak frankly to the Governor particularly regarding the need for civilian control of the refugee camps.

When I saw General Seneviratne the next day, his reaction to my proposed initiative was generally positive. But as for Trincomalee district, he tactfully alluded to the communal problem: for such a project to obtain essential political support, it would have to be seen to be multi-ethnic in approach, and it would be much easier to implement in Mannar, where there was no ethnic problem to complicate matters and the civil administration was strongly behind us.

9. The war zone and the LTTE

*Mannar war zone – safe haven on Mannar island? –
displacement dynamics – LTTE encounters*

Mannar war zone

Immediately after leaving Government-held Vavuniya we –
Mahmud Hussein, the administrative officer, my driver
Patmanathan and I – were in the war zone, facing one problem
after another. The first obstacle was a blown-up bridge on the
Anuradhapura–Mannar road, where by dint of placing some rocks
in the deepest parts, we eventually managed to get the Landcruiser across to the formidably rocky terrain on the other side.
While we were working, a small boy from a nearby village, pushing a large bike, stopped by the river bank to watch these strange
visitors and their even stranger activity. Probably no more than
eight years old, he was alert, clearly fascinated by what we were
doing and able to express himself well enough with a very little
English supplemented by expressive gestures, summarizing his
view of the conflict as: "Sri Lanka Army ... me," and then with the
hand that wasn't holding the bicycle, he made a big sweeping
movement and shouted at the top of his voice, "*INDIA!!!*" Next
we came across a small village where the jungle tracks crossed,
which was entirely deserted and very largely burnt out. But not
entirely so, as there were one or two houses here and there which
hadn't been burnt. What had saved them? Later someone
suggested that they might have belonged to Muslims. After winding our way backwards and forwards over very bumpy side roads
in dense dry jungle, we eventually arrived at a large clearing in
the midst of the jungle, with water tanks and a church. This was
"Madhu Church", the historic Roman Catholic shrine. It had long
been widely respected by Sinhalese Buddhists and other religions,
and in normal times its annual festivals attracted large numbers of
pilgrims, for whom there was accommodation for up to 3000.
    IDPs were everywhere (from 7000 to 9000 according to the priest
we spoke to). Since the arrival of the Army in the neighbouring area
in recent days, they had been streaming into Madhu and then
moving on to points from which they could cross to Pesalai, the

[124]

fishing village on the northern coast of Mannar island which was the final point of departure across the Palk Strait to Rameswaram in South India (some 3000 persons had recently left that way).

Finally, we arrived at Talladi, the Army camp on the mainland, commanding the three-kilometre causeway to the island. There we met Brigadier Upali Karunaratne, a friendly Sandhurst-trained officer, who had pushed up from the south at the head of his troops. Soon the Bishop of Mannar came and together with Patrick Vial of MSF, we all discussed the situation. Thereafter, we were dropped in the middle of the causeway, at the bridge – or rather what was left of it after the LTTE had blown it up. A boat pushed out from the far shore and we clambered aboard. The Bishop pointed up at the wiring running along the side of the causeway. "Mines," he said, making a wry face.

Shortly after we landed on the beach, I saw four LTTE cadres, in Tiger camouflage fatigues and armed to the teeth, kneeling in prayer at a shrine, and reflected that whatever their politics or faith, Sri Lankans were very religious people.

"Sunny Village" (Chapter 6, p. 79) was now serving both as a small refugee transit camp and a temporary *kachcheri*. Where there was no housing or cover, IDPs had erected temporary shelters or even flimsy screens of cloth and palm leaves around tree trunks. Former UNHCR local staff members and their families were occupying most of the field office rooms, and the radio – now the only link with Colombo – was functioning from a small back room. Mr Croos was as welcoming as ever, but clearly exhausted with all the extra work that the conflict brought his way – and also reproachful, saying: "You have taken so long to come!" The next day, he took us to a number of villages, each of which was being affected by the conflict in very different ways. First, there was Thalvupadu, a mainly Catholic fishing village with a very large church. Some shells had fallen there a few days previously, since when more than half of the village had decamped to the other side of the island, from where they had probably crossed to South India. Those who had stayed did not have youngsters – those who did had usually thought best to get them out before the Army arrived, as they feared that even the very young would be rounded up, questioned and possibly sent away for interrogation at the Boosa Army Detention Centre.

Next we visited Tharapuram – a Muslim village whose normally rather quiet and sleepy streets were now bustling with activity.

Many non-Muslims were there; those who had Muslim friends were staying and leaving their movable possessions with them, while those who hadn't were selling their belongings to traders. As during the '83 troubles, the Muslims were feeling sufficiently secure with the Government to stay put rather than follow the general move across the Palk Strait. Finally, we arrived at Pesalai, the large fishing village and strong Catholic centre on the north coast of the island from which many of those in flight made the short crossing of the Palk Strait in small boats. The priest in charge was dynamically tending to the flow of people on the move from the mainland.

Most of those questioned had fled with little more than the clothes they stood up in, and quite a number were in pretty poor shape, especially those who had been several days en route from the east. There was a high proportion of families headed by the mother, suggesting that the father had either been killed or stayed behind to fight. In any event, most were fleeing the fighting, many having stories of shelling near their villages and some of bombing and strafing from helicopter gunships. But mention was also made of the fear that the Army might use against the Tamil civilian population the cruel methods said to have been used against the Sinhalese JVP supporters in the South.

The priest said that on average, 15 boats were leaving Pesalai daily between 1800 and 2000 hrs, with small trawlers taking 30 adults and glass fibre boats 20, at an average daily departure rate of 1000 persons. He also spoke about the anxiety of parents with young children as to what would happen to them when the Army arrived, as very young boys were joining the LTTE and the Army tended to consider youngsters as potential, or even actual military personnel. He pleaded strongly for assurances that the military would not take children away for questioning. (I took this matter up with Brigadier Karunaratne when I passed by Talladi camp on the way back to Colombo – sadly without success, as he reiterated that youngsters had to be questioned, and if suspected of LTTE activities, taken away).

Safe haven on Mannar island?

The situation was nightmarish: fleeing Tamils from throughout the north east were already streaming towards departure points to get on boats for the crossing to India (12,000 were estimated to have left so far, and many more were on the way).

Government forces were consolidating on the mainland opposite the island with the declared intention of taking it with full force and then commencing "clearing operations". The worst scenario was that there might be one or more major engagements there between Government forces and the LTTE. If that happened, everybody – displaced mainlanders as well as islanders (with the probable exception of the Muslims) – would rush en masse to the departure points, desperately trying to board boats for India. All the dangers of "boat people" type movements anywhere in the world were already present – overloading, some unseaworthy boats and many passengers who couldn't swim and other hazards – all of which risked being magnified into a large-scale humanitarian disaster with heavy loss of life. A less dramatically calamitous, yet nonetheless dire, scenario would be if, for one reason or another, there was no fighting on the island, but the Army started "clearing operations" which got out of hand and triggered many, if not mass, departures.

Following talks with *kachcheri* officials, it seemed that there might be a solution worth suggesting: for the island to be demilitarized and in effect become a safe haven for persons fleeing the conflict, whether refugee returnees or internally displaced persons. But what was so dangerous was that the civil administration (the GA and his *kachcheri* team), who knew the situation infinitely better than anyone else, were cut off from the authorities in Colombo, save for the UNHCR radio link (a vital humanitarian lifeline, but one which obviously could not be used for sensitive communications). I believed that the Government, in which at least some influential elements were currently in a humanitarian damage-limitation mood, might think twice about ordering the Army to take the island with full force, if it fully understood the ground situation, and in particular the attitude of the civilian population and the likely consequences. Then, it might decide to hold back for long enough in the hope that the LTTE themselves would withdraw before major hostilities on the island became inevitable.

On return to Colombo, I would be briefing the Minister of Defence, Ranjan Wijeratne, when I would argue strongly for the need to avoid military confrontation on the island. But in order to win acceptance of this line, I would also have to have some independent support for my views – which wouldn't be difficult, if only I could get the right people to see for themselves. So, I intended proposing an official fact-finding mission comprising Charita

Ratwatte and Devanesan Nesiah, the top two officials in charge of Essential Services and respectively from the majority Sinhalese and minority Tamil communities, whose report on conditions would have undeniable authority.

* * *

Fighting on the mainland delayed our departure, but finally died down sufficiently for a boat to take us to the Government-held side of the causeway, where I was met by an agreeable young subaltern, with whom I chatted as he escorted me to Talladi camp. Then an improvised ambulance approached with its headlights on, bringing in two corpses and some wounded. "O, this bloody war!" he said, speaking from his heart for both of us.

I hadn't wanted to bother the brigadier, as I thought he would be too busy to see me, and said so as I was ushered into his office. "Not at all," he replied, saying that in the midst of a battle, a general should be calmly in command of the situation. There was then a deafening roar with a strength that could have taken the roof off, which seemed to come from only a few yards outside the wooden building where we were sitting. Apparently, there was still fighting at Mantai, a few miles up the coastal road to Jaffna, and the Army troops in action there were getting artillery support from Talladi.

I told the brigadier what I thought about the dangers of civilian casualties on the island once the Army attack commenced. He confirmed that the intention was indeed to take it with full force (artillery, helicopter gunships and from 3000 to 4000 men). I then gingerly broached the sensitive question: whether it might be possible to delay the attack until such time as I had had a chance to brief the Minister of Defence in Colombo and float my idea of a fact-finding mission by the Essential Services chiefs. Fortunately, the brigadier took it positively: he knew them both, welcomed the idea and said that for his part he would do his best to hold the attack until such a visit could take place.

* * *

Back in Colombo, there was a wide range of meetings in all of which great interest was shown in the conditions I had found in the war zone, together with varying degrees of support for the ideas I was floating. First, I debriefed with Charita Ratwatte and Devanesan

Nesiah at CGES. Both strongly supported my proposal that they make an official fact-finding mission at the earliest possibility, accompanied by me and also, if he would agree, by the chief ICRC delegate, with a view to exploring the possibility of a safe haven on the island. But they said that the support of Ranjan Wijeratne, the hardline Minister of Defence, would be essential and so wished me good luck in my forthcoming meeting.

Next, I went to see Philippe Comtesse at the ICRC to discuss the safe haven idea and share my misgivings, which were at least as strong as my hopes. What I heard from him was a big surprise: the idea of turning Mannar and part of Vavuniya district into a "zone of peace" to be set up by the ICRC was already being pushed strongly by – astonishingly in view of its traditional reticence with international humanitarian organizations – the Government of India, which was also prepared to pay. Comtesse described ICRC practice in similar situations when areas were demilitarized. But he was far from enthusiastic: he hadn't the resources (in particular, not enough staff). It would be a last resort. We both fully agreed that we had to keep up the moral pressure with the objective of saving civilian casualties.

The critical meeting with the Minister of Defence was held at the parliamentary complex, on an island in the lake at Kote, outside Colombo. As I drove through a tropical downpour to the impressive building spectacularly shrouded in mists at the end of the causeway, I had misgivings as to the outcome. But in the event, they were unjustified, as despite his formidable air of authority, Ranjan Wijeratne was interested in my account of conditions on the island and open to the safe haven idea I was floating. He explained what Comtesse had already told me about the Government of India requesting the ICRC to set up no-combat zones. I said that UNHCR had a particular interest in Mannar because of the high concentration there of refugee returnees for whom the High Commissioner had legitimate concern, the close relations we had developed with the civil administration in the district and the facilities we had provided under our returnee reintegration programme. He then suggested that we might like to be associated with the ICRC in such an arrangement, at which I made the obvious and for UNHCR fundamental point that we could not be a party to anything which might in any way prevent persons fleeing their country pursuant to the fundamental human right to seek asylum. He gave some assurance that the intention was indeed to provide a *voluntary* alternative to flight. (However, I retained some doubts as to how this might eventually work out in practice.)

[129]

Thereafter, there was increasing activity on the safe haven concept. The ICRC view was that it was *"un piege a cons"* (a trap for fools) – but that we should continue talking. My own view was very similar: namely that problems from the protection angle were immense and would probably preclude its adoption, but that it was vitally important to keep the discussions going in the hope of defusing the potential humanitarian disaster of major hostilities on the island while it was full of IDPs. At the very least, we were buying time. At the UK High Commission, David Gladstone's view was that it would be "a concentration camp", but that international reaction would depend entirely on how it was presented (Western governments were primarily concerned with the prevention of civilian casualties and so would be likely to support any scheme which aimed to do that). At SCF, which had a programme in Mannar, Shirley Allan and Marion Birch had reservations that there might not be not enough water on the island and they didn't like the idea of regimentation into camps. In the latter respect, I quoted one senior official's perhaps inelegant use of the term "free-range chicks" to emphasize the Government's acceptance that nobody would be confined in camps on the island.

The feedback from Charita on the meeting with Ranjan was positive – apparently he had been impressed with the idea of turning Mannar island into a safe haven. But I was quick to explain that while I was flattered at having obtained such influential political support, my own position as the UNHCR representative in relation to it was sensitive. This was, first, because it was essentially only an idea that was being floated as a possible way of averting an impending humanitarian disaster; there were major protection problems involved that would have to be solved before it could be seriously considered by UNHCR. My second reservation was that purist upholders of the mandate in Geneva would be likely to be nervous, if not hostile towards such innovation. To the latter point, he commented memorably: "Yes, we both have problems with those behind us." This was indeed true for most of us in Colombo who were thinking at that time, whether for Charita as a sensitive and politically influential Government official or myself as the UNHCR representative in a historically unique and challenging situation. By comparison, I thought enviously of the ICRC with its healthy tradition of responding with sober pragmatism to whatever came up.

When I called at the Indian High Commission, Mr Raath, the Acting High Commissioner, said frankly that it was his Government's objective to dissuade refugees from leaving Sri Lanka for India. At this, I reiterated the fundamental UNHCR position on the right to asylum. I emphasized that I had no instructions to raise matters specifically, but felt that it was my duty as UNHCR representative – and indeed the only relief agency official to have seen the conditions on Mannar island – to take the initiative in sounding out possible ways to avoid what looked like an impending humanitarian disaster. His initial surprised reaction was quickly followed by his saying, with some warmth, that he hoped I would continue to do so. In fact, he told me much less than I already knew about Indian intentions through the ICRC. But this meeting passed off in a much more positive atmosphere than usual.

It soon became clear that the Sri Lankan Government was supporting the safe haven idea. At the regular briefing of the diplomatic corps in the Cabinet Office, Ranjan said: "We have decided to leave Mannar island to the refugees under the care of the ICRC and UNHCR." This caused something of a stir, and after the meeting broke up I was waylaid by a number of ambassadors who wanted to know more. Of course, the congratulations I received didn't reflect support for the position I had taken so much as acknowledgment that I had obtained powerful political support from the Government. And there was the common need of diplomats for information to report to their capitals. Nevertheless, in the context of the general, but incoherent wish of the donors to do something to reduce civilian casualties, the proposal was well received.

* * *

However, the more closely the ICRC delegation and the UNHCR office examined the safe haven idea, the more clearly unworkable it appeared. There was a serious question as to how and by whom internal security could be provided, and there were problems on the technical level over modalities for entry and exit controls. But the clearly decisive issue was that not even a combination of international humanitarian organizations such as the ICRC and UNHCR would be in a position to guarantee safety in the haven; in the highly likely eventuality that there were serious differences with one or other or both of the combatants, there would be little or nothing we could do about it. And in any event, there was increasing divergence between military and humanitarian objectives for the safe haven's usage. So, by the end of July, the idea was dropped.

Displacement dynamics

Thereafter, we returned to the original plan to develop a small protection-orientated relief programme as an alternative for refugee returnees and displaced person would-be refugees, who would otherwise feel that they had no choice but to flee by boat to India. Further intensive field trips concentrated on observation and analysis of the ground situation, particularly as regards the motivation and pattern of civilian displacement in the war zone. During the first half of August, I made two further field trips to the Mannar war zone, where conditions were changing and the shape of an appropriate UNHCR response was emerging.

The journey from Mannar back to Vavuniya was a grim and eerie testimony to the effect of the war on the civilian population. We stopped at Nannadan, a village lying back from the coast, where there was a badly bombed administrative headquarters and a large housing cluster that had once been a showpiece of the UNHCR returnee programme. It was now entirely deserted, with the houses boarded up and abandoned by their former inhabitants, who had fled to India. Further down the road we were stopped by a small crowd, who told us that they had two wounded brought from a village in the interior which had been attacked by helicopter gunships. A mile or so further on, there was a group of three men by the roadside, moving personal possessions out of a house and onto a pick-up. Very nervous and talking excitedly to one another, they were obviously hell-bent on getting away from trouble.

In mid-August, I was back on the island, meeting a group of about a thousand families from Vankalai on the mainland. They had left after the Army had moved in a few days previously, and had made the two-hour crossing to Thalvupadu fishing village, where they had now taken refuge. They recounted how an Army chopper had flown over firing its guns as a detachment began to advance towards their village. Fortunately, the LTTE had already withdrawn by the time the Army arrived and the latter had behaved quite well. The colonel in charge had called a meeting of the villagers in the large church, during which some of the troops had begun looting the empty homes. But the honour of the Army had been saved on this occasion by the colonel eventually managing to retrieve the loot and have it returned through the parish priest.

Vankalai had been a prosperous Catholic fishing village of some 5000 to 6000 persons before the Army arrived. By the time we passed through it en route for the island a week earlier, there were no more than 300 families, and these were mainly old people who spent the nights in the relative security of the church. Most of the inhabitants of Thalvupadu, on the island, had left for India some six weeks before, when the Army camp at Talladi on the mainland had started shelling. The knock-on effect was that the Vankalai population (from the mainland) was now camping out on the verandas and in the kitchens of the islander Thalvupadans, who themselves were in India.

The Vankalai group said that they didn't want to go as far as India, simply because they would thereby lose everything they possessed. By staying on the island in a location such as Thalvupadu, where they could watch what was happening on the mainland across the water, keep in touch with their home village and occasionally go back for short visits to see for themselves. They said that all those who had property or possessions felt the same way. The only reason why they had left their home village was to distance themselves from the Army. They gratefully acknowledged that it was behaving well now, but believed that it might not always do so in future – and certainly would react when the LTTE attacked Army installations there – as it obviously would – and the vicious spiral of intensifying conflict began to turn.

* * *

Back in Colombo, when I discussed the situation with Neelan Tiruchelvam, we commiserated over the current situation in the north east and I explained my view that the best that could be done at present in the humanitarian field was for aid agencies to work pragmatically in small sectors, where imagination and intelligent hard work could make an impact. He reacted very positively to our proposed project in Mannar. Later, I debriefed with Charita at CGES and extolled the virtues, as I saw them, of relief centres – as opposed to camps – in the particular conditions on the ground. He agreed and asked me to contact Bradman Weerakoon, the Presidential Advisor, and brief him as soon as possible; the Government's idea of setting up a mega-camp at Vavuniya was gaining support and the issue was likely to be decided at the National Security Council meeting that very night. When I phoned the Advisor, he was as receptive as ever, especially of my ideas for using Madhu as a relief centre.

However, as regards my emphasis on the need for military restraint on the island, he remained silent – I feared ominously so.

LTTE encounters

"Baby brigade" in the jungle

We came up to an Army post in a strategic position where jungle tracks crossed. The officers were cordial, but redirected us onto another road. Neither Mahmud nor I was very pleased, as it would take us out of our way, but we took the advice proffered. Events were soon to justify our unease, as when we were no more than 50 yards down the recommended road, we saw an LTTE patrol ahead, running for cover. Then we heard a couple of shots cracking into trees in the jungle at our side. At that point, the patrol signalled to us to get out of the Landcruiser and walk towards them. This we did, wondering whether the shooting would resume. When we came closer, we soon saw that this was one of what the Army called "baby brigade" patrols. They were in no way hostile towards us; indeed, the group's commander (unlikely to have been more than 17) quite courageously dashed forward to pull us out of the line of fire. He had a no. 2 (probably about 14) with a walkie-talkie radio and some five patrolmen (none of whom looked more than twelve, while one or two might have been less and seemed not all that much bigger than the weapons they were carrying).

Nevertheless, they were certainly not to be taken lightly: very keen and efficient and obviously fearless, they went off into the surrounding jungle to see if any Army soldiers might be lurking there. Fortunately for us, there were none. The young commander was worried because his patrol had fired – though not at us – when we appeared on the road and this would have alerted the Army post as to their whereabouts. He didn't know what to do with us. As the Army could have opened fire at any moment, we suggested with some urgency that he let us continue on our way – which he did.

We moved on quickly, resolving to be more cautious in future with Army advice to re-route – and also reflecting on our encounter with the "baby brigade" patrol which, although brief, had made a strong impression. From the human rights standpoint, it was undeniable that the use of children to fight in wars of any nature anywhere in the world was a flagrant violation of the rights of the child, and deeply sinister in effect. Nonetheless, our experience on that occasion served as a reminder that in the heat of a fierce, ethnically driven civil war in which a minority perceived itself to be fighting for its survival,

[134]

such a view did not necessarily reflect the whole truth. Of course the kids involved were brutalized thereby, and certainly the youngest the most. But the patrol came over as a very keen young team, led by a seemingly less than brutal commander.

The child with the large bicycle whom we had encountered while trying to ford the river by the broken bridge only a couple of hours previously had been representative of most young children in the villages of the *Vanni* at that time in thinking – albeit incorrectly – that the Sri Lankan Army's objective was to force them to flee to India. And as the young do in such situations the world over, they wanted as soon as possible to join the force which was fighting the just cause of defending their homes. Unlike in many other places, particularly in the east, I would have been surprised if anyone in that particular patrol had been forcibly conscripted. Evidently, there were several facets to the truth.

A patrol on Mannar island

When we had problems with soft sand on the dunes, we noticed an LTTE patrol approaching. It was made up of seasoned veterans, most of whom were in their twenties and carrying either RPGs or sub-machine guns.

We had no trouble with them, as they kept their distance save for sending over a rather taciturn cadre to help drive us out of the soft sand. Aziz got out and the cadre got in. Once behind the wheel, he accelerated rapidly and the vehicle shot forward. Our "saviour" gave a shy grin, as he slung his automatic rifle back over his shoulder and trudged off along the beach to rejoin the rest of the patrol. Later I took a group photo of them, which they quite liked. But our guide was not so fortunate, as they called him over and evidently he was in trouble. When we caught up with him, he was nervous and rather crestfallen, explaining that he would be punished for having brought foreigners such as ourselves into a restricted area. But when he said his sentence was "one month's cooking for the LTTE", he joined in as we all burst out laughing.

Area leadership in Mannar

I met Suresh, the political leader for Mannar, and two of his colleagues. I explained that UNHCR wanted to start a small relief programme that would take some of the pressure off the people to leave, particularly with the objective of avoiding civilian casualties, but that this would require military restraint on sides. At this point, I waited for the outburst I anticipated. And sure enough, it came – although it was not delivered aggressively: the Government had been murdering Muslims in the east and saying it was the LTTE just in order to get arms from the Middle East.

There was quite a lot of hot comment of this nature. The LTTE didn't like the idea of a safe haven because they thought that the Government would use it to trick them by letting large numbers of displaced persons onto the island – and then attack it. They didn't want people to go to India, but to stay and come to terms with the situation. Nor did they want any part of the country to be given a special status. As to my proposal for limited humanitarian relief, they liked it: "*a little!*" In other words, they would tolerate it. I knew that this was all we were likely to get out of them at that stage, but it was enough for us to start putting a programme together.

I also raised the proposal for a fact-finding mission by Charita in his capacity as Commissioner General for Essential Services, to let him see relief needs for himself at first hand. Suresh and his colleagues had obviously known that this question would be coming up and had taken advice from on high. "No" they said. They had no objection to Charita himself, but they feared that the Government would use any such move for propaganda purposes by saying that they had sent a representative to the island.

Mission to Jaffna

Despite the Government forces now beleaguered in bases on the outskirts (the Army in the fort, the Navy in Karainagar and the Air Force at Pallaly), Jaffna town was the LTTE's stronghold – a base from which its leadership controlled the rest of the peninsula and other areas in the north east. While it had a developed structure of military commanders and political leaders in such areas with some measure of operational autonomy, it was in Jaffna that the major decisions were taken.

The local leaders in Mannar were becoming increasingly uneasy about the relief programme in general, and in particular the provision of temporary shelters in the centre at Madhu. They evidently feared that shortcomings might have negative repercussions on their political control in the villages. It therefore seemed necessary for us to go to Jaffna and put our case to the top leadership – a sensitive move in the current state of the fighting in the north. This did not upset the local leaders, as I had feared it might – quite the contrary: they were glad to be relieved of a tricky political question.

Getting to Jaffna – through what was for the time being the largely deserted arena of the war zone – was not that difficult. With Patmanathan driving, Binod and I pushed off as unobtrusively as possible through the dense dry forest north of Madhu along the western coastal road to Pooneryn. The landscape was flat: sandy soil with scrub, punctuated occasionally with erect and austere palmyrahs, growing either alone or in small clumps. Traditionally the crossroads for traffic from Jaffna across the lagoon and over to the east below the strategic entry to the peninsula at Elephant Pass, Pooneryn was now a rather miserable memorial of more tranquil and prosperous days. Some magnificent shade trees survived in the middle of the village, but otherwise it was scruffy, with little left of the small seventeenth-century Dutch fort except some blown-up ramparts lying sadly in the middle of its stagnant moat. Of course the ferry service across the lagoon was no longer operating, though individual traders and others were getting across during the night.

Eastwards on the southern edge of the great Jaffna lagoon was Paranthan – a small trading centre on the Colombo–Jaffna road south of Elephant Pass. Paranthan had witnessed heavy fighting on the resumption of hostilities in June and the Army post had been overrun by the LTTE. The few shops that had been built in permanent materials were now either heaps of rubble or contortions of reinforced concrete posts. Overhead electric cables had fallen down and lay in twisted knots – grim sculptures of war. All of us felt relieved at getting away from such a hauntingly devastated place as we continued towards the east coast. By now we had reached a part of the lagoon which was dry: a brown landscape of sand and occasionally clay, dotted with scrub bushes.

Clumps of tall palmyrahs on the horizon marked the distant shore to the south of Jaffna. We followed the tracks in the sand, turning this way and that and accelerating in patches where it was soft, while a very long and sinuous line of cyclists heavily loaded with jerrycans was winding its way towards us from the direction of Jaffna (mostly itinerant vendors carrying diesel smuggled from India for sale at a handsome profit in the interior to the south of the peninsula). All seemed fairly quiet when we drove up out of the bed of the lagoon and onto the straight metalled road which led towards Jaffna town. But as we passed through the built-up area, we saw the people in the streets looking up at the sky, where there was an Air Force chopper flying over at about 3000 feet, leaving behind it a trail of some white substance. Just what this was we were soon to see, as small pieces of paper began to float down into the street like snowflakes. We stopped by a large man who was trying to catch them. Before rushing forward to grab another, he handed us one of the notices.

FINAL WARNING

THE SECURITY FORCES ARE NOW CLOSING IN ON ALL TERRORIST POSITIONS ... DO NOT DELAY; GET OUT NOW AND AVOID GETTING KILLED ... HURRY MOVE OUT NOW.

(sgd) SECURITY FORCES

So much for the seeming quiet of Jaffna, which now seemed more like the calm before the storm.

We drove straight to what we expected to be the bombed-out remains of the UNHCR field office at Nallur, near the Kandaswamy temple. But despite the ICRC report that it had suffered a direct hit a month back, it was still standing and indeed looked in reasonable condition, except for the window panes and ceiling panels which had been blown out by blast. We sent for Ashokumar, the courageous colleague who lived nearby and who had stayed on to man the field office radio which had been discontinued since the reported bombing of the field office. He explained that the bomb had in fact fallen in the next but one compound and hadn't caused much more damage than we could now see for ourselves.

After contacting the ICRC, we went in search of Anton Alfred, the Government Agent. When I had met him in Colombo the previous month during one of his periodic visits on a returning ICRC food boat from Kankesanthurai harbour, he had described one of the most strenuous experiences a civil administrator had to face anywhere in the world: keeping essential public services going in times of insurgency, when rebel forces had taken over, but the link with the central Government remained – albeit only tenuously. He had then spoken with tears in his eyes of the effects of the aerial bombing on the civilian population and how on 5 August he had seen the first child casualties: six of them up to 13 years of age, stretched out on the hospital floor – he had thought they were asleep.

Government food supplies were getting through to Jaffna – very much to the credit of Essential Services and the ICRC. The LTTE didn't interfere with food distribution, which he and his *kachcheri* team handled through the Multi Purpose Cooperative Societies network. The GA described their position as one of "negative popularity" – in reaction to Government policy and particularly the aerial bombing. When I told him of the bombing of our field office on the previous Sunday, he was badly shocked, especially since his essential and humanitarian services work largely depended on the radio link with Colombo which it had provided (ICRC regulations did not permit their radio to be used for other than their own purposes).

We had some difficulty in finding him on this occasion, as he was no longer living in the official Residency but staying with some colleagues in a safer place. When we caught up with him, he greeted us very warmly. But when we gave him the warning notice dropped by the chopper a few hours earlier, he seemed dismayed. The position of the GA in Jaffna was very special – more complex than in Mannar, where his counterpart had a pivotal function in the life of his district, whichever side was in control. Anton Alfred was popular with the people in Jaffna, because of his influence with the central Government in keeping essential services going. With the LTTE, he had a good relationship, but kept his distance – as ever, the position of GAs in the north throughout the conflict.

Binod and I ate and slept in the office, Patmanathan with his relatives in the town. All of us were tired after the strenuous day's travelling, but slept well, aroused only by the sound of an Air Force plane, which fortunately didn't drop any bombs.

* * *

While waiting for an appointment for the requested meeting at leadership level, we took the opportunity to visit the war-scarred city, where a white UNHCR Landcruiser with big blue UN markings had not been seen since the outbreak of hostilities.

In several respects, Jaffna was strongly reminiscent of early childhood experiences of the London *blitz* in 1940: the debris of bombed houses and office buildings right and left, but cheerful courageous people on the streets. The downtown commercial area was devastated – as were the areas surrounding the fort, although the latter was more understandable in view of the efforts of the security forces to relieve the beleaguered Government garrison inside it. It was widely believed that there were from 800 to 1000 civilian casualties, and sources always hastened to add that there would have been many more but for the "bunkers" – mostly home-made air raid shelters in the compounds or gardens, to which each family retreated at the sound of Air Force planes – again like London in 1940.

The casualties had not only been human: Jaffna had lost much of its architectural heritage dating from the Dutch colonial period. I hadn't realized that there had been so many spacious Dutch villas until I saw remains of the unmistakeable brickwork in the devastated areas surrounding the fort.

Apart from essential services – the most important of which was Government-supplied food, delivered mostly by ICRC food boats and distributed by the GA – the civil administration was hardly functioning. Some food was also getting through on lorries driving up from Vavuniya, which took the road around the lagoon, but that route would shortly become impassable with the rising water level at the onset of the monsoon. The banks were not open: pensioners, of whom there were many in Jaffna, had been unpaid for four months, although Government servants were paid by cheques which could be cashed with traders – sometimes at a discount as high as 5 or 6 per cent. With the "quit Jaffna" notices being dropped by the Air Force, it now seemed unlikely that the banks would re-open shortly, as had been planned. Departures were on the increase especially from the middle and upper middle classes, who were trying to get their children out.

* * *

When our meeting eventually came, it was with "Yogi" Yogaratnam, at that time Secretary General of the Popular Front for the Liberation of the Tamils (PFLT), the LTTE political wing. Previously, he had headed the team in the negotiations with the Government aimed at bringing the LTTE back into the political mainstream which had started in early 1989 and continued until the outbreak of hostilities in June 1990. He also dealt with external relations, functioning in some respects as foreign minister.

Binod and I duly attended at the LTTE reception compound, rather tastefully laid out with a small, round, thatched structure in the centre which was open at the sides and contained a conference table and chairs. There was a definitely non-military atmosphere;

most personnel there were in civilian clothes and courteous and friendly. After a while Yogi arrived in a blue Pajero, which he drove himself, accompanied by a single bodyguard. Unlike the other cadres around the compound, they were both in tiger-stripe fatigues. I had seen photos of him in the Colombo press on a number of occasions when he had been leading the LTTE delegation to the ultimately unsuccessful talks with the Government, and so was prepared for someone who was intelligent and probably in his mid-twenties. He carried himself well, with a certain modesty and mildness of manner, apologizing for being late as he greeted us and we sat down at the table.

I opened up, in essence saying that we had come not because of any problems with the LTTE leadership in Mannar, but in order to be quite sure that there were no misunderstandings about who we were and what we were trying to achieve: we were the UN with all its advantages and disadvantages, UNHCR with the resource limitations inevitable in its present period of worldwide financial crisis and, finally, motivated UN humanitarian fieldworkers, who already knew Mannar and wanted to help the people who were caught in the conflict there. As such, we needed the full under-standing and support of the LTTE to establish our essentially neutral operational role. He listened attentively throughout, occa-sionally asking a question, giving the impression that we were making a good case and had his support. At the end, he asked if we had our lorries clearly marked and said that he would want to speak to the area commanders.[1] Binod and I drove off, filled with cautious optimism that we had achieved what we came to do: henceforth it would be unlikely that there would be significant ambiguities in the attitude of the local leadership in Mannar towards us or our programme there.

* * *

On the way back, we reached Madhu by lunchtime, where Danilo had laid on a great meal of wild boar and elk. He came with us to Anuradhapura, where we caught up with the logistics team of Aziz and Nihal. But we were all tired and fairly on edge – I'd left my last bottle of scotch in Jaffna with Anton Alfred, whose need was greater than ours.

10. Engagement in Mannar, controversy in Geneva

Innovative engagement – mines – monsoon logistics – expulsion of Muslims – Army takes Mannar island – resignation of High Commissioner – challenge and controversy

Innovative engagement

> In Colombo, they talk a lot about protection without saying what it is.

With its implication that we didn't really know what protection was, nor indeed what we were doing, the above observation typified much of the carping criticism that UNHCR Colombo faced in Geneva when putting together its innovative programme in response to the protection challenge in northern Sri Lanka in the early part of *Eelam War II.* But in reality, by August 1990, we were six weeks into the war and had benefited from close observation and analysis of displacement dynamics during several field trips in the war zone. We thus had a very clear idea of what was needed there in the way of protection, and indeed how to go about delivering it.

The highly volatile and fierce hostilities of the early days had by then stabilized somewhat into conditions of low-intensity conflict on the Mannar/Vavuniya front. As a result, both security conditions for the affected Tamil civilian population and the nature of their humanitarian needs had changed sufficiently for a relief organization such as UNHCR, which already knew the ground well, to be able to consider a number of protection-orientated initiatives on their behalf.

As regards security, the overall reality as ever was that, without military support on a decisive scale, neither UNHCR nor any other humanitarian agency could be in a position to provide assurances for the physical safety of Tamil civilians in the war zone, whether they were refugee returnees, internally displaced persons or endangered local residents. This had been one of the conclusions of the intensive study in July of the very tentative proposal to use Mannar

[142]

island as a safe haven. It had since been vindicated by the experience of displaced groups in the war zone asking for assurance that it was safe for them to return to their villages. As experienced fieldworkers, we knew that we could not possibly give any such advice, simply because the dynamics of the conflict were too volatile for prediction. The highly dangerous situations into which it would lead could well be imagined. For example, the local commander on one side might say that a village would not be attacked, but he might then be killed or replaced, or the other side might take provocative action there – which in the nature of such a conflict would be very likely sooner or later. Moreover, there might be a top-level political decision involving a change in the direction and intensity of the war, the effect of which would be to override all previous undertakings that might impede implementation of the new policy.

Nevertheless, the ground situation in Mannar was now such that there were several places sufficiently removed from the principal areas of engagement to provide some relative and temporary measure of safety – a development of particular importance in relation to the changing motivation of the mass of displaced Tamil civilians. Thus, although they were still in danger and on the move, there were now fewer of them and they were less desperate to flee. This was partly because many families with young boys whom they feared the Army would interrogate – or worse – had already crossed the Palk Strait to the security of South India. But it was also because many of those who still remained but had not yet been directly affected by the fighting were reluctant to flee headlong to India or beyond. Rather they wished to move no further from their homes than the immediate situation demanded, and to find somewhere with a relative degree of safety from which they could watch the changing security situation in their own localities, and particularly in their own villages; they hoped to be able to keep an eye on their property and possessions and during quiet periods, even make short trips back home to take the temperature. This was particularly noticeable among those from the rich farmland around Adampan and the prosperous fishing villages of the mainland littoral, as in the example of Vankalai (Chapter. 9, pp. 132–3).

Altogether, such elements argued against the setting up of camps in the traditional sense, in which civilians in flight were more or less confined and controlled in a delimited area. They favoured a flexible system of centres where essential relief items such as temporary shelter, water, health care and most importantly food were provided at key points along the strategic route for the movement of the displaced who were fleeing the country. Moreover, in line with the conventional wisdom that, from the outset of a refugee situation, the possibility of voluntary repatriation for all or part of a group should at all times be kept under active review, these centres would also be available for refugees eventually returning from India. The displaced people could move into these centres, and stay indefinitely or leave entirely on their own judgement of the changing local security situation. This was the core concept of what soon came to be known as "open relief centres" (ORCs), which distinguished them on the one hand from safe havens or protected areas which the inhabitants were encouraged to remain in or enter on the basis of some form of international assurance as to security, and on the other from enclosed areas controlled by government authorities, whether civil or military, which were in effect, even if not in name, concentration camps.

All that the very meagre funds available for Sri Lanka from the unexpended balance of the previous programme would permit were two such centres sited at the principal junctions on the refugee route: on the mainland at Madhu, the traditional Roman Catholic shrine at the crossroads of the tracks through the dense jungle to the coast, and at Pesalai, a fishing village on the northern coast of Mannar island which was the principal point for crossing the Palk Strait to South India.

Food – the assurance of regular supplies and the capacity to establish buffer stocks for periods when regular convoy deliveries were disrupted by fighting in areas along the supply routes – was fundamental to the functioning of the centres. Ironically, there was some measure of common interest between the combatants in ensuring food supplies for the destitute displaced Tamils who were passing through or congregating there, as if they went hungry they would be sure to flee to South India, which did not suit the respective political objectives of either side. The LTTE wanted the Tamils to stay and face up to the war, while for its part the Government, for reasons of both national politics and relations with the international community, also did not want the Tamils to flee aboard. And as it had sufficient supplies of food in the south, greatly to its credit – and shrewdly in its interest – it had accepted the responsibility to feed them. As regards the centre at Pesalai, food delivery was not a problem, as the Government's Essential Services could send food barges to Mannar island. But deliveries to Madhu, in the midst of the mainland jungle controlled by the LTTE, was politically as well as logistically problematic.

At that stage in the war, not even Tamil government officials could take the convoys through LTTE-controlled territory. The ICRC, which was already shipping Government food to Jaffna, did not have sufficient staff to handle additional overland convoys to Madhu. And as the Government was not prepared to entrust such a politically sensitive function to one or more nongovernmental organizations, UNHCR undertook the financing, organization and supervision of the convoys.

* * *

The most controversial aspects of international protection – essentially, what it is and how far it can be said to have been provided in the particular circumstances of the ground situation during the early part of *Eelam War II* – are considered in the concluding part of this book in the light of the role that UNHCR was playing in the Mannar war zone at that time, which is the principal subject of the mostly contemporary narrative account that follows. For present purposes, suffice to say that international protection consisted, on the one hand, of the High Commissioner's legitimate concern for and right of unhindered access to the relatively small group of Sri Lankan Tamil refugee returnees whose repatriation and reintegration he had been monitoring, together with, in accordance with established field practice, those Tamil civilians among whom they were now living in identical conditions of destitution and danger. Protection also – at the manifest wish of the Government – concerned the reinforcement of national protection for displaced and endangered persons which, owing to the conflict, the competent authorities were not themselves in a position to provide.

In terms of mechanisms and modalities, the principal components of the proposed programme were:

- *Open relief centres*: these would be located at Madhu and Pesalai, respectively on the mainland and the island, key points on the route along which the displaced were moving where essential relief items, particularly food, could be provided.

- *Food convoys*: the Government would provide food stocks from the south, and UNHCR would transport them on a fleet of lorries supervised and led by its international staff without military escorts through no-man's-land on an ongoing basis in order to ensure that the centre at Madhu was adequately provisioned to feed the displaced persons who sought refuge there.

- *Protection:* both as regards the permanent presence of international staff in the war zone and their active functions there. Field officers were to be outposted in both centres, where they would supervise the programme. At Madhu, they would help with convoy duties to and fro across no-man's-land and eventually, if and when the Army landed on Mannar island, operate procedures to monitor military access to the centre at Pesalai.

As originally formulated, these proposals were limited to the end of the year, in order to utilize funds left over from the now-defunct refugee reintegration programme. The total financial obligation was below US$ 1.5 million – altogether an exceptionally modest and economical country programme for UNHCR in a major refugee-producing situation. By the end of August, the High Commissioner had given his outline approval, and we had to move very rapidly with the bureaucratic processing in order to start the programme on the ground. In particular, there was urgent need to truck enough food through to Madhu to establish a two-month buffer stock at the open relief centre before the rains made the jungle tracks impassable.

* * *

During the next two weeks, support for the proposed programme grew strongly in most quarters in Colombo. At the Presidential Secretariat, Bradman Weerakoon was enthusiastic at the news of a small relief programme in Mannar, saying that it was what was needed and was also in line with the President's thinking. He promised full support and also confided that the Government would be leaving Mannar alone militarily – which, if it were true, was the best news I had heard for a long time. The effect of strong Presidential support was soon to be seen throughout the structure of Government – even in the foreign ministry, which seemed to have tempered somewhat its habitual anti-UNHCR line.

At the ICRC, Philippe Comtesse was not unfavourable to a UNHCR programme in Mannar which would leave the ICRC free to concentrate on the Jaffna peninsula. Most importantly, Olivier Rouleau of MSF, with whom I had been coordinating closely, was fully supportive and ready to come in and implement the health and medical side of the programme. Initially, SCF was not so happy, feeling that we would be queering its pitch in Mannar, where it had already been efficiently active in relief work. But with the acute sensitivities all round, particularly of the Government/military and the LTTE, SCF had neither the mandate nor the clout to run the actively protection-orientated programme we had in mind. Of course, we wanted and needed to cooperate closely with SCF and would do all we could to coordinate our functions with all NGOs within the overall programme framework. But in such a sensitive and highly volatile situation, it would not have been feasible operationally to run such a programme in an NGO open forum where essential rapid decision taking and response would inevitably have been problematic. Moreover, with such an arrangement there would have been credibility problems with the combatants on the ground.

Significant support was beginning to emerge in the professionally cautious diplomatic corps. At the Canadian High Commission, Nancy Stiles was strongly supportive, as was the British High Commissioner, David Gladstone who, in passing, commented that the UNHCR mandate seemed to have expanded somewhat in launching a relief operation within a refugee country of origin – to which I replied that in the particular circumstances where we had already been helping to reintegrate refugees who had returned during the previous two years, there was sufficient legal basis pursuant to the relevant Executive Committee Conclusions on international protection. Klaus Francke, the German ambassador, was very interested, noting that our project might encourage potential refugees to stay at home (although indeed this was not its primary objective). At the Indian High Commission, they were asking for confirmation of numbers of refugees and displaced persons with the intention of supporting us with donations in kind. There was notably strong support at the Swedish embassy, where the Charge d'Affaires, Mai-Brit Amer commented: "So UNHCR is creating a zone of peace!" I was careful to stress that we were not doing anything so ambitious, but that there would be plenty of

scope for pragmatic humanitarian initiative within the framework
we were setting up.

The new, mostly young and Asian team, which included some
colleagues of outstanding motivation and ability, was swiftly taking
shape. Binod Sijapati, the Nepali programme officer, and Mahmud
Hussein, the Pakistani administrative officer, were already in place
and Aziz Ahmed, the senior Bangladeshi colleague, and Nihal de
Zoyza, the Sri Lankan national officer, would run the logistics unit.
As a Philippino Catholic, Danilo Bautista was ideal for the open
relief centre at Madhu on the mainland, and for the centre on the
island at Pesalai, Pipat Greigarn, the devout Buddhist Thai who had
been so well trusted in Mannar under the former programme, was
willing to stop building his house on the banks of the Mekong in
order to come back and help. With no more than seven international
staff, it would be an extremely small team for such active operational duty in hazardous conditions, and with no reserve capacity
we would be stretched to the limit. Strong motivation, resourcefulness and flexibility, particularly the readiness to stand in for one
another as from time to time unforeseen needs would be likely to
require, would be of the essence. Although we would be tried to the
limit, there was a sense of solidarity in being able to show what a
UN field team could achieve in difficult conditions.

* * *

In Geneva, however – despite the go-ahead given by Thorvald
Stoltenberg, the High Commissioner – there were difficulties particularly on staffing. In that regard, the competent committee decided
to discontinue certain lines, such as the programme officer posts
and related local staff. Although not a knock-out blow, in that the
staff members concerned would stay in place and receive their
salaries for the time being, it was a serious setback. It meant that
those concerned, notably Aziz and Binod, had the insecurity of
working without contracts. Disappointing though this was for all of
us in Colombo, we believed sufficiently in what we were doing to
carry on, mindful of the fact that in the last resort, we had the
support of the High Commissioner.

The Ministry of Defence was doing its best to see that units in the
war zone at least tolerated UNHCR, and for our part we were trying
to be diplomatic. Even so, frequent missions by UNHCR staff from
Colombo to and from LTTE-held areas both on the mainland and on

the island – where Government forces were shelling Tiger installations – were causing tension with the Army command in Mannar.

This had been only too apparent in mid-September 1990, when I met the command at Talladi camp on the mainland, which was evidently trying to do its professional best to handle this difficult visitor who had suddenly appeared among them. As I had just come across from the island, it wasn't difficult to get the conversation round to the effect that the Army shelling was having on the civilian population there. In that context I managed to slip in the suggestion that if it might be possible to avoid shelling the town, the population who had taken refuge in the surrounding villages would be able to return, and so make a much needed contribution to restoring civil confidence. At this, there wasn't an explosion, as I had half expected, but only the terse response that they would fire at the LTTE in the fort at the end of the causeway, but not beyond the Bank of Ceylon building by the entry to the town. In the circumstances, this was a major concession, at which I expressed due appreciation, although it would still have been unwise for the inhabitants of the town who had fled to return. Irritation at this unwanted intervention was understandable, and at a subsequent meeting at which I was not present, I was not surprised to hear that there was pointed comment that certain UNHCR people were coming down from Colombo and trying to exercise their options for them! True enough, but the point had to be made, and I was the only person in a position to make it.

Mines

In any event, friction with the Army was developing over our insistence on exercising our own discretion as to which tracks were safe rather than accepting its say-so. The Army view was that the LTTE was controlling our movements, whereas what was happening was that the Tigers would mine a stretch of road and tell the neighbouring villagers, who would then tell us. The military would carry out mine clearing operations and then declare that a road was safe, but this was by no means certain, as mine clearing operations were open to technical as well as human errors. And in any event, LTTE mine layers were quite up to following the Army mine clearers at a discreet distance and then re-mining. Mining, de-mining and re-mining was usually a daily ongoing process, and it was therefore no more than minimal prudence to decide for ourselves whether a road might be mined and should therefore be avoided.

Just how easy it was for friction to develop in such conditions was illustrated when together with the MSF coordinator, Marie-Rosaire, and Hjiell Gottfriedesen of the Norwegian Refugee Council, on mission from Oslo, I was going by boat from Mannar island for a pre-arranged meeting with the military. The one and a half hour's crossing was made over a black sea and under grey clouds with pelting rain that soaked us to the skin, but morale was high. It needed to be, as when we landed on the beach outside the Army camp at Vankalai the reception we got was very different from normal; we were kept waiting in the rain before the major in charge came to tell us to proceed by road to Talladi camp further along the coast. It was generally known that that particular section of road was often mined by the LTTE – and we said so. This, the major brusquely denied, refused to discuss the matter further and then left us standing in the rain again. After a discussion in which Hjiell contributed a bloodcurdling account of the perils of mined roads from his own experience in Afghanistan, we all decided to return to the island without our scheduled meeting with the Army.

Monsoon logistics

The arrival of the monsoon rains brightened up the landscape on Mannar island, as the white sand beds of the wide lagoons on which one could drive with such ease and speed in the dry season soon became expanses of silvery water with fringes of bright green grass at the edges, while the sandy flats around Mannar town on which innumerable wild donkeys grazed were covered with a thin film of verdure. But by early November, the incessant rains were turning many roads into soft mud. On the jungle tracks to Madhu, food lorries were frequently breaking down and getting stuck in deep ruts from which they could only be extricated by the combined efforts of villagers who would unload them, so that a small tractor could then be used to pull them out. With such daunting daily logistical hazards, it was by no means certain that we would be able to continue the regular food convoys to Madhu on which continuance of the open relief centre there depended.

One of the worst sections on the convoy route was in no-man's-land at Poontotam, just outside Vavuniya. Returning from Madhu one day in early November, I found a scene of chaos and multiple mini-disasters there, with heavy trucks stuck and broken down and even oxcarts turned over in the mud. The saving grace was the remarkably high morale of the crowd in which people were laughing and helping each other with obvious enjoyment. As soon as a vehicle got stuck, everyone started shouting their own ideas as to what should be done. But reaching a consensus was very rapid, as we all got down together to the common task of shoving and pulling in the communally agreed manner. Evidently, a cheerfully purposeful dynamic took over in such disastrous conditions, in line with the spirit of the traditional village. I left the scene feeling that all of us who had been engaged in wading knee-deep through mud the consistency of chocolate sponge in order to extricate the vehicles that were stuck were better for the experience – it helped release some of the pent-up tensions that were inevitable in all of us living in such conditions. Nonetheless, we were relieved to get out of no-man's-land, past the Army checkpoint and into Vavuniya, half an hour before the curfew deadline, especially as the security forces, both Army and Police, were becoming increasingly nervous when the light began to fade. We pushed on to Anuradhapura, where by contrast, away from the war zone, the tranquillity of the sacred city was immensely soothing.

Expulsion of Muslims

"Not a single Tamil supports this move against the Muslims – they have always lived here in peace with us." Such was the comment of a Roman Catholic priest on the abrupt decision of the LTTE high command that by 1 November all Muslims were to quit Mannar (where they had indeed been living in harmony with their Hindu and Catholic Tamil neighbours for centuries). His remark implicitly drew a distinction with the east, where there had been bitter fighting between Muslims and Tamils. And it seemed that the LTTE were aware of the unpopularity of the expulsion among the Tamil population in Mannar, as they had moved in a contingent of hardline cadres from Batticaloa to enforce it.

At that time, the prevailing attitude in UNHCR headquarters in Geneva was one of deep unease. It was perceived that the agency's mandate was being exceeded by extending protective relief to Tamil IDPs, although in fact only to those who were suffering the same insecurity and hardship as the much smaller number of refugee returnees living among them. According to such a view, the only possibly valid argument in favour of this action was that this group was being offered an alternative to flight abroad, thus reducing the scale of international refugee exodus. As the Muslims expelled by the LTTE were in internal flight to refuge elsewhere in Sri Lanka, such a consideration could not apply. So the UNHCR team on the ground had the chagrin of having to witness what was in effect ethnic cleansing LTTE-style, without being able to protect or even relieve the plight of its victims.

We stopped at the beach where the LTTE had told the Muslims to assemble while waiting for boats to take them off before the 1 November deadline. There, we found some 5000 men, women and children without shelter in the heavy monsoon rain. Several near us were showing signs of fever and a small child was shivering convulsively. Over 60 trawlers had been promised by the trustees of the largest Muslim village on the island in order to evacuate their people to Kolupitiya on the mainland coast to the south. But as yet, there was little sign of boats arriving in anything like that number.

A group of Muslim leaders came up to Mr Croos – impressive men with their bushy beards and skull caps, dressed in white shirts and sarongs. They behaved with great dignity, bearing up under the difficult circumstances and not giving way to despair. He did his best to reassure them and then got on with the task of doing what he could to alleviate their conditions. He went first to SCF to get plastic sheets in order to provide some protection from the rain, and then to the LTTE to negotiate for the group of 5000 to move to Thalvupadu, where they could wait in relative comfort in the extensive church buildings. Finally, he set about organizing meals – altogether a heavy load for one man with little support – but typical of the work of SLAS officers in the northern *kachcheris* during the war.

Next day the atmosphere on the beach where the Muslims were assembling for evacuation had greatly improved. The inaction and generally depressed air of the day before had gone. The scene was now of hustling, indeed buzzing activity, as they boarded a number of 18-ft boats that were being pushed out to sea and heading for the horizon. I counted more than 20 such boats in a line stretching out in the distance.

This was not nearly enough to take off everyone who was waiting. But even such a relatively modest movement had spread a mood of cautious optimism among the anxious crowd. Now there were people who were smiling, some at times even laughing. Later in the morning, we saw distant specks on the horizon: boats coming from the south heading towards us – I counted 22 – an immense morale booster for the crowds on the beaches. Not an Armada, nor even a Dunkirk of small boats – but withal, a flotilla of hope for a courageous people.

On the crossing back to Vidattaltivu, the sea was calm but the sky was ominously forbidding, with a constant succession of military helicopters flying in and out of Talladi camp, as the build-up for the expected invasion of the island progressed. Passing rapidly through Madhu, we saw several lorries packed with Muslims getting out in time before the expulsion deadline. Finally, after a trip of 14 hours, we made it to Colombo, where I called on Bradman Weerakoon at the Presidential Secretariat and recounted what I'd seen. He looked worried and said that the Army had decided to go onto the island. Then I went to Charita Ratwatte at Essential Services, who was trying to get more trawlers to Mannar for the evacuation. In the evening, Anton Alfred, the Jaffna GA, back for a couple of weeks, came by the house for a drink. With all that was going on, there was much to talk about.

Army takes Mannar island

November opened with the Army landing on Mannar island with full force, involving much tension, displacement and insecurity among the civilian population. In Colombo, we could only try to follow events over the still-functioning radio, on which there was grim news on 2 November: the Army was landing on the island with artillery barrages and chopper gunships in action. It sounded as though there was some fighting near Sunny Village, which was now both refugee camp and temporary *kachcheri*. Later, Mr Croos came on to say that Sunny Village was OK, but that the security forces needed to be informed of the various locations in and around Mannar town where the naturally terrified population had taken refuge (mostly in Government buildings and churches), which he specified and asked me to pass on to the Ministry of Defence.

I then went round to the JOC and saw the principal staff officer in order to pass on the information and to make known UNHCR concern for the safety of refugee returnees on the island. He explained that it was normal Army practice when "clearing" an area to separate men from women and screen them with the help of hooded informers. Later, he phoned to say that he had spoken to the field commander and passed on instructions to do their best to heed UNHCR concerns. Good cooperation at our end – but I was deeply apprehensive as to what was going on the ground. At the end of the day, however, Mr Croos again came on the radio to say that two Army officers (including a lieutenant colonel) had come to Sunny Village and assured the people they would be all right.

For the next few days, there were no communications from Mannar. But on 6 November, Mr Sebanayagam, the GA, came on the radio early and asked me to come up as soon as possible, as there were some "bad elements" and UNHCR influence was called for. Unfortunately this was impossible because, as mentioned below, I was already preoccupied with the crisis in Geneva, and in any event I doubted if I would have obtained security clearance from the Ministry of Defence to visit Mannar island at that stage.

However, several weeks later, I was able to put together from various non-military sources the following account of what happened when the Army landed on the island. Artillery shelling and action by helicopter gunships had preceded the troops landing. By then, the population of Mannar town had long since been evacuated to various centres, such as schools, churches and convents outside the town, while the GA had been holed up in the old Dutch residency. There were several witnesses to widespread looting by troops who broke open the boarded-up shops with axes and helped themselves to the contents, which were then loaded onto lorries and driven to waiting boats. Reportedly, looting extended to the *kachcheri*, where chairs and clocks were carried off, and to the church at Palmunai, where the gold-plated siborium was taken. When the GA complained to the Army, the response was that there were only orders not to shoot, indicating that looting couldn't be stopped.

Then the screening of the civilian population began, by making them file past a hooded informer. Not a single LTTE cadre was identified, however (the Tigers had decided not to fight in the town area and so had shaved, exchanged their uniforms for sarongs and slipped away to the mainland). Meanwhile, the civilian population stayed at various locations outside the town where the *kachcheri* and local NGOs distributed food, until the President arrived by helicopter to give the impression that all was back to normal under central Government control. But in fact the situation remained very tense, although mercifully at least the humanitarian nightmare of major hostilities on the island had not come about. The Army consolidated for several days in the Mannar town area before moving out to Pesalai on the northern coast.

Resignation of High Commissioner

In mid October, for the second month running, there were serious problems with our budget (miniscule though it was) and another cliff-hanger on renewal of most staff contracts, with only days left before they were due to expire at the end of the month.

Although the High Commissioner had approved our programme, some elements evidently didn't wish it well and were indeed seriously impeding its progress, mostly by dragging their feet on bureaucratic procedures such as due processing of staff contracts and the transfer of funds, which in themselves were the essence of procedural simplicity, but without which we could not function.

These problems prompted reflections on the way UNHCR was going. While there was often the commitment and professionalism that such a humanitarian mandate required, lack of appropriate imagination, *arrivisme* and other less than professional attitudes were widespread in the agency's bureaucracy, as the approach towards responsibilities in Sri Lanka was currently illustrating. Of course all large institutions have their weak points. But UNHCR's trouble was that the frequent indifference of its internal adminis-tration was in stark contrast both with the high ideals of its mandate to which most of the staff were strongly committed, and with its vital function in the changing world. However, as regards the leadership, Doug Stafford, the new Deputy High Commis-sioner was a good-hearted, assertive American technocrat from the UNDP, albeit with a strongly Washington-centric view of UNHCR's role. And of critical importance Thorvald Stoltenberg, the new High Commissioner, was good – the best we had had since I joined UNHCR in the mid-seventies. He was thinking deeply about the role of the agency in the rapidly changing world of the post-Cold War era, with on the one hand the relaxation in tension, but on the other the number of ethnically-driven internal conflicts, not to mention the cheapness of air travel and the conse-quences of such developments for international responsibilities for refugees. In Sri Lanka, we felt a particular loyalty to him as it was he who had approved our programme and upon whom we had felt we could rely in the last resort.

Within a couple of weeks, however, there was a late night tele-phone call from Geneva which came with a bombshell that stunned us all: Stoltenberg had resigned. In Colombo, we all felt that he had let us down badly. When I radioed the sad news to our two teams on the ground at that time, the reaction from both was the same: after a stunned silence the word "Irresponsible!" came crackling angrily back. No doubt similarly fraught conversations were taking place between UNHCR offices throughout the world. Now that Stoltenberg had gone, an interim administration would be in charge and until the General Assembly elected a new High Commissioner and whoever it might be eventually settled in, we would be fair game for any one who wanted to have a crack at us.

The following day, I attended a dinner given by the US ambassador, which was quite relaxed. But when I mentioned that Stoltenberg had resigned, everyone professed to be shocked at the news – although I was sure they already knew.

Challenge and controversy

"You're setting up camps."
"An open relief centre is not a camp."
"A camp's a camp, whatever you call it."
"'ORCs in Sri Lanka don't function like that."[1]

Sure enough, the programme's critics lost no time in upping the ante after High Commissioner Stoltenberg's departure. We were subjected to a barrage of detailed questions, demands for statistics and documentation and other requirements that would have been more appropriate for a formal inquiry into a morally reprehensible matter than a small emergency programme duly approved by the High Commissioner that was meeting undeniably imperative humanitarian needs on the ground. And from the type of questions being asked, it was evident that it had not been appreciated that open relief centres were neither safe havens (purporting to guarantee the security of refugees and displaced persons who entered them), nor concentration camps (where the freedom to leave at will was restricted). Nonetheless, the programme's principal backers in headquarters – the Asia regional bureau – soon judged it necessary to call me to Geneva to help them defend it against the increasingly shrill criticism it was attracting. While I was there, there would be meetings at which the various points would be discussed and a decision taken on the programme's future.

Prior to leaving, I briefed and consulted our strongest supporters in the Government, the diplomatic community, and among leading Tamils outside Government – most notably Neelan Tiruchelvam – all of whom were deeply concerned that a programme they considered to be necessary and effective was under such negative pressure. I then left for a brief field visit to Mannar, the purpose of which was twofold: to be able to report the latest developments in the ground situation when I got to Geneva, but also to have the benefit of the return journey from Mannar to Colombo in which to prepare my defence of the programme. Since I first arrived in Sri Lanka, I had found that with the combination of several hours of enforced idleness, the physical discomfort of being jolted from side to side on jungle tracks and the pleasure of passing through changing scenes of unequalled natural beauty, a return journey from the field in a four-wheel-drive was much more conducive to sorting out ideas, clear thinking and concentration on formulating solutions to difficult problems than sitting in my office in Colombo. On this occasion, the result was the following list of conclusions on various points, which served as a personal aide-memoire in Geneva.

Broadly, the challenge derived from funding, geopolitics and the mandate.

Funding

There was indeed a fairly acute funding crisis at that time, largely as a result of "compassion fatigue" among the donor community. But during my previous 15 years in UNHCR, there had been several such cliff-hangers, each of which had been said at the time to be much more serious than before. Yet each had been resolved miraculously at the last minute – to the extent that such grim forebodings of imminent financial disaster had become somewhat suspect, at least to my mind, as contrived opportunities for manipulation practised by special interests, both in-house and particular donor governments.

Moreover, the idea that there was only so much cake to cut up in the form of funding available in the international community for UNHCR's programmes – an argument invoked to justify the decision to refuse to accept funding for the Sri Lanka programme – was less than persuasive, at least as regards emergency relief funds. (Several embassies of donor countries in Colombo had indicated that they would have been glad to recommend funding

UNHCR for relief work at the outset of the fighting, but that in the absence of a programme they had instead allocated their available funds to the ICRC and NGOs.) In any event, the cost of the Mannar relief programme, with a projected budget of US$ 1.5 million, was an unprecedentedly small, economical and cost-effective country programme. As regards motivation for an attack on the Sri Lanka programme, the funding crisis seemed to be more of a pretext than substantive.

Geopolitics

Geopolitically, there was a superpower preference for shifting more donor support to underfunded programmes in areas where there were vital strategic interests, such as in the Horn of Africa. This in turn led to a tendency to discourage activities perceived to be on or beyond the limits of the agency's mandate, as in Sri Lanka, where there was an important bilateral programme. But such a policy ignored the fact that there were many donor countries which were hosting large numbers of Sri Lankan Tamil refugees and asylum seekers and so – unlike the United States – were ready to consider supporting an agency initiative for protective engagement, which would also reduce the push factor at the source of the refugee outflow.

The mandate

Although the funding crisis and complexity of the geopolitical situation were important contributory factors which the critics were using to strengthen their case, the substantive issues which were generating such heat were mandatory: the conceptual parameters within which UNHCR existed, operated and evolved as a unique international organization with sensitive responsibilities and an institutional life of its own. In particular, the programme's unwelcome challenge to conservatively minded elements in Geneva related to the UNHCR protection role in a refugee country of origin – the legitimacy of such a programme and its operational content in the midst of an internal conflict that was generating an exodus of international refugees.

* * *

Unsurprisingly, there were tough meetings in Geneva and a great deal of discussion in the corridors before and after them, together with some signs of increasing support outside the Asia regional bureau as the days went by and the significance of the programme began to emerge in the wider conceptual debate on how – if at all – the UNHCR mandate should be applied to provide appropriate protection in a conflict.

During the final meeting, it was conceded that there was some moral and political justification for the programme. However, the meeting ruled that the legal case for the programme had not been proved, claiming that the relevant Executive Committee Conclusions applied only to rehabilitation and not to relief. This, I considered to be a technical position that was devoid of merit in a humanitarian organization when there was imperative need on the ground, and when the Conclusions provided a legal basis to support the High Commissioner's response. But I had to let it pass with no more than a comment that the essence of the UNHCR mandate was indeed the moral authority of the High Commissioner who, if he considered that he had sufficient support in the international community for action he deemed necessary in a particular refugee-related situation, could go ahead and take it – which was precisely what former High Commissioner Stoltenberg had done in approving the Mannar relief programme.

It was agreed that the programme would to continue for one year, but be subject to (unprecedented) quarterly reviews, while every effort would be made to find some other agency which might be prepared to take over its functions. The more extreme critics would have liked to suppress the programme outright. But as several Western governments on whom UNHCR relied for significant funding were supportive, the imposition of such conditions of limited tolerance was the furthest they could go.

In contrast to UNHCR's idealism and the professional commitment of most staff members, opportunism, intrigue and crude bilateral pressures were some of the negative facts of life in its headquarters, as indeed in various degrees in any international organization at any time. But with its quasi-monarchical constitution in which protection was mandated to the High Commissioner rather than the agency, UNHCR was particularly vulnerable in an interregnum, and even during a relatively short period, it had reached near-dysfunctional levels as regards Sri Lanka.

The state of play at the end of the first round of the contest between the programme's supporters and its critics was thus a draw – but with feelings running high on both sides. To the former, the exercise seemed to be more of a tendentious critique than an appraisal of the legitimacy and need for the programme, while the latter had clearly resented the robustness of its defence. The bureaucratic foot-dragging and other unprofessional pressures would therefore be likely to continue. The next round would be the first review, which was clearly intended to be tough. But in the meantime, we could carry on.

Part IV

Protective neutral engagement

October 1990 to December 1991

11. Rising tension on Mannar island

*Second open relief centre – a "gentlemen's agreement" –
voluntary repatriation and human rights – Air Force shoot-up*

After nearly two weeks of the intense bureaucratic atmosphere in Geneva, it was refreshing to get back to the reality of protection challenges in the volatile Mannar war zone, where with minimal material resources available, such strength as we had lay in the intangibles: motivation and field skills, the credibility of operational neutrality with the combatants, and the effectiveness of protective mechanisms.

"We've so missed UNHCR influence during the last two weeks!" was the polite reproach of the Roman Catholic priest that left so much unsaid when I arrived at Pesalai, the site on Mannar island intended for the second open relief centre. He then went on to describe the first visit of the Army on 17 November, when he had been in trouble because the LTTE flag was flying at the entry to the village. The Army immediately ordered him to take it down, but left shortly afterwards. The LTTE then re-emerged, and he had problems with them because he had removed it. When the Army came back again to take possession of Pesalai, there had been an incident when they went in hot pursuit of some cadres who ran through the fisheries departmental buildings intended for use as accommodation in the centre. Several families were already living there, from among whom 16 youths were arrested and taken away for questioning.

By now, the team had received two badly needed reinforcements in the persons of Pipat Greigarn, the dedicated and effective field officer in Mannar under the previous programme who had come back from his native Thailand to help, and Patrick Vial, the former MSF administrator in Colombo, who was joining us for a few months between contracts to help get the convoys to Madhu going. On the way up to Mannar, as soon as we had left no-man's-land behind and entered LTTE-controlled territory, the roads were bedecked for mile after mile with the red and yellow streamer flags of the Tigers and their political wing, PFLT, together with lines of pale green young coconut leaves strung across from one side of the road to the other. This was the tail end of the LTTE Heroes Week celebrations in honour of more than 2000 LTTE cadres who had died in action. The Colombo press had reported the festivities as having "fizzled out" – but Danilo, who had seen them earlier in the week described celebrations in the villages as "exuberant".

Now that the rains had subsided somewhat, the jungle track to Madhu was much improved. No longer were we struggling through oozing chocolate sponge, but surging through deep puddles of frothy milkshakes. We only got stuck once and were pulled out easily enough. In the meantime, conditions in the centre at Madhu had been improved with the replacement of most flimsy shelters either by *cadjan* sheds for several families, or small houses for three or fewer families. We carried on down to the coast and onto the causeway, driving as far as the blown-up bridge in the middle, where there was now a makeshift structure of planks which, although not strong enough to bear the weight of the Land-cruiser, enabled us to walk across the gap. A pick-up was waiting on the other side and took us through the deserted town to Sunny Village, now once again a busy refugee camp. For Pipat, returning after a year's absence in which so much that was so sad had happened to the people of Mannar, this was an emotional event. Many people recognized him and came round to talk, drawing no small comfort from his presence.

The UN flag went up at Pesalai on a pole improvised from two palmyrah beams lashed together, from which it fluttered proudly in the sea breeze high above the buildings. On principle, there was no perimeter fencing round the open relief centre compound. But big blue and white UNHCR banners were extended across the approaches to it so that no outsiders could have any doubt as to where they were.

Pipat quickly established his quarters in the office, where we all camped out and in the evening sat outside in the moonlight discussing the situation, drawing conclusions that were not encouraging. The Army was behaving well by comparison with the past (especially '83, when there had been many killings). But this had been so elsewhere before more negative practices had developed. We all felt uneasy about its general approach in trying to identify LTTE supporters and sympathizers on the island, when the reality of the Tigers' control there had been that virtually everyone was under pressure to show support and sympathy for them. If the Army carried on that way, the islanders would certainly be antagonized and much more likely to stick by the LTTE than to abandon them, although for a number of reasons the Tigers were pretty unpopular at that time.

We started early from Pesalai, driving into the rising sun, with palm trees silhouetted by the seashore, the lagoons dark green and silver shimmering in the half shadows, and two wild donkeys playing on the roadside. Paddy cultivation was continuing with difficulty – there was virtually no diesel available for tractors, so that farmers had to resort to traditional methods, notably picturesque but slow ploughing with buffalo.

However, some fertilizers were slowly coming through (largely thanks to the efforts of NGOs such as CARE and SCF). At Madhu, the numbers at the centre had risen to 17,000, as more Tamils arrived from areas where there was fighting.

A "gentlemen's agreement"

As UNHCR representative, I needed to have ready access to General Denzil Kobbekaduwa, General Officer Commanding in the north, as this was fundamental to successful working relations with the Army in the conflict-affected areas, particularly in relation to security at the new open relief centre at Pesalai in the midst of Government-controlled Mannar island. After passing numerous guards and aides at his headquarters in Anuradahapura, I got to see him – a stocky, broad-shouldered and athletic man, whose appearance did not belie his reputation as a keen rugger player in the tradition of Trinity College, Kandy, and subsequently Sandhurst. I had also heard that he was a very well-intentioned man, who planned to retire early from the Army and go into development work once the war was over, which in effect would have led him into politics despite his known distaste for politicians. Although obviously very much an officer who was professionally preoccupied with winning the war, he gave the impression of sincerity and sensitivity and seemed to have little of the aloof reserve so often found with the military wherever in the world. As he put it, at least half of his job was to win the hearts and minds of the people in the *Vanni*,[1] for whom he had previously been responsible during the mid 1980s. In particular, I raised the sensitive question of security in the newly established open relief centre at Pesalai. As a result, after a very full discussion, we eventually agreed on the following protective procedures governing access by the Army in what came to be known as the *"gentlemen's agreement"*, which was honoured by the Ministry of Defence at the highest level and used subsequently as the basis for successfully defusing several incidents:

A. The Army would not intervene in the centre otherwise than in consultation with the civil administration and UNHCR [the only exception being in cases of "hot pursuit"].

B. Any such intervention by the Army would be carried out under the command of an officer of the rank of major or above [this was designed to prevent unauthorized initiatives being taken by junior officers, non-commissioned officers and ordinary soldiers].

C. If such intervention should lead to the arrest and removal of any one or more persons from the centre, then they would be formally signed for by the officer in charge [this was of the utmost importance in that normally when the Army arrested and detained civilians, it was impossible to trace them thereafter because no records had been kept].

D. UNHCR's duty to follow up and request information on the cases of any persons who had been so arrested and removed from the centre would be respected.

E. The competent Army authorities and UNHCR would maintain an ongoing dialogue on the security of the centre.

F. Should the centre become a major source of terrorist subversion, UNHCR would be consulted on appropriate measures

At the end of the meeting, the General asked if we could extend our activities into neighbouring Vavuniya – to which I could only regretfully reply that we hadn't sufficient resources. Finally, he said that the presence of UNHCR field staff had a restraining influence on his men.

On the way back to Colombo, I called on him again and raised the problem of the 16 detainees from Pesalai; he listened carefully, took the list and said he would take the matter up with the brigadier at Talladi camp. What hope was there for their release? The problem was, I reflected, more one of finding out if they were still alive.

* * *

After Christmas leave in Australia, the jungle was refreshingly different, although the bird life seemed to lack the brightness of the cockatoos, jezelas and such exotic birds. But no sooner had this thought occurred than a peacock, the king of birds, flashed its brilliant plumage and was followed by several families on the move, circumspectly picking their way through the long grass by the roadside. As we drove by, they quickened their pace to distance themselves from us, while one uttered a screech of alarm and flew up into a tree. And then there were the pelicans. If the peacock was the king of birds, then the pelican must surely be of distinguished nobility – clearly a courtier of high rank. There were several on one of the now-flooded lagoons, strolling with an air of courtly dignity and discretion. There were also flocks of geese on seasonal migration from Siberia. One of the compensations for the tensions of the conflict in Sri Lanka was the beauty of the flora, fauna and scenery, the contemplation of which helped impart some small measure of badly needed equanimity to fieldworkers in their midst.

Voluntary repatriation and human rights

By late January 1991, there was more than enough evidence of conditions on the island since the Army had landed for UNHCR to be able to take a view on the wisdom or otherwise of organizing voluntary repatriation of Sri Lankan Tamil refugees from India, which the Sri Lankan and Indian authorities were known to be discussing bilaterally. Rumoured human rights abuses had been checked and confirmed, and the civilian population was both scared and alienated by the Army's practice of searching for individuals' past connections with the LTTE – an easy enough task in view of the previous long period of LTTE domination. While the civil administration headed by the GA was the appropriate channel for such complaints to be taken up with the Army, it had been warned off and was now hesitating to follow up reported cases of abuse. At the same time, it was proving increasingly difficult to hold meetings at the level of UNHCR representative–Army commander, at which such cases could also have been raised. Moreover, a large part of the island had been classified as security "no-go" areas for the civilian population.

All of this was critically relevant to plans for organizing large-scale voluntary repatriation. "Spontaneous" repatriation by individual refugees who might have their own reasons for wanting to return was another matter. For refugees who wanted to make their own arrangements, the open relief centre facilities at Pesalai and Madhu were available. But in no way could UNHCR be involved in promoting or organizing voluntary repatriation for refugees in conditions that demonstrably failed the minimal "safety and dignity" test.

As ever in highly sensitive situations, I sought a meeting with Bradman Weerakoon, the Presidential Advisor, in order to make known UNHCR preoccupations. In view of the very short time available to see him, I had put down as briefly and factually as possible in the form of a "non-document" my deep misgivings at the prospect of voluntary repatriation onto the island in such conditions, together with an annexe summarizing the principal human rights abuses that had come to UNHCR's notice. When the meeting came, we read these papers through together and at the end, he said that it was clear that there could be no more than spontaneous repatriation for the time being.

Thereafter, there were two versions of the security situation on Mannar island circulating in Colombo: the local Army command's, which reported the situation to be calm and ready for large-scale repatriation movements – and the UNHCR view to the contrary. In order to find out which was correct, Ranjan Wijeratne, the tough State Minister for Defence, typically decided to go and see for himself – a visit which he intended making by chopper at the week-end, together with a team of high level officials from Colombo.

Subsequently, Binod, who was there at the time, described how two Air Force helicopters had landed in the centre at Pesalai, carrying Ranjan Wijeratne accompanied by Mr Ashraff, the Muslim minister, and much of the Army top brass from Colombo and Northern Command, plus Charita. Ranjan started off by saying that he wanted "to receive my people back from South India" and to see how far advanced UNHCR was with the necessary preparations on the island. This had been foreseen when Binod and I had discussed how to handle the meeting before he left for Pesalai, and so he very politely expressed the agreed UNHCR position: namely, that conditions generally were not such that refugees could return in "safety and dignity" and that we were firmly against any idea of using Mannar island as a holding centre. This didn't go down well – indeed Ranjan's immediate reaction was to suggest that as he had been in the country for two years, it might be time for him to go back home to Nepal! But the atmosphere had improved gradually, as both Binod and Pipat gave a factual briefing on the difficult conditions in which the islanders were living. Both felt that they had been listened to patiently and treated with respect. And it was very much to the credit of the Government delegation – particularly of Ranjan himself – that they understood that the situation had to change.

Air Force shoot-up

Danilo came on the radio at 1600 hrs from Madhu, insisting on speaking to me personally, and then started talking in French. But the reception was unusually poor and after several efforts at getting him to repeat what he was saying, all I could understand was that four UNHCR-marked lorries at Tambani – the point in the middle of the jungle where the food sacks had to be unloaded onto tractors for the last leg into Madhu – had been fired on; luckily there were no casualties. Reception was so bad that further transmission had to be deferred until later. I discussed with Binod what could have made the LTTE do such a stupid thing, and we both concluded that it must have been an accident. However, in the evening, he phoned me at home to say that the shooting had been from a chopper. So, it wasn't the LTTE. The possibility of an accident or mistake was negligible – the lorries were clearly covered with very big blue and white UNHCR markings on top of the cabin and the military well knew the route we took to Madhu – indeed their JOC had approved it. Evidently some ill-disposed elements in the security forces were trying to discourage us.

At CGES, I phoned Charita on the basis that "I was investigating a report that ...". He grunted with concern and asked me to confirm as soon as I could. Later in the morning, at the Presidential Secretariat, I got through to Bradman Weerakoon, who was shocked, saying "this is no way to fight a war!" He agreed that I should most certainly protest through official UN channels. I spoke to the field security officer at UNHCR headquarters in Geneva, who confirmed that there should be a clear and firm formal intervention. I then contacted Robert England at UNDP Colombo and we agreed to intervene jointly in accordance with UN security practice.

Thereafter, there were calls on European embassies and Commonwealth High Commissions, all of which were shocked and said that they would bring the matter up at the Human Rights Task Force, which they would be attending at the Presidential Secretariat the next day. Nancy Stiles, the Canadian High Commissioner, was well able to understand the importance of the incident, as we had stopped at Tambani on our joint trip to Mannar only a week back.

Then in the midst of this intense activity, Pipat came on the radio from Pesalai to report that the Army had surrounded the centre compound and moved in, with the brigadier landing by chopper. The troops were said to be behaving correctly, but they wanted to screen on the suspicion that there were LTTE cadres there. I told Pipat to see that the provisions of the "gentlemen's agreement" that General Kobbekaduwa and I had made were strictly adhered to. Later in the day, he reported that the screening had been carried out without violence and that only one person had been arrested as a result of it. The brigadier had himself been present throughout and been quite cordial. But later, three more people had been arrested when Pipat was not there. Moreover, he said that the situation was increasingly tense in Talaimannar as a result of the continuing Army practice of arresting people at night and then subjecting them to torture by a ne'er-do-well lad in the village with the intention of getting them to admit to belonging to the LTTE. (A description of these goings-on had been included in the "non-document" mentioned above.) The villagers were now very scared, with a group of 30 families moving into the open relief centre at Pesalai, while there was a general petition to UNHCR to set up another centre at Talaimannar itself.

The intervention comprised a formally written protest which Robert England and I delivered to General Cyril Ranatunga, the Secretary for Defence, at the ministry where we were joined by the Air Force commander, Air Marshal Terence Gunewardene, whose principal excuse was that UNHCR markings were insufficiently visible. I had the impression that both the Secretary for Defence and the Air Force commander were decent professional officers who would not be party to dirty tricks.

Discipline, or rather the lack of it, once the troops went out on operations was part of the problem in Sri Lanka – as of course with armies anywhere in the world. The truth in the present incident – at best – was that disciplined command control of chopper pilots was weak. At worst – well, UNHCR had recently been getting in the way of the Army in Mannar. The manner in which the situation was becoming increasingly complex, with the compounding of one problem after another – the negative human rights situation on the island, the tension between the Army and UNHCR there, the Government's mooted plans for large-scale repatriation from India and now the Air Force shooting up a UNHCR food convoy – was in itself a cause of concern.

Unsurprisingly, there was much talk of the UNHCR convoy incident at the India Day reception on 26 January, particularly among the donor community ambassadors, who had attended the Human Rights Task Force meeting the day before, immediately after my own meeting with the Secretary for Defence. Apparently, one ambassador had launched into an attack in uncompromising terms, talking of "provocation", which some others had thought to be too strong. In any event, the incident appeared to have been roundly condemned and the point that such action weakened the basis for humanitarian aid was underlined. On the Government side, I again saw the Air Force Commander, who was full of further technical possibilities to account for the shoot-up. But I also chatted with another key official whom I had increasingly got to know and trust in recent weeks, who confided that he didn't believe the incident had been a mistake and said that he would try to find out what had happened. I doubted if he would succeed – either it was a crass error resulting from indiscipline and ineffectual command structure or a "shot across the bows" – metaphorically, of course, as the bonnets of two lorries had indeed been hit, although there was no one inside them at the time.

Fortunately, I also saw the Secretary for Defence again and took the opportunity to ask him if we could move aside and discuss human rights problems in Mannar. This General Ranatunga kindly agreed, adding that as a commander in the field and later at the Ministry he had always told his men that they had to treat civilians in the conflict in the north the way they would their own families. I said that I fully appreciated that, but this unfortunately was not how some elements in the Army were behaving in Mannar. I quoted the Talaimannar situation with the latest detail. He didn't say much, but looked concerned.

[171]

After the reception, I went home with a troubled mind and eventually dropped off to a restless sleep during which I never really turned off, but from which I awoke after a few hours with a fairly clear mind as to the nature of the situation and what needed to be done in order to try and influence it. I jotted down the main points as follows:

- The protection situation was increasingly difficult, but there could be no question of giving up, packing up or in any way abandoning what we were doing.

- The best way out of current difficulties would be to exploit to the full while it lasted a certain diplomatic strength we had recently acquired that derived from:
    - sympathy and support over the convoy shoot-up incident
    - the Indo-Sri Lankan bilateral need for UNHCR services, if they were to resolve their common refugee problem
    - the shock in Government circles now that the reality of events on the island was known in Colombo.

- Thus, the objectives we needed to pursue were:
    - to press at a high level for the Army command in Mannar to have due respect for human rights in the context of facilitating the Government's efforts to promote voluntary repatriation
    - *amnesty*: however it might be called, what in effect would be an amnesty for all persons on the island who have past connections with the LTTE – no one could have lived there during the previous two years without coming to terms with the Tigers – in order to stop the ruthlessly cruel practice of torturing people into confessing such links. (Of course this would be a highly sensitive objective and one that would more appropriately be handled bilaterally through the embassies of countries with strong traditions of friendship and support for Sri Lanka than by UNHCR directly. But in any event, some such measure was essential).

The next day, I got up with what was for once a fairly clear and confident mind as to what was required to influence events, which we so badly needed to do at that critical juncture. I discussed and made plans with Binod and Pipat, both of whom were now back from Mannar, and then called on David Gladstone at the UK High Commission, who was preparing for his visit to the island. I raised with him the question of possibly suggesting an amnesty to the Government, which he quite liked, and in the afternoon, I managed to get to see the Indian Foreign Secretary, Muchkund Dubey, who was in Colombo accompanying his minister. I briefed him fully on the situation in Mannar, the UNHCR position and other aspects, emphasizing that the military-style planning of large-scale return movements was premature in view of the unstable security situation. What was required, I suggested, was an improvement in human rights on the island. The Government now seemed to accept this and was understood to be considering certain options – of course he knew much better than I what these were.

There still needed to be a tempering of policy towards the islanders in the direction of an amnesty, however, and an end to the current practice of chasing after people on suspicion of past involvement with the LTTE, which was proving to be heavily counterproductive in driving the people towards the LTTE for protection. Specifically on repatriation, I stressed the importance of letting the Sri Lankan refugees in South India decide for themselves without overmuch encouragement, as they alone could assess individually whether the security situation in their home areas was safe enough for them to return.

He asked me if the UNHCR programme was capable of expanding to cope with a large-scale repatriation movement. I said " No" – but if the refugees started coming back on their own initiative, UNHCR would have no choice but to provide the resources required for expansion. In that respect the de facto repatriation monitoring mechanism we had established at the Pesalai centre (with returnees coming back of their own accord and registering with UNHCR on arrival) would provide the necessary information with which the programme could be developed progressively according to needs.

When the joint statement of the Governments of Sri Lanka and India on the repatriation of Sri Lankan Tamil refugees to their home areas in the north east came out the following day, the influence of our ideas was clear. For once, we seemed to have got our views across – at least as regards repatriation, although the human rights situation on Mannar island remained what it was. However, a week or so later, there was also some encouraging news in that direction which was delivered at another Sri Lanka–UK Association dinner when at the table of my host, Ananda Chittambalam, I found myself sitting opposite the Army C-in-C, General Hamilton Wanasinghe, a good-humoured, Sandhurst-trained soldier of massive build. Neither of us was very good at small talk, so we soon found ourselves talking about Mannar, which he knew well – non-military things such as the natural beauty of the jungle, the island, the abounding wildlife. At one point when the conversation seemed to lag a bit, he gave me a broad wink and said with military incisiveness, "We are sending Lal to Mannar."

I had first known Brigadier Lal Weerasooriya in mid 1988, when he was local commander of Sri Lankan troops in Mannar at the time of the 1987 Accord, which required them to remain in barracks, while the IPKF was responsible for security. However, such a low-profile position had not prevented him from being very helpful with advice and support. Later, I had known him when he was coordinating officer for Trincomalee district shortly before and after the IPKF withdrawal. With his clipped moustache and quiet reserved manner, he was outwardly very much the correct regimental "officer and gentleman" in the best professional sense. But there was much more to him than that – someone of exceptional personal qualities, he was sensitive, intelligent and religious (a member of an evangelical sect). I had heard that there was to be a change of command in Mannar following the Minister's recent visit, but this was the first confirmation. What immense relief there would be in the *kachcheri*, where he was very highly respected and trusted. Of course, this didn't mean the end of human rights problems on the island – these there would always be to some extent wherever the military were in effect performing the role of an army of occupation in a civil war. But if it would not be possible to eradicate entirely cruelly vindictive practices, at least they would be curbed and the civil administration would no longer be scared to take up cases of abuse with the Army.

* * *

At a meeting for the donor countries on reconstruction plan funding, several Western ambassadors asked sharply what the Government's war aims were in the north: to eliminate the enemy or to destroy civilian infrastructure? A negotiated political settlement had seldom seemed further off, with the Army thinking they had got the LTTE on the run and keen to use their newly acquired Chinese weaponry (mostly planes and some tanks). The President, who wanted peace, had given the military until June to prove their case. Last September, it was said to be until Christmas.

* * *

One day in mid-February, I phoned a colleague in one of the support services in Geneva for some advice. This he readily gave, but then bluntly advised me to get out of Sri Lanka, saying: "The programme is controversial and messy, and if you hang in there the perception of you is the same!" As we usually got on quite well, I didn't react with the broadside such a comment deserved. "Messy" – what did that mean? More a reflection of the limited minds which thought that way than professionally valid criticism of a programme for which there was such acute humanitarian need – one which UNHCR was obliged to address in the circumstances of its involvement in Sri Lanka. The truth was indeed quite the contrary – in terms of applied skills, commitment and caring, our programme had a lot from which heavily funded and overstaffed programmes elsewhere could usefully learn. I didn't doubt that such criticism reflected accurately the view of many bureaucratic courtiers in the corridors at Geneva. It was just that the ideals of the international civil service – let alone the additional commitment required of UNHCR staff under its Statute[2] – would have been better served by less trimming conformity and more dedication and imagination.

12. Food is neutral

Convoy rationale – logistics – security – non-food items

Convoy rationale

Why did internationally supervised food convoys across no-man's-land on the Mannar/Vavuniya front operate without military escorts? First, because there was no impartial military force available for UNHCR to call on for such a purpose. Second, because, paradoxically in view of the callous cruelty with which both combatants so often waged the war, neither wanted Tamil civilians affected by the conflict in the north – and particularly the displaced and destitute group in Mannar – to face starvation with the inevitable consequence that they would flee across the Palk Strait to India and beyond. Apart from some well-intentioned individuals on both sides, the reasons were at least as much political as humanitarian: it was shrewd policy.

On the one hand, the LTTE wanted Tamils to stay in Sri Lanka and face up to the conflict. But it had been losing the argument because there was insufficient food in the north. The difficulty of its position in that regard had been illustrated graphically at the height of the exodus in the early days of *Eelam War II*, when Tamil displaced persons were massing on the northern beaches of Mannar island and trying to get on small boats to cross to India. At that point, some LTTE cadres had tried to stop them leaving by removing the engines from the boats. The robust reaction of the Tamils was to say that if they were to stay, the LTTE would have to feed them; and as it was in no position to do so, they left.

On the other hand, because of both national politics and international relations, the Government also did not want Tamils to flee the country. As there were sufficient stocks of food in the south, it had shrewdly accepted its responsibility to feed them, but owing to the conflict, it could not itself deliver the food. (Even the assignment of Tamil civil servants for duty on the convoys would have been unacceptable to the LTTE at that stage.) The ICRC already had its hands full with shipping food to Jaffna and did not have sufficient staff available to take on the additional task of running overland convoys to Madhu. And as the Government was not prepared to entrust such a sensitive function to one or more NGOs, UNHCR undertook it.

The ground situation in the north was much more conducive to a system of ongoing relief convoys than the subsequent conflict in Bosnia, where the restriction or prevention of food supplies getting through to beleaguered Bosniac civilians was a tactical objective of the Bosnian Serb Army and its paramilitary associates.

In Sri Lanka, however, it was possible was for an international humanitarian agency such as UNHCR to feel its way gingerly with both sides in order to identify common ground between them, formulate its own programme on a back-to-back basis to take account of their respective sensitivities – and then sell it to each of them separately.

Of course, there were weaknesses in our position. Without military back-up, we were walking a tightrope of bare tolerance by both sides, whose acceptance of our neutral function depended largely on the even-handed way in which we managed ongoing operational relations with them. If we had at any time abandoned that strict neutrality, the entire programme would have collapsed as the regular supplies of food, which were the lifeline for the open relief centre, would not have got through to Madhu.

In the event, however, UNHCR's position of operational neutrality proved in two ways to be more a source of strength than weakness. First, the introduction of an additional, albeit impartial, military party would inevitably have further politicized the ground modalities for the delivery of humanitarian relief, as both sides would have continually been trying to influence its disposition and movements to their tactical advantage in the war zone. Second, the patent operational neutrality of the food convoys enhanced UNHCR's credibility and thereby made it more able to insist on protection priorities when the situation so required.

Nevertheless, despite the benefits of a normally acceptable neutral function, it was far from easy to get food convoys across no-man's-land on an ongoing basis to ensure an adequate food supply at the continually expanding open relief centre. At times of particular tension and crisis, both combatants were inclined to forget their enlightened self-interest in having such a programme in the war zone. And there were major day-to-day problems as regards logistics and security.

Logistics

Logistical modalities for the food convoy project had to be devised within the parameters set by the meagre available resources, both financial and human, and the hazards of operating in the war zone. Thus, UNHCR could not acquire a fleet of trucks to transport the food, on account of both the expense and the uninsurable risks of losing such a costly asset, not to mention the exposure which it might bring from time to time to politically motivated pressures from both sides.

Instead, the convoy comprised a team of up to 20 individual lorry owner-drivers who for relatively high payments were prepared to take the personal and commercial risks of working in the war zone. Convoys were loaded up with food at the Government warehouses in Anuradhapura under the supervision of (mostly national) UNHCR professional staff, who led it to the final checkpoint on the Government side of the line at Vavuniya. There it was subjected to very thorough searches by the Army and Police in order to ensure that there was no smuggling of prohibited items that could be turned to military use. (Prohibited items included candles, camphor, matches, batteries and soap, which could be used in the manufacture of explosives – but also, with no justification, antibiotics and painkillers). International field officers then took over and escorted the convoy across no-man's-land, through the LTTE checkpoints on the other side and finally over the rough jungle tracks to Madhu. This last leg was usually by far the most difficult logistically, as the tracks were unsuitable for heavy transport even in the best of weather and were frequently flooded during the rains, resulting in many breakdowns on the way. Two to three days later the same lorries were escorted back empty the way they had come and again loaded up at the Anuradhapura warehouses. And processing for the next convoy recommenced.

Convoy duties were a major strain on an already overstretched small team, with the result that initially the lorries were supervised and led across no-man's-land by a single international staff member. When this arrangement had to be revised in the light of a security incident (see below, pp. 182–4) to provide for closer supervision with two colleagues – one leading and the other bringing up the rear of the convoy – the only way in which the convoys could be run effectively was by using expatriate staff not normally involved in operational duties. This meant the programme officer (Binod

Sijapati), administrative officer (Mahmud Hussein) or the representative (myself) standing in from time to time when, for one good reason or another, regularly outposted field staff were not available.

* * *

SEPTEMBER 1991

"I take over the convoy of 16 lorries at a checkpoint on the southern outskirts of Vavuniya – the last Government-held town before no-man's-land – where Luis Riviera, a young Swiss colleague recently arrived from Geneva, has come through from Madhu early in the morning to bring up the rear.

A soldier then takes us to his officer, who in turn takes us to another officer, who telephones someone and finally says we can proceed. But on the far side of the town, we are again stopped by the Army and Police, who insist on checking the drivers and their 'cleaners' (mates). This is done as the lorries are called up one by one and searched. Individual checking takes a long time and one driver has over the permitted number of soap bars, so there are piles of yellow bars by the roadside. Nonetheless, this is a problem and a lieutenant colonel and a major come up, saying that their brigadier wants us to make a statement into a dictaphone. This we refuse. But finally, in order to get the convoy moving, we compromise by leaving behind the driver who had exceeded the permitted number of soap bars, together with his lorry.

Then, with Patmanathan and I in our Landcruiser leading and Luis at the back, the convoy of 15 vehicles, each covered with large blue and white UN markings and banners, proceeds slowly past the final Army checkpoint and along a side route into no-man's-land. Unlike the northern exit from Vavuniya, which is usually full of civilians crossing on foot or wheeling their bikes, this stretch is eerily deserted.

Proceeding slowly for two or three kilometres, we arrive at a lonely spot where four big diesel cans form a primitive barrier beside a *cadjan* building. Outside, a small knot of lorry drivers is thronging round a young lad seated at a table, who is trying to register and issue them with the pink passes they need to enter LTTE controlled areas. This 'border official' – unlikely to be more than 15 years old – is not wearing Tiger jungle fatigues, but he does have an AK-47 slung over his shoulder as he sits and writes. I hand in copies of our lorry load specifications. As I turn back to the Landcruiser, I see that an LTTE guard has been watching me all the time, with his AK-47 at the ready. He looks like a seasoned veteran and could be as old as 18.

He half smiles – more than one normally gets from an LTTE cadre. In my case partly because he has seen me around and is amused at my grey hair – at 58, I'm more than three times the age of many of the surrounding LTTE cadres.

A couple of miles further on, we see a young LTTE cadre of not more than 16 or 17 cycling slowly towards us. He asks for our papers and lists of drivers, which we do not have. Patmanathan then addresses him as 'Thambi' ("young brother" in Tamil) and suggests that the particular papers demanded are not really needed. This does the trick and we proceed.

Later on, there is a large tree across the road, which on examination appears to have fallen rather than to have been felled. So we find a way around the side and the lorries follow, swaying drunkenly from side to side over the uneven ground. Back on the forest track, with the sun streaming through the tall trees, they jolt along, each trailing clouds of billowing red dust. At last, six hours after departure from Anuradhapura, the convoy makes it into the centre at Madhu, where the local civil administration unloads the lorries and puts the food in the store.

Before starting out on the return journey the next day, we find that there is a big problem with the convoy lorries and their drivers. When they set out from Anuradhapura, the Army had reduced their diesel supply to below the level required to get back – and had sealed the tanks. So, we take this up on radio with JOC, asking permission to break the seals and replenish the diesel sufficiently to get the lorries back to Vavuniya.

Finally, JOC agrees to our breaking the seals and the convoy is ready to set off, with Patmanathan and I in the Landcruiser leading, Luis bringing up the rear, and both of us in two-way radio contact with one another. It is an uneventful journey, except for two lorries breaking down, for which Luis waits behind until they are repaired. The rest of us stop at a tea bar on the edge of the jungle, where we relax by the roadside in the leafy shade of the forest and refresh ourselves with tea, *tosai* and sweetmeats. The lorries are parked closely together sideways across the road in order to make the most of the shade. En masse, they resemble another dense forest, but of towering UN blue and white banners instead of trees. The drivers, cleaners and all of us are very much at ease and making the most of the opportunity to relax while we can.

The drivers are colourful characters, up to all sorts of dodges to fiddle the diesel and beat the Army controls in petty ways. But they have plenty of guts and are justly proud of being drivers in the war zone and doing the food convoy runs to Madhu.

When Luis and the last two lorries finally catch up, the convoy proceeds to the LTTE checkpoint, where the usual 15- or 16-year-old cadre, is giving instructions with quiet and rather dignified authority, as the drivers hand in their pink passes.

Moving slowly into no-man's-land with the first lorry following us, we finally stop some 300 yards before the Army checkpoint. I get out and begin to walk towards the post in the heat of the early afternoon. But about a hundred yards from the checkpoint, there is still no sign of anyone. Then I hear voices and a soldier comes out and waves some papers as a sort of greeting. I continue walking towards him and he is soon joined by four or five others. I hand over my papers and say: 'UNHCR convoy of 15 lorries coming back empty from Madhu.' The soldier in charge grunts with military gruffness and then waves to Patmanathan in the Landcruiser and the first lorry to come forward to the checkpoint.

When the lorry arrives, the driver and cleaner get down and the team of Army and Police – now increased to ten or twelve – begins the work of checking, taking out the seats, tapping the tyres, looking under the chassis and all the rest. They find nothing and the lorry is passed through in less than five minutes. In carrying out the inspection, they seem to be relatively relaxed. The same processing is repeated another 14 times as the other lorries come up and are passed through.

We've been lucky. With the last convoy, the atmosphere was much more tense: the Army personnel involved were quite aggressive from the outset and the drivers were scared of being beaten. Luck comes – and goes – and we might well not be so fortunate next time."

* * *

Some tension was inevitable at most checkpoints most of the time, but particularly north of Vavuniya when a convoy was re-entering Government-held territory from no-man's-land on a return run from Madhu. Very largely, the atmosphere depended on the political and military state of play, and on chemistry with the security personnel at the time and place in question – two potentially volatile variables.

The convoy described above was also fortunate in the weather – it was outside the monsoon – and in the relatively low level of intensity of the conflict at that moment – there were neither Army offensives nor exceptional LTTE operations at that time. During the monsoons, the heavy rains created what seemed to be near insuperably daunting logistical problems for the heavy convoy lorries trying to get across the low-lying flooded quagmire outside Vavuniya and over the dry-weather tracks in the jungle around Madhu.

Normally, hostilities were of sufficiently low intensity to permit the twice-weekly food convoys to Madhu to proceed as a matter of operational routine. But convoy modalities were disrupted from time to time by sudden attacks from one side or the other, consequent counter-attacks and ensuing periods of intense fighting. The range of problems during an intensification of conflict was illustrated in March/April 1991, when the Army launched an offensive to push the LTTE back from the northern periphery of Vavuniya town and jungle areas immediately beyond no-man's-land.

The attack continued for several weeks, during most of which the convoys had to be suspended, while the population in Madhu was rising by a daily average of 250 to 350 persons. Eventually, the problem was resolved by getting together a very large convoy and sending it by a circuitous route up north towards Jaffna and across to the western littoral in order to avoid the fighting. In the event, the convoy did arrive safely in Madhu. But it had not been without risk because of the rapidly moving hostilities in the jungle, which at one point had seemed likely to catch up with it.

However, operational difficulties with the convoys in times of intense conflict were only one side of the coin – the other being the evident effectiveness of the centres as a protective mechanism for civilians in the war zone in times of danger and insecurity.

Security

LATE APRIL 1991
"There was the unmistakeable 'Tack! Tack! Tack!' of an AK-47 burst 200 yards or so away, as Binod and I entered no-man's-land on a return from Mannar. A thin line of civilian pedestrians and cyclists walking their bikes was wending its way from the checkpoint on the Government side. On the other side of our Landcruiser, the corpse of a cyclist was lying beside his bike. I told Patmanathan to turn round, back in the direction of the LTTE checkpoint which we

had passed only a few minutes previously. As we turned, the driver of the burnt-out convoy lorry ahead of us which had been caught in the crossfire suddenly appeared with bad hand injuries – a gory mess on the fingers of his left hand. We took him aboard and then another man – nothing to do with UNHCR – limped forwards with leg injuries. We all set off back to the LTTE checkpoint and headed for the nearest health centre to get treatment for the wounded. Eventually, we found a doctor at Omantai several miles up the Jaffna road, who examined the two injured and said he couldn't operate to remove the bullets from their wounds. He gave them some temporary treatment – which made them scream – and told us to take them either to Jaffna or Anuradhapura hospitals.

Back at the LTTE checkpoint, we radioed to the Army post on the other side of no-man's-land and told them that we were coming, and then drove very slowly across the eerie wasteland until we reached the Army side where I greeted a rather dazed Danilo and tried to comfort his driver who was overcome with shock. We went to the Army headquarters, where we saw a major we knew who was fairly cordial, and another who was less so. Binod then took the wounded off to the hospital.

Later on, we all met up at Tissawewa rest house to take stock of the near-disastrous events of the day. Binod argued forcefully that this was only an isolated mishap; Yvan agreed; and Danilo also said we must continue, though he had been more directly affected by the strain of events earlier in the day than any of us. Early next day, Nihal – our logistician and a former Sri Lankan military man – arrived from Colombo and we held a council of war, the main objective of which was to get the convoy drivers, who were stranded either on the LTTE side or in no-man's-land, safely across to the Army side and then bring their lorries back. Binod stayed behind with Yvan and Nihal to do the job and I pushed on to Colombo to face the Ministry of Defence and the press. The former was tight-lipped but correct, the latter mischievous, with *The Island* printing a report saying that 15 LTTE cadres had ridden in the back of a UNHCR lorry from which they had killed two PLOTE (pro-Government militia) cadres in no-man's-land – and that it was uncertain whether UNHCR knew it was carrying the LTTE! (In fact, what had happened was that unbeknown to the colleagues who were leading this convoy on the return run from Madhu, an LTTE patrol had in effect used our lorries as cover to move stealthily through no-man's-land to a position where they could fire on PLOTE, whose rapid fire response had knocked out some of our vehicles)."

Non-food items

During the five-month period in 1993–94 when UNHCR international staff were withdrawn from Madhu pending an improvement in the security situation, the task of organizing food deliveries was undertaken directly by officials of the civil administration, an arrangement which was continued after the international field officers returned to Madhu, save that UNHCR carried on transporting non-food items such as medical supplies, building materials, *cadjan*, blankets and clothing.[1] At the time, it no doubt seemed a sensible move for UNHCR to divest itself of the logistically onerous, staff-intensive and tricky function of getting food convoys across no-man's-land. But in the event, it proved to be at the price of reducing the agency's influence in the war zone, as the organization of the convoys and escorting them from the south to the north required the functional engagement of international staff with both combatant parties day in, day out in the tense and highly volatile areas within and on the fringes of no-man's-land. It had thereby enabled UNHCR to establish its moral standing by being seen both to uphold international humanitarian standards and to be acting in accordance with arrangements of trust which were otherwise alien to such an intensely partisan situation.

This was of particular importance in *Eelam War III*, when food deliveries in the *Vanni* were being reduced by the Army for avowedly strategic purposes, for although UNHCR continued to press for humanitarian levels of food to be maintained for Madhu, it was clearly in a weaker position to do so than if it had itself still been organizing and leading the food convoys.

The operational significance of having UNHCR directly involved in running the convoys had indeed been noted by Charita. He explained to the UNHCR programme review mission in April 1991 that although the Government fully accepted its responsibility to feed the Tamils in the north, having an international agency in charge of organizing and leading the convoys across the battle lines greatly facilitated the CGES task of ensuring that, even in difficult times, adequate food supplies were pushed through to where they were needed.

13. Protection crises

During March and April 1991, the crisis management aspect of UNHCR's role was illustrated by volatile events relating to both centres, at Madhu on mainland Mannar – in areas dominated by the LTTE – and at Pesalai, on the Army-controlled island. At Madhu, the Army's plan to evacuate the centre triggered a crisis of political dimensions over a period of three weeks. At Pesalai, the crisis related to an exceptional incursion into the centre by unauthorized Army elements with potentially grave consequences, which occurred and was defused within a single day. The resolution of both crises through close interaction between UNHCR, supportive elements in the Army, central Government and the diplomatic community is described below.

Madhu

"Well, Mr Clarance, I have a bit of a bombshell for you – we want you to move the refugees out of Madhu!"

"Where to?"

"We are not sure – somewhere south, to a temple, *kovil* or church where they would feel safe."

"Who authorized this? Is it an order from the President, the National Security Council or what?"

"I don't think it was the President. The Secretary for Defence told me to tell you. Perhaps it's only preliminary military thinking."

"UNHCR is strongly opposed to any such move. Please go back to the Secretary for Defence and ask him to clarify the position and then come back to me. Only then will I inform my headquarters."

"Who takes the decision, you or Geneva?"

"The High Commissioner in Geneva, personally. But she would be most unlikely to react any differently. UNHCR has a duty to protect the beneficiaries of its programmes."

The "bombshell" had already burst on the way back from the field to Colombo, when I had called on General Kobbekaduwa at his headquarters in Anuradhapura. Evidently, there was something up because he had been untypically on edge, and when we ran out of conversation and I got up to go, he asked me to wait for tea. Then the telephone rang and he sprang across to his desk to answer it and said to the person at the other end of the line: "Yes. he's here sitting in front of me." Clearly, he had been expecting the call and handed the phone over to me, saying "It's Charita Ratwatte," who in turn said rather tensely, "Bill, we want you to take the refugees away from Madhu!" As we had always had excellent straightforward relations, I simply replied: "My gut reaction is that it won't work – if the Army wants to conduct military operations in the area, the natural inclination of the people will be to crowd into Madhu for protection rather than to quit it." I said I would phone him back to discuss further when I got to Colombo.

After Charita rang off, the general and I discussed the matter briefly and rather uneasily. I insisted that if UNHCR were to decide to move the inhabitants of the centre at Madhu elsewhere, they would certainly panic and it would end up as a humanitarian disaster. Towards the end of our discussion, he said that it might be all right – he would personally undertake that Madhu would not be bombed nor indeed would the Army enter it – other than he himself, together with me to reassure the people there. He might get other instructions from on high, but he would interpret them that way. We parted with our good relations intact, but both ill at ease at the potentially tragic turn of events.

I then picked up Ann Skatvet of the Norwegian Refugee Council and Malcolm Rogers of the British Refugee Council, with whom I had been travelling in Mannar, broke the news to them and we all drove back to Colombo together, pretty depressed and unable to relax and enjoy the bucolic serenity of the last stages of the *maha*, with the now mostly brown fields of stubble and harvested paddy at the edges, either piled in irregular mounds or already arranged in small round stacks awaiting collection. However, I had time to prepare for the next moves in Colombo, of which the above telephone call to the principal staff officer at JOC was the first.

By then, however, the drawbridges at the UK and Canadian High Commissions had been pulled up for the weekend – appointments only on Monday. And at the Indian High Commission, Mr Jha asked if it couldn't wait until Monday – I said not and went straight there. Unsurprisingly, he was very concerned, but most opportunely, had invited the Foreign Minister, Foreign Secretary and Army commander to dinner that night and said he would have a go at them after a couple of drinks. "India won't pay if they insist on moving them," he said. We agreed to keep closely in touch.

On the Monday, Charita phoned to say that it wouldn't be necessary for us to move out of Madhu – there might be some restriction of movement, a curfew or something like that which I would have to work out with the military commander on the spot. It seemed that the pressure was off. Great relief. The following day I called on Nihal Rodrigo, one of the two director generals at the foreign ministry, who seemed rather vague about what was happening – possibly quite genuinely so. As regards the rumour that Madhu was going to be bombed by the Air Force, he said that this was excluded because of its status as a national shrine respected by all religions. He thought that the matter could be sorted out. Shortly afterwards, I saw the Indian High Commissioner, who also thought that the heat was off, at least for the time being, although he was not certain that there might not be a move to start it up again once the current session of the UN Human Rights Commission was over.

A couple of days later, there was a series of telephone calls in the morning: the first from Chris Morris of the BBC, which was quickly followed by another from Thomas Abraham of *The Hindu*. They had both attended the press briefing given by Ranjan Wijeratne, the Defence Minister, who had said that the refugees and displaced persons would have to leave Madhu because of military operations to remove the LTTE from the area, and that leaflets to that effect had already been dropped by the Air Force. The third call was from David Gladstone, the UK High Commissioner, with whom I briefly discussed the matter. The telephone continued to ring most of the day, as I tried to draft a full report describing the situation and recommending action by headquarters.

Later, I phoned General Ranatunga, the Secretary for Defence, who said that he had written me a letter "two or three days ago" – which I confirmed I hadn't received. Then in a more donnish than military style, he tried to play the matter down: it was only "temporary" action, taken out of humanitarian concern for the refugees and displaced persons themselves. At times I felt sorry for him in his professional efforts to give a positive spin to some of the dirtier actions in the war. Most importantly, he confirmed that the date for implementing the decision hadn't been decided – "it could be in five, seven or even ten days". I asked that nothing should be done until I had been up to Madhu, had a look at logistical feasibilities and spoken to the inhabitants of the centre.

In the late afternoon, I picked up Chris Morris and Thomas Abraham and drove in the light of the full moon to Anuradhapura, where we checked into Tissawewa rest house, had a drink on the terrace and chatted about the grim turn of events before turning in.

First thing next day, I tried to contact General Kobbekaduwa at his headquarters; at the other end of the line somebody said that he was in Colombo. Whether true or not, I had done my duty and asked that my call be noted. Then a bomb burst – not in the rest house, nor even in Anuradhapura, but in Colombo in the upmarket residential area of Havelock Road. Thomas received a call from his wife, who said that there had been a very strong blast not far from their house. When I phoned the UNHCR office, there was no further news, except that some ceilings had come down and that the tea boy – smart lad – had cycled off in the direction of the explosion to find out what he could. We waited for a while, then there was an unconfirmed report that Ranjan Wijeratne had been killed by an immensely powerful car bomb, with much loss of life for persons in the vicinity. Chris and Thomas left immediately for Colombo to cover the Ranjan story, and I pushed on, anxious to get through Vavuniya before the news broke, when I anticipated truculence from the military at the checkpoints. In fact, there was none – indeed no more noticeable signs of tension than usual. But both Patmanathan and I felt easier when we had crossed the line.

Shortly after we arrived at Madhu, a crowd of some 3000 persons assembled outside the field office. As expected, there was an eloquent petition pleading for UNHCR to stay. First, I spoke to the leaders, then briefly to the crowd, using one of the interpreters. When I had finished, there were shouts of rejoicing from the assembled multitude and much throwing up of toffees, as was the local custom in celebrations. In fact, all I had said in English was that I had noted what the people wanted and would faithfully report it to Geneva. Possibly, my remarks had been embellished somewhat in Tamil translation. In the afternoon Pipat and Mr Croos arrived from the island for consultations; apparently, my opposition to the Army's plans for the evacuation of Madhu had been headlines in the Jaffna papers and covered in the BBC Tamil service. In the latter, I was reported as having "condemned" the move; I had indeed expressed strong opposition to it, but in more diplomatic language.

It was clear that the inhabitants of Madhu would not leave voluntarily. Time and again, the same argument came up: "If UNHCR goes and we have to move out, we will be in great danger, as we were before we came here. Better we die here than elsewhere." Such resolve was undoubtedly strengthened by a miracle. A miracle? Yes – a miracle: in times of trouble, the statue of Our Lady of Madhu was popularly believed to move as an expression of divine concern. And this was precisely what was reported to have happened during the night, as a crowd which had assembled before the statue to pray had witnessed tears coming out of her eyes, her head shaking and her outstretched arms hands moving. I felt sure that my citing such a happening in support of the case for UNHCR to stay in Madhu would not only be likely to infuriate some colleagues in Geneva, but also give them an opportunity to further rubbish the Sri Lanka programme on the basis that I was now asking them to believe in miracles! So I made a mental note to introduce the matter in my report with the comment that the views of international civil servants as to the credibility of the story were irrelevant. The only point for consideration was whether the inhabitants of Madhu believed it – which they certainly did, and that belief had strengthened their resolve to stay, come what might.

* * *

In order to get back to Colombo in time for the lying-in-state and funerary arrangements for Ranjan, I had to leave Pesalai very early. It had been raining heavily during the night, the ground was wet, and here and there goats and cattle had taken refuge on the few vestigial scraps of tarmac. Reluctantly, the goats got up to let us pass and trotted off with their big ears flapping. But the cattle, luxuriating philosophically in the warmth of the early morning sun, were more steadfast in holding their ground – they stayed put and we had to drive round them. The police were yawning at the checkpoint, as they drew back the barbed wire barrier to let us cross over the temporarily repaired bridge and onto the causeway from the island to the mainland across a seascape of gently rippling water. On the northern approach to Vavuniya, I counted over 130 empty lorries waiting to cross the line – most of which had been there for over a week.

I arrived in Colombo around 1600 hrs, immediately showered and changed and went to Ranjan's official residence in Horton Place to pay my last respects to his coffined remains, which were lying in state. While paying condolences to his family, I met his brother, who spoke of his decency and straightforwardness, which people outside the family didn't sufficiently know. I didn't doubt that Ranjan was a decent fellow in his personal life; the only time I had dealings with him, he had struck me as being without the small-mindedness of so many politicians, and I said so, which seemed to be sincerely appreciated by his family members and those who had worked with him closely.

Among other members of the diplomatic corps paying their respects at Ranjan's residence was the US ambassador, with whom I had a passing exchange. He was going on about not being sure that it was right for me to oppose the Government's decision to evacuate Madhu, in words to the effect that by so doing I was telling it how to wage a war in its own country. I replied briefly that I was not doing that, but was trying to protect people who were of UNHCR concern.

Fortunately, I had fairly strong support elsewhere, at least morally, for the stand I had taken from several other leading Western embassies, the Indian High Commission, my ICRC counterpart, and, most importantly of all, a number of key Sri Lankan officials in the upper levels of governance, who for their part, continued to do what they could to prevent a doomsday scenario at Madhu. Significantly, they regarded UNHCR's efforts positively. Indeed, a full briefing I gave to one very senior official in the midst of the crisis had concluded with his saying: "Please carry on with what you are doing."

A "Day of National Mourning and Public Holiday" was declared for the state funeral for Ranjan, which was held with full military honours on 6 March 1991: an awesome occasion of deadly solemnity, with the funeral cortege, a 21-gun salute, and finally the lighting of the pyre and its all-consuming conflagration. Ranjan had always been a highly controversial figure. On the one hand, to the Sri Lankan establishment and upper middle class of Colombo 7 and those officials and security service personnel targeted by the JVP, he was the saviour who had maintained the established order against all odds. But on the other, to many ordinary people such as one old man I knew – whose limited English didn't prevent him from hotly denouncing Ranjan as "very bad man, killed so many people!" – he was near diabolical. Undeniably, he had pursued a highly successful political career with flagrant disregard for human rights and the suffering caused to those directly affected and their families. However, there was the personally decent side of his character within his family, in which I had no difficulty believing. As so often in situations of conflict as complex as Sri Lanka's, the truth about leading actors was multi-faceted.

What would happen now? There was a vicious reaction immediately after the event, with intensive bombing of Jaffna by the Air Force in which some 23 civilians lost their lives. But there were some enlightened professional officers who must have been hoping for a less bloodthirsty war policy. The first indication of the future direction of the war would be the appointment of Ranjan's successor as State Minister for Defence. Who would it be, a hardliner or a moderate? The President would decide.

On the day after the funeral, Mr Wijetunge, already Prime Minister and Minister of Finance, was given the additional portfolio of Defence. A very distinguished and nice man among politicians, he was as different in style from Ranjan as could be imagined. But would the war policy change? In the medium-to-long term, it could not fail to. With Ranjan's demise, the war effort had lost too much momentum and morale. There might well be vicious reactions in the short term but they would be likely to peter out, although in Sri Lanka nothing was certain.

Later, I saw Bradman Weerakoon at the Presidential Secretariat, when he spoke well of the President's perception of the UNHCR role and indicated that it had to continue. Most importantly, he referred to the avoidance of military intervention in Madhu and of the need for what he called "sanctuarization". Straws in the wind? Just possibly, which tended to confirm my personal view that the President was – indeed always had been – unfavourable to the move against Madhu, with the deep offence and divisions which it would inevitably have caused among a people as religious as the Sri Lankans, whatever their faith. Constitutionally, the President was the Minister for Defence and Ranjan had been his subordinate Minister of State. But in the politics of the conflict after mid 1990 and with someone as strong-willed and gung-ho as Ranjan, it would have been very difficult for the President to directly countermand the move without a confrontation. Governance in Sri Lanka was complex and had its ways of reflecting political pressures that were not always apparent to the outsider, but I would have been surprised if the President did not now succeed in influencing it in the way he wanted.

Later in the afternoon, however, events didn't seem to be going that way. I received a call from Thomas Abraham, who had just come from the weekly press briefing where the Secretary for Defence had said that the Madhu operation was still on. This quite alarmed me. But when I spoke to the Indian High Commissioner, Mr Jha, he was not quite so pessimistic, indicating indirectly that the President might not be in favour. When I called on General Ranatunga, he said that force would not be used to evict the inhabitants of Madhu, but that UNHCR and/or the NGOs would be expected to persuade them to get into buses provided by the Army! Either the Ministry of Defence was being naive or it thought that UNHCR was. What irked me most was the lack of "thinking through" – the whole plan was either a non-starter or a large-scale disaster in the making in which many people would be killed.

* * *

As the decision to evacuate the centre at Madhu was still Government policy, further discussions on contingency planning were required with the Army commander who would be responsible for implementing the decision, General Kobbekaduwa. Also, another fact-finding visit to Madhu was needed in order to ensure that the Government was fully aware of the intentions of the people it intended to move, and the consequences. I arranged to call on the General in Anuradhapura and then to go on to Madhu to join Chris Morris and Thomas Abraham and resume our earlier visit which had been interrupted by Ranjan's assassination. When I arrived at General Kobbekaduwa's headquarters in Anuradhapura, he was wearing medals and dressed for a parade later in the day. Perhaps as a result, our meeting started off rather too formally. He said that he had received two calls from the Secretary for Defence in Colombo about my visit. The first had been made before I left Colombo when I was actually with General Ranatunga at the Ministry of Defence, and the second had no doubt explained what a difficult fellow I was – or so the rather sticky atmosphere now seemed to suggest.

In any event, we made some progress. General Kobbekaduwa said that nothing had been decided about how to handle the question – only that there would be military operations in the Madhu area. There were, he explained, basically three options: (a) for the refugees/IDPs to move out, (b) for them to stay put, or (c) the possibility of military operations avoiding Madhu. He said that if as a result of my forthcoming visit to Madhu I could confirm that the refugees refused to move, then I should say so clearly to the authorities in Colombo and military operational plans would be likely to take account of that fact. He reiterated to me personally that he would neither attack nor bomb Madhu, and when he entered it he would do so in coordination with UNHCR, repeating that he would personally enter Madhu unarmed, together with me in order to reassure the inhabitants. Even if a bit edgy, the meeting was fairly reassuring in that evidently the Army was now approaching the whole question with much greater caution. I suspected that this reflected the President's prompting and that humane professional officers such as General Kobbekaduwa were more than a bit relieved.

Leaving no-man's-land behind us, we saw a bare corpse on the road, with two LTTE cadres keeping the crowd back. Patmanathan asked them who it was, but they refused to talk. By the time we arrived in Madhu, Chris and Thomas were hard at work interviewing. Exhausted after a full day, I went to bed early in the small cramped quarters that served as UNHCR field office, Danilo's quarters and a rest house for visitors such as, on this occasion, Thomas, Chris and I. In the small hours, I awoke to the sound of the flimsy wooden house vibrating with multiple soft snores and through the window and beyond the sentinel-like silhouette of a tall tree, saw a sky more star-studded than any van Gogh painted in Provence.

In the morning, I locked myself in the tiny room that served as the office and drafted my full report on the attitude and conditions of the refugees and displaced persons in the centre. Formally, it was addressed to UNHCR headquarters in Geneva, but more importantly it was intended to be shared with the Government in Colombo. With the exception of a group of 25 families who had decided to return to their homes at the fishing village of Palmunai on the island before the Army's decision to evacuate had been announced, the rest of the centre's inhabitants were adamant in their decision to stay. It had been taken on the basis of undeniably forceful logic: they were in Madhu because they had fled the conflict, and they would be safer sitting it out there than moving elsewhere where they would once again be caught up in the fighting. Then there was the "miracle" of 2 March. Objective considerations of credibility were irrelevant – the people in Madhu, whether Catholic or Hindu, certainly believed it and it had powerfully strengthened their resolve. Another point of relevance to Government intentions was that if refugees/displaced persons felt that they had no other protection, they would flee to the LTTE – especially, the most vulnerable (and in military terms critical) group of young boys.

Particular emphasis was placed on the fact that no humanitarian organization could attempt to remove persons otherwise than on a strictly voluntary basis from a place where they perceived themselves to be secure to somewhere else where they feared for their security. The report concluded that the only feasible solution seemed to lie in the direction of further negotiations with the competent military authorities to ensure that any operations in the Madhu area would be conducted with maximum regard to security safeguards for persons who would be crowding into the centre. Some agreement would have to be negotiated on the spot between the competent general (Kobbekaduwa) and UNHCR representative (me). I consulted with Danilo and Pipat and then set off back to Colombo, too preoccupied to appreciate the bucolic tranquillity of the countryside at the end of the *maha.*

On 13 March 1991, I was working late in the office, feeling pretty grim with fatigue, but forcing myself to get on with replying to headquarters' multiple questions for the forthcoming review mission. To the outside world, I said I was sick, which was true – but it didn't stop a call from the Indian High Commissioner, Mr Jha who said: "Madhu is off! The National Security Council decided last night." We both expressed mutual thanks and immense relief. He then laughingly said that there would be "many Fathers of Success", both in the embassies in Colombo and in UNHCR headquarters, who would be rushing to claim credit. The truth of his comment didn't stop me falling asleep that night feeling really great.

First thing next day, Chris Morris and Thomas Abraham phoned to ask if it was true. I said I wasn't reporting to Geneva until I had confirmation from the Government. This soon came by way of a statement from the Secretary for Defence, that the proposed evacuation of refugees and displaced persons from Madhu was being shelved.

Reference was made to a long dialogue with UNHCR and to my fact-finding missions in Madhu. Military operations would go ahead otherwise as planned, but with safeguards for civilians. So, after all the cliff-hangers of the past three weeks, the crisis was over.

* * *

The Indian High Commissioner's dry comment that there would be "many Fathers of Success" following the successful resolution of the Madhu crisis would have been true enough of UNHCR headquarters in normal times. But the unpopularity of the Sri Lankan programme in influential quarters in Geneva was still such as to ensure that the role of the Colombo office was minimized; consequently the institutional view was that the successful outcome had been entirely a result of Indian pressure – a simplistic judgement that ignored some of the more complex dynamics of the situation. Certainly, the Indian part had been very important, and UNHCR Colombo had throughout appropriately coordinated closely with their High Commissioner in view of the coincidence of international humanitarian concerns with the bilateral interest in avoiding another mass exodus of Sri Lankan Tamil refugees to South India. Influential roles had also been played by a number of Western High Commissions and embassies – though not the United States, which alone among the diplomatic community had queried the UNHCR position. But the most effective, albeit necessarily unsung, "Fathers of Success" were Sri Lankan – the highly intelligent and principled individuals who had throughout been working round the clock to get the Government off the hook.

Much of the next two days was spent in calling on various high officials, thanking them for the support, and in some notable cases the strong encouragement, they had given me throughout the Madhu crisis. The response I got was surprising – my interlocutors were in fact warmly thanking *me* for what *I* had done. One eminent official referred to the bitter debates in the National Security Council. Someone else said that General Kobbekaduwa, with whom I had been rather tensely negotiating contingency plans in case the doomsday scenario had actually transpired, had been deeply unhappy about the decision – which I had more or less understood, although he was far too professional a soldier to admit it to me personally. In particular, I had not looked forward to calling on General Ranatunga, the Secretary for Defence, in view of the sometimes rather cold exchanges we had had during the previous three weeks. But in the event, he was much the same as the others – relieved, relaxed and friendly in tone, talking about peace and what the LTTE would accept and several other such things. It was altogether a marked change of tone from previous encounters. I could have been talking to one of the President's advisors – but then indeed the President's influence had slowly but surely emerged to resolve the crisis. Obviously, I was being pumped and sounded out. But at least it was clear that my fears about relationships with the Army and the Ministry of Defence in particular as a result of the stand I had taken over Madhu proved to be unfounded.

The conventional view was that governments were often ready to accept UNHCR interventions in support of international standards in crises as a convenient cloak of international respectability with which to cover crude bilateral pressures. There had been an element of this in the present situation. But overall, such a view did less than credit to the universal standards to which many influential Sri Lankans aspired, or indeed to the complex processes at work in their national governance to resolve sensitive issues.

Pesalai

Early one morning in April, Pipat radioed from Pesalai that an Army detachment had entered the centre without any reference to him, rounded up all the men and taken them away. He had informed the unnamed lieutenant in charge that he was acting in contravention of procedures agreed with General Kobbekaduwa and accepted by the Ministry of Defence. The response from the lieutenant had been that he didn't know anything about that and that Pipat had better see his captain who was staying at a village nearby. When Pipat went there and explained the situation, the captain had agreed to release the men he was holding and Pipat returned with them to the centre. But as he was checking them back in, he found that 26 were missing! And when he tried to find out what was happening, he was told that the missing men had been taken off to the jungle – and that it was not safe for him to follow.

This was precisely the type of situation that the "gentlemen's agreement" had been designed to prevent and on an emergency basis, I immediately got through to Bradman Weerakoon at the Presidential Secretariat. I explained how agreed procedures had been contravened, but much more importantly that dire consequences would follow for the future of the UNHCR programme if any of the refugees taken by the Army was harmed, let alone killed. He understood the situation and said he would do what he could personally through the Secretary for Defence.

I then told Pipat to request the Army detachment which was still in the centre compound to leave it, to collect Mr Croos, the Additional Government Agent, and go together with him to see Brigadier Lal at Talladi camp. But about half an hour later, he reported that Brigadier Lal wouldn't be back for another 24 hours. In his stead, he had seen the major who was in charge of the island, who appeared to be aware of the situation and had assured him that he was "giving the matter his urgent and personal attention" – whatever that might be it wouldn't have been enough to avert the looming disaster. Later, I heard that while Bradman Weerakoon was with him, General Ranatunga had spoken directly by radio with the Army in Pesalai and ordered them to see that the 26 missing men were returned immediately to the open relief centre safe and sound. Shortly afterwards, Pipat radioed that the order from on high had indeed been obeyed and that the men were back in the centre.

It had been a close call. But the way in which the situation had been swiftly defused said much for the goodwill for UNHCR at the top level of Government in Colombo, and even in the Army itself, without which we could not have played an effective protection role.

14. "Open relief centres are working"

Issues: state of programme – ORCs work – repatriation into conflict? – survival: governance in conflict – the LTTE – geopolitics – "servitude et grandeur humanitaire"

From time to time, there was a need to stand back from events, to discuss, reflect and brainstorm. And in brief interludes before and after field trips, the ancient Sinhalese Buddhist city, Anuradhapura – outside the war zone and with its atmosphere of timeless serenity – was the most convenient and conducive place for humanitarian thoughts on the conflict being fought out so bitterly only an hour's drive to the north.

Issues

State of the programme

One year into *Eelam War II*, when we were fatigued by the pace of events and more than usually depressed by the vicious circle of a dirty war going round and round without any glimmerings of a way out, we decided to check in at Tissawewa, the old colonial rest house at Anuradhapura set in the seclusion of a park of tall trees by a small lake, to take stock of the programme and to try to answer the question why, with the odds on the ground and in Geneva stacked so heavily against us, it was surviving, when failure – naïve or heroic, according to whether one was against or for it – would have seemed a more likely outcome.

At that time the situation in the war zone was worsening as the Army seemed to think that with its newly acquired Chinese weaponry it had the LTTE on the run and could finish the conflict by the end of the year. But we were working in Tiger-controlled areas and didn't see things that way. Indeed our impression was that, although the Army was better equipped, the LTTE was by no means weak, and certainly not about to crack. Morale was high, there was no place for defeat in its mindset, and individual cadres had a deadly determination to fight to the end regardless of the likely cost to their lives and were tactically smart. Rather than anxiously awaiting the

[198]

next Army offensive, it seemed more likely that they were planning their own deadly strikes against military installations at key strategic points such as Elephant Pass, which controlled access to the Jaffna peninsula, and locations along the trunk road to the north and the coast of mainland Mannar – an impression which seemed to be confirmed by the grisly rumour that several hundred coffins had been ordered. So, rather than the decisive victory by the end of the year which President Premadasa had been promised, the likelihood was of another round of fierce fighting with heavy loss of life on both sides that would be inconclusive, and so further perpetuate the stalemate on the ground.

Meanwhile, perhaps rather surprisingly, the position of the operation seemed to be consolidating rather than disintegrating under the impact of events. For although we were facing crises and challenges by the day, each time we came through one, the programme gained field credibility and we felt more confident of being able to weather similar storms in the future. But this was having an unexpected impact in Geneva: not mollifying the critics, but on the contrary causing them to redouble their efforts to have the programme closed down. In this regard, the new tack was to put up uncommitted colleagues with whom I had good relations to say that I was ruining my professional future by hanging in with a programme which, so they said, was "messy". (There had been a couple of such approaches in recent weeks.)

On the way to Anuradhapura, we passed through the rich rice-growing country south of Kurunegala, where the *yala* season was in full swing, happily remote from the conflict only a couple of hours drive to the north and far removed from the bureaucratic shenanigans in Geneva. The landscape was a patchwork of irregular quadrants of bright green shoots and watery mirrors of flooded mud that often reflected overhanging palm trees, while the bucolic scene was completed with the sight of cultivators busily transplanting green paddy seedlings into brown irrigated fields, and yoked water buffalo with their wide horns, thick snouts and bodies as muddy as the waterlogged fields they were ploughing – a view of timeless serenity which seldom failed to raise the spirits of fieldworkers such as ourselves on the way into and out of the war zone.

Once we were settled in the unusually relaxed atmosphere of Tissawewa, discussion flowed freely with a fruitful exchange of views on the role of protective neutral engagement we were playing in the conflict, and reflections on why we were surviving. The former included themes such as the protective impact of open relief centres and the agency position on joint Indian and Sri Lankan plans to repatriate Sri Lankan Tamil refugees from South India in the midst of the conflict. The latter mostly comprised thoughts on Sri Lankan civil governance in the conflict, relations with the LTTE and the growing support for the programme in the international community.

All these were questions which we didn't have time to discuss in our day-to-day work, nor indeed in any great depth in as short a time as a weekend. But even such a rapid review helped clear our minds.

ORCs' effectiveness

Following a review of humanitarian needs and action in Mannar, the primary conclusion was that as a model for self-regulating refuge in conflict – providing it was combined with an actively functional UN presence – the open relief centres were working pretty much as intended, bearing in mind the rationale for setting them up, their operational modalities and their territorial impact within the war zone and adjacent areas.

After the Madhu crisis, the Army had been honouring its pledge not to interfere with the centres and, as the commander in Mannar, Brigadier Lal Weerasooriya, observed: "When UNHCR is involved, both sides think twice before they take action which might harm the civilian population." Nevertheless, intensification of the conflict as a result of the planned offensive in Mannar had soon put the soundness of the centres' modalities to the test. Persons displaced by the fighting, not only in the vicinity but also further afield in and beyond the *Vanni*, headed towards Madhu and increased its population with a daily intake of some 300 to 400 persons. Those living nearby moved in with as much of their movable possessions as they could transport, while some even brought their livestock. This resulted in what Brigadier Lal called the "concertina effect" – a graphic description of the way in which the centre's population expanded rapidly during periods of intense engagement and contracted when the fighting died down, whereupon most of the new arrivals went back home.

This was a time of concern over the food supply owing to the interruption of the regular convoys by fighting in and to the north of no-man's-land, as stocks at the centre were being consumed more rapidly than they could be replenished. But in the event, through a combination of pushing through convoys when there was a lull in the fighting, increasing their size and re-routing them, things had worked out. Outside the centres, the network of decentralized sub-centres, where food was distributed regularly, was enabling many Tamil families to stay put who would otherwise have had to flee for fear of destitution. And as for protection, as one leading Tamil put it, "you can remain in your village ten miles away if you know that UNHCR is in the centre and you can move in there in times of trouble." Another put the distance at "50 miles up the coast". Whatever the calculation of their territorial extent, the ORCs' protective impact was evidently proving to be broadly effective and helping to reduce the strain on civilians living in the war zone, whether in the LTTE-dominated jungle on the mainland near Madhu or even at Pesalai on Mannar island which was controlled by the Army. In the latter area, the situation had improved since the incident in April (Chapter 13, pp. 196–7), as the Army was now observing the provisions of the "gentlemen's agreement" (Chapter 11, pp. 165–6) whereby UNHCR monitored access to the centre.

Repatriation into conflict?

Since the assassination of Rajiv Gandhi and the pressures it had been generating in India, the question of repatriation of Sri Lankan Tamil refugees from Tamil Nadu – simmering since the early days of *Eelam War II* – had now rapidly come to the boil.

As so often in the Sri Lankan conflict, UNHCR's position in relation to this question was complex. On the one hand, the promotion of voluntary repatriation was one of the High Commissioner's functions; but on the other, verification of the voluntary nature of the refugees' decision to return in conditions of safety and dignity was a fundamental prerequisite for the agency's involvement. Promoting repatriation should properly have been carried out in India as the country of asylum, but at that stage the Indian authorities were not prepared to permit it. And verifying that the decision to return was voluntary could in practice only be done on the ground in Sri Lanka. We were deeply uneasy from what we already knew of conditions, and so decided to defer judgement until we could make another visit to the area most likely to be the focus for receiving refugees from South India: Talaimannar, on the western-most tip of Mannar island and at the narrowest point of the Palk Strait, with its pier and spacious former immigration facilities.

Talaimannar

The scene was full of haunting mementos of previous engagements and disquieting evidence of the current situation. As we drove along the coastal road with a newly installed blue beacon flashing on the roof while the Army mine-clearing teams got on with their work, the tension was palpable. At the pier, there were battle scars, bunkers, roadblocks and bomb-shattered buildings; and as we pushed on slowly over the grotesquely potholed road, it was under the glowering gaze of the tall palmyrah palms, blackened, split and stunted – grim surviving witnesses of the fierce fighting which had raged at their feet.

The nearby fishing village, with its wide sandy streets of red-tiled houses leading up to a large Italianate-facaded church cheered us up somewhat. But the relief was only visual, as in the presbytery the priest recounted the tribulations of his much reduced flock of some 300 or so parishioners. His tale included the nightmarish days when nine villagers had been taken in the night by soldiers from the camp and tortured by a ne'er-do-well lad from the village with a grudge against everyone until they confessed to being LTTE, where-after they were categorized as "disappeared" – that customary euphemism for death at the hands of the security services. After mass each week, their wives and families stayed on at the church to share their grief and weep.

Both the priest and the chairman of the Citizens' Committee acknowledged that there had been some improvement since those days which they attributed to Brigadier Lal – a most remarkable soldier, who bore the professional strains and hardship of an active field command in the midst of the conflict with evident stoicism. But there were limitations to the extent to which even a commander of his exceptional calibre could improve the lot of civilians, largely because he was perforce preoccupied primarily with fighting the war.

This was only too apparent when we called on him: he had recently beaten off fierce LTTE attempts to overrun his camp at Talladi on the adjacent mainland and explained that he had just lost a number of his men in two incidents. The first, he said, was just "bad luck": a soldier at Vankalai sub-camp had been bitten by a snake during the night, so a party of ten men had set out to escort him to the main camp at Talladi, where basic medical treatment was available. But they had been ambushed by an LTTE mine-laying patrol which had been hiding nearby. Nine of the ten men who had set out (including the snake-bite victim) had been killed in the attack. The second loss had been from the explosion of a small "Johnnie" pressure mine which had triggered an adjacent heavy landmine. When I asked how many casualties there were, he held out the fingers of one hand.

Another concern for the villagers was the "Muslim factor" – the use of specially recruited Muslim guards from among those expelled from the island in order to identify civilians whom they considered to be LTTE supporters – which was causing widespread fear. The classification of large areas as security "no-go" zones also increased the difficulties of daily living on the island.

By no stretch of imagination did these conditions satisfy the "safety and dignity" test for UNHCR to actively promote voluntary repatriation, and we could not therefore be associated with the bilaterally organized movements for which the Indian and Sri Lankan authorities were preparing. However, the political reality was that with or without UNHCR, and one way or another, repatriation would go ahead. The best we could do was to try and avoid some of the most likely negative developments, including the use of the island as a holding centre for all or most of the refugees repatriating to the north east, which would inevitably result in many having to stay there indefinitely in conditions which were already unhealthy. We had to be very clear on that score, both with the President's Office and at the Indian High Commission.

Survival

The question why the programme was surviving was answerable primarily in relation to governance in the conflict, the LTTE and the geopolitical situation.

Sri Lankan governance in conflict

Leaving aside fundamental criticisms of the Sri Lankan polity made most trenchantly by some Sinhalese writers,[1] and in spite of its often grim record on human rights in the war with Tamil separatists in the north east – not to mention the suppression of the Sinhalese insurgency in the South in 1988–89 – Sri Lanka was a democracy that was often distinctively liberal in the ethos and structure of its governance.

The working conditions for an international humanitarian agency in Sri Lanka contrasted sharply with those I had experienced during postings elsewhere in Peoples' Socialist states. There, although the relief services were bureaucratically and structurally well-organized (indeed better than in many non-socialist states) the attitude of the competent authorities was very different. In the everyday working life of a United Nations agency, contrasting conditions related primarily to matters such as the strictness of control, restriction of access, movement, freedom of expression and other limitations – in effect the space within which the agency was permitted to carry out its humanitarian functions.

In these respects, as a UNHCR representative leading a small field team with an innovative protection role in the midst of a volatile conflict, I had constant cause to appreciate the many liberal aspects of the Sri Lankan authorities' approach to the problem of relieving the plight of the civilians who were caught up in it. This was to be seen in the access we were given to all levels of competent authority, the freedom to move in the war zone with only minimum security controls, and the flexibility allowed to our programme. It was shown too in the tolerance of frankly expressed comments during some highly sensitive situations. Such latitude would have been very difficult if not impossible to achieve in a democracy which was not significantly liberal in outlook. The consequence for governance in the conflict was a certain flexibility and open-mindedness as to the ways and means to relieve civilians in the war zone on the part of officials responsible for relief: principally, CGES in Colombo and the GAs and senior SLAS staff in the *kachcheris* of the northern districts. This greatly facilitated the close working relations with the competent authorities that a humanitarian agency such as UNHCR needed in order to be effective on the ground.

CGES was led by high-calibre officials from both communities – Charita Ratwatte, the able aristocratic administrator with political connections, and Devanesan Nesiah, the intellectual former GA in Jaffna during the earlier troubles – who had overriding emergency authority to requisition goods and provide and effect delivery of food and essential supplies in conflict-affected areas. As regards mainland Mannar, this resulted in its procuring supplies to feed civilians in the war zone through the open relief centre network at Madhu, which UNHCR delivered by pushing its convoys across no-man's-land whenever ground conditions permitted.

The SLAS was at the core of civil governance. The direct descendant of the prestigious Ceylon Civil Service, which in its day had been the equivalent of the better known Indian Civil Service under the raj, the SLAS was an elite corps of professional administrators, recruited through open competition, with a traditionally high level of commitment to public service. Although it suffered from some overly politicized governance after independence, it had nevertheless managed collectively to maintain its position as the service from which key positions such as the GAs and their senior staff who ran the *kachcheris* were filled. Governance could not have continued during the conflict without their professionalism and flexible pragmatism. They were always walking a tightrope – and their task was particularly hazardous when control of their district was passing backwards and forwards between one side and the other (three GAs were killed before and during the IPKF period). On the national scale, they provided the tenuous link which helped to keep the country together; internationally, they deserved recognition as exemplars of enlightened civil practice in conflict which countries in the throes of civil war wherever in the world would do well to emulate.

In Mannar, UNHCR was fortunate in having outstandingly committed SLAS counterparts. Neelan Tiruchelvam helped explain why: as professional civil administrators, officers in the *kachcheris* had been deeply demoralized by the highly volatile and intensely partisan conditions of the war, and so when UNHCR arrived with a humanitarian programme which needed to be implemented by the competent authorities, it had been strongly appreciated for reintroducing the basis for soundly professional functions.

However, the most impressive evidence of the liberal aspirations of Sri Lankans during the conflict came from key actors, some military as well as civil, who understood UNHCR's protection concerns and supported them at critical junctures. The "gentlemen's agreement" (Chapter 11, pp. 165–6) that set out protective procedures to monitor Army access to the open relief centre at Pesalai was negotiated directly with General Kobbekaduwa, the General Officer Commanding in the north and thereafter provided the basis for defusing several difficult incidents. He was also the officer with whom I had subsequently to negotiate contingency plans at the height of the Madhu crisis, when his hints as to how best present the case in Colombo were a helpful contribution to the eventual solution. And in the background, there were always the strongly supportive Governor of the North East, General Nalin Seneviratne and, critically near the apex of government, Bradman Weerakoon, the Presidential Advisor on International Relations, that shrewd and highly principled official who was always accessible and supportive in times of crisis. It was largely because of Weerakoon's influence that the President regarded UNHCR's role as being in Sri Lanka's best interest. And when it came to the crunch during the Madhu crisis, the way in which enlightened public servants such as these and others supported the UNHCR position in the intense debates which were going on behind the scenes illustrated the liberal fibre of Sri Lankan governance in action.

Although, as professionals rather than politicians, these public servants were not in a position to stop a war they mostly deplored, their personal commitment helped to reduce its impact on civilians. To say more might seem to suggest that the conflict was a less tragically disastrous form of national evisceration than in fact it was. And the danger of giving the impression that such enlightened individuals were in the majority or were prevailing has to be avoided. Indeed the opposite was nearer the truth: they were a small minority fighting against the odds to maintain civilized values in a situation where they were being violated most of the time. Nevertheless, the existence of a leaven of individuals of that calibre throughout national governance greatly facilitated the task of an agency such as UNHCR in developing and operating an innovative protection programme in the midst of a complex internal conflict.

The LTTE

Appropriately for international civil servants carrying out an impartial humanitarian function, UNHCR never established close relations with the LTTE. Yet from time to time we had to meet and discuss with cadres at the area leadership level, when our interlocutors were usually tense and suspicious and could be quite difficult (Chapter 9, p. 135–6). But they were never impossible, and at the other end of the scale there were occasional passing contacts with the LTTE rank and file as part of ongoing UNHCR field activities from which I had gained a number of impressions which were not entirely negative. The overall impression was of well-disciplined and highly motivated young people fighting a war which they firmly believed to be just and which they knew would very probably claim their lives. To condemn them out of hand as terrorists was to fail to understand the

[206]

nature of the complex problem which had made them like that – of which they were the symptom, not the cause. Essentially, their history was one of a culturally proud and very able minority which was politically insecure, humiliated and unable to do much about it within the prevailing framework of the unitary Sri Lankan state (Chapter 3, pp. 38–40). Historians in the future may be better able to judge whether the LTTE was a liberation movement fighting a just cause or a terrorist organization. Meanwhile, the view of this particular fieldworker was that it was both, but in different measures. That is to say, it was primarily a liberation movement – and justly so in view of the history of insecurity and humiliation which had been the fate of the Tamils since independence – but also one which from time to time, to its total prejudice in the eyes of the interested international community, committed heinous acts of terrorism.

Although the LTTE could not itself hope to win the war outright, neither could it be definitively beaten. It was there to stay. That was the raw reality upon which appropriate humanitarian action, not to mention peace strategies, had to focus in 1991 – as indeed it still is today in 2006.

Geopolitics

Long after the passing of maritime imperialism, Sri Lanka had remained of key geopolitical interest to powers both regional and global. As the regional superpower, India had been closely following events in its strategically placed southern neighbour and doing its best to broker peace negotiations – while at the same time providing military training for Tamil separatist groups. After the effective failure of its intervention through deployment of the IPKF under the 1987 Peace Accord, however, it was most unlikely to take another such initiative. And any other external military involvement was excluded – even in the diluted form of UN peacekeeping – as unacceptable to both Sri Lanka and India.

On the other hand, there was the United States as a global – albeit not yet sole – superpower, which had a large USAID programme in the country, was wary of Indian moves, and indeed had not been overly pleased to see UNHCR there. In between, there were the other industrialized states of the first world – particularly Canada and the Western European countries – to which Sri Lankan Tamils had been fleeing since the earliest days of the conflict. Although initially some had had doubts about the innovative UNHCR role in the war zone, these had disappeared when it steadily gained credibility on the ground as a constructive humanitarian programme. The geopolitical interplay between the various interested parties had been illustrated during the programme's first periodic review which had been conducted by an independent consultant during April 1991.[2] In view of the negative briefing on the programme he had received from its critics in Geneva before his departure in the hope that he would recommend its discontinuance, on his arrival in Colombo he was surprised to find how strongly supportive were Canada and the Western European countries.

The Canadian High Commission had spoken with authority as its High Commissioner had seen all aspects of the programme on the ground, and the consultant's queries had been dealt with quite sharply: if UNHCR activities at the source of a refugee problem were outside its mandate, then what about northern Iraq, where the situation was analogous? For Canada, Sri Lanka was the number one country of origin for refugees and asylum seekers. It made sense for UNHCR to remain in Sri Lanka, at least for monitoring and evaluation purposes, and in view of eventual repatriation, it would be "very silly for it to shut down". Admittedly, the programme was not without risks. But it had important advantages, such as facilitating the international community's efforts to stand up for better treatment of civilians and to provide a good alternative to flight (eventual return home would be much easier for displaced persons from the open relief centres in Sri Lanka than it would be for refugees from camps in South India).

The UK High Commission, where David Gladstone, the High Commissioner had also made a field visit to Mannar island, took a similarly firm line, saying that there were no conflicting signals from London, which was strongly behind the programme. There was a large group of Tamil civilians who did not want to flee to India, but could not yet return to their homes. Without the open relief centres they would be leading a very precarious existence. UNHCR had achieved a position which was accepted by both the Government and the LTTE, and very much appreciated by the Tamils. If UNHCR were to withdraw, it was dreaded what the consequences might be.

The Netherlands embassy, which also spoke for the European Economic Community (EEC), said that the open relief centres were not only important for the people benefiting directly from them, but also because they were one of the very few instances during the conflict

where trust had been built up on both sides and that this was important for the future. There was strong support among the diplomatic
community in Colombo for UNHCR and MSF working together in
this programme. If there was a funding problem, something could be
arranged bilaterally and the EEC was quite supportive.

At the US embassy, however, both the position and tone were
different. Nonetheless, even there, change was on the way, as within
a few weeks, Court Robinson, a senior analyst at the US Committee
on Refugees – an influential NGO – came on a special mission to
Mannar. As a result he wrote *Sri Lanka: Island of Refugees*, a report
which recommended US Government financial support for the
programme, and even suggested an extension of open relief centre
practice to the Government's welfare centres in the east.[3] In itself,
Court's report did not shift policy in Washington, but he had taken a
video camera with him and the resulting film – once it had been
shown around – did. Several individuals including Sarah Moten, the
Deputy Assistant Secretary of State for Refugee Affairs, who had
previously been non-committal about the programme, thereafter
decided to support it. When next I met the embassy interlocutor at a
reception in Colombo, he commented wryly that I seemed to have
some friends in Washington who were "quite supportive of what
[I was] doing". Several years were to pass before Richard Holbrooke
was to articulate the robustly commonsensical view that UNHCR
should take over responsibility for IDPs worldwide. Nonetheless, at
that stage this was a great improvement in the US position, and
helped to reduce some of the pressure on the programme.

Moreover, the review mission had concluded in April with the
consultant saying that he would do his best for the programme in
Geneva, albeit on his terms: recommending its short-term extension
rather than accepting its conceptual significance. However, I later
heard that in Geneva he had spoken up strongly in support of the
quality of the programme. And even the customarily anodyne annual
report to the UNHCR Executive Committee noted his evaluation
judgement that it had "met with considerable success in achieving all
of its original objectives and clearly provided a valuable alternative
to further flight".[4] Although on the ground we felt that this was a
rather disappointingly cautious judgement on an exceptionally
economical programme which was having a beneficial impact in a
highly sensitive refugee related situation, it represented significant
progress in what was still was still a relatively hostile institutional
climate.

* * *

From Anuradhapura, we drove off into the warm languor of a Sri Lankan Sunday morning, with a few villagers slowly beginning to go about their business: ladies in saris strolling with umbrellas open to shield them from the sun, motorcyclists in brightly coloured crash helmets chugging by, wide expanses of pink and white lotus in the tanks and the rustic activity of the *yala* in the countryside in full swing – altogether a tranquil scene that had been powerfully conducive to reflection on the dramatically different scenario of civilians in the midst of armed conflict which we had been discussing over the weekend. Of course armed conflict was the ultimate disaster for civilians who had the misfortune to be caught up in it anywhere in the world – a continuing series of catastrophes, tragedies, dangers and intense personal suffering. For an international agency team such as ours which was trying to protect them in such troubled circumstances, any claims to success would have been vain.

The programme was not so much succeeding as surviving, essentially because we were performing a much-needed humanitarian function which other relevant actors were either unwilling or unable to take over – and this was appreciated by an impressive array in the international community.

Servitude et grandeur humanitaire[5]

Towards the end of 1991, most of us who had been in Sri Lanka for over three years were feeling the need to move on. We had fought hard, and eventually successfully, to prevent UNHCR withdrawing from the country at the outset of *Eelam War II*, as powerful interests in Geneva had wanted – an option which would have left in the lurch the refugee returnees whose reintegration we had been monitoring. And in the particular conditions on the ground, the resulting protection-orientated programme for that relatively small group which was within the UNHCR mandate had also benefited larger numbers of IDPs and endangered local residents who were outside that mandate – but who as potential refugees were nonetheless closely related to it.

Although with less meagre funding and better back-up we could have achieved a lot more, both the focus of the programme – the war zone in a conflict at the source of an exodus of refugees from their country of origin – and the practical methodology devised to respond to it were significantly innovative. Nevertheless, with the deeply entrenched conservatism of international bureaucracies and the external interests powerfully represented within them, we were sceptical that the lessons to be learned from the Sri Lankan experience would in fact be learned.

By early 1992, we were all on our different ways to new assignments in the challenging refugee crises of that time: Sudan, Cambodia, the Gulf, Former Yugoslavia and the new Commonwealth of Independent States.

Part V

Protection and the UN in 2006

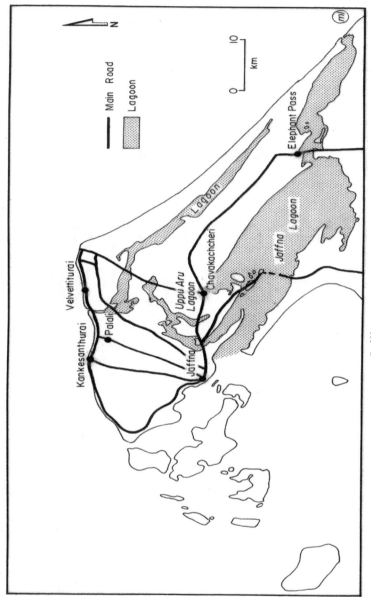

Jaffna peninsula

15. In and between Sri Lankan warfare

*Eelam Wars II and III – ceasefires and peace processes – protection
practice evolves – UN Guiding Principles – Eelam War IV?*

Eelam Wars II and III

Eelam War II 1992–94

Warfare continued in 1992 with bitterly fought offensives and
counter-offensives between the combatants to control strategic
locations on and at the entry to the Jaffna peninsula, which
inevitably endangered and displaced further large numbers of
Tamil civilians. From Jaffna, the LTTE maintained territorial
control of most of the peninsula and the *Vanni* north of Vavuniya,
which in effect functioned as a mini-state. In the east, however,
where it was unable to retain control in urban areas, the Tigers
carried on guerrilla warfare with the mining of strategic roads,
ambushes and lightning attacks on Army camps and police
stations, mainly from bases in the jungle interior. For tactically
more important strikes, they were strengthened with cadres
moved from the *Vanni*.

This was also a time of leadership assassinations in Colombo: first,
Lalith Athulathmudali (the leader of a breakaway faction of the then-
ruling United National Party (UNP)) was shot dead at an election
rally on 23 April 1993; eight days later, President Premadasa was
blown up, together with 24 others, at the May Day rally; and on 24
October 1994, Gamini Dissanayake, by then the UNP Opposition's
Presidential candidate, was killed in an explosion which altogether
ended the lives of 60 people. It is some indication of the political
atmosphere in the south at this time that opinions differed as to
whether some or all of these killings were carried out by the LTTE, or
originated in conspiracy.

From September to November 1993, there were bitter engagements on both sides of the Jaffna lagoon to the south-west of the
peninsula on the strategic route from Jaffna to both the *Vanni* and
the east: at Kilali, a crossing point held by the LTTE on the northern

shore, and at Pooneryn, a key Government military complex on the southern side.

In the former, an Army column of 3000 men pushed into the peninsula from its major base at Elephant Pass and after a six-day running battle with the LTTE succeeded in taking Kilali. But instead of pushing on to take Chavakachcheri on the road to Jaffna, as had been intended, it withdrew to Elephant Pass after two days – thereby vindicating the widely held view that while greater firepower and far superior numbers enabled Government forces to take positions and territory, they were often over-extended and so unable to hold them. Both sides suffered casualties and many civilians were killed in the accompanying air raids and shelling of Jaffna and its surroundings. Thereafter, the LTTE launched its operation Thavalai, an assault by night across the lagoon, when Tiger frogmen captured the Navy base at Nagethevanthurai, while its crack commando brigade attacked the Army camp at Pooneryn. The objective of this assault, in which the LTTE captured a great deal of arms and equipment, was to try to halt attacks on the Kilali crossing. In Colombo, there were reports of very heavy casualties on the Government side. The LTTE admitted losing 411 cadres.

Eelam War III 1995–2002

Following the collapse of the peace talks in April 1995, the Government launched what was then its biggest offensive, with the objective of taking Jaffna pursuant to its newly declared policy of "war for peace". By early December 1995, the national flag was flying over the city, while much of its population had been displaced, including large numbers of civilians who, with some measure of coercion, followed the LTTE across the Jaffna lagoon to Kilinochchi in the *Vanni*, where the Tigers relocated their headquarters. Hereafter, the war was fought primarily on two fronts in the north and the east, with occasional LTTE strikes at economic targets and selective acts of terrorism perpetrated in Colombo and anywhere else in the country under Government control where there were individuals whom the Tigers perceived that it was in their interest to eliminate.

In the north – the Jaffna peninsula and extensive *Vanni* region north of Vavuniya – the strength of Government forces was primarily in their superior firepower, which enabled them to prevail in engagements such as the taking of Jaffna in late 1995 and early 1996,

Kilinochchi in September 1996 and Mankulam in September 1998. But, as ever, they were disadvantaged by their being – strict legalities apart – an alien army of occupation holding relatively isolated positions, with over-extended lines of support which ran through mostly hostile territory. In contrast, after its withdrawal to the *Vanni*, the position of the LTTE was correspondingly strong, as its principal bases were protected in the depths of the Mullaitivu jungle, it controlled territory commanding the vital land routes between Jaffna and the rest of the country – particularly the east – and the jungle was its own formidable battle terrain, the natural advantages of which the Tigers were already well experienced in turning to their tactical advantage. (During the IPKF period, Indian forces failed to catch Prabhakaran in the jungle, and it was indeed there that they incurred most of their relatively high casualties.)

Each side was launching colourfully named offensives and counter-offensives to take or re-take key locations, routes and territory. The names reflected their different military styles, such as Certain Victory for the Army and for the LTTE Unceasing Waves, which was reminiscent of Viet Minh tactics in Viet Nam. The Certain Victory offensive, launched in May 1997 to open a land supply route to Jaffna from Vavuniya through LTTE-controlled territory, illustrated some of the comparative strengths and weaknesses of the two combatants. By September 1998, the Army had taken Mankulam (the temporary LTTE headquarters at a strategic crossraods on the road to the north) But the early stages of the campaign had seen serious setbacks, as in June 1997 when the rear of its advancing columns was devastated by the LTTE in human-wave assaults in which over 600 troops were killed.

Following the recapture of Kilinochchi by the LTTE, Certain Victory was terminated and the Army launched two new operations. The first, Sun Power, began in December 1998 and aimed to capture the LTTE stronghold in Mullaitivu in the north east of the *Vanni*. The second, Battle Cry, was launched in March 1999, striking north west from Vavuniya through mainland Mannar to the coast. In both of these offensives, the Army took vast expanses of territory previously controlled by the LTTE. However, in November 1999, in another Unceasing Waves operation, the Tigers threw back Government forces, recovering in a matter of days most of the *Vanni* territory they had lost over the previous 18 months. And in April 2000, in yet another such operation, the LTTE captured the strategic Government base at Elephant Pass at the eastern end of the Jaffna lagoon, and then followed up with an advance westwards along the northern shore, taking several Army camps, including Kilali. With Elephant Pass, the Tigers took control of entry to the peninsula; with Kilali, they gained protected access to the northern shore of the lagoon, which facilitated the transport of supplies from their bases in the *Vanni*. The Government garrison in Jaffna of 40,000 troops was now directly threatened and its evacuation was mooted, although by July the immediate threat of the city falling to the LTTE had been averted.

Meanwhile in the east, there was a stalemate between the Tigers in the jungles and the Army in the towns and security installations, whether camps, police stations or Air Force and Navy bases. This often gave rise to the classic result of insurgency situations around the world, that government forces were in control during daylight and the separatists after nightfall. Of greater strategic significance, however, was that the east was a sideshow for the war in the north; the LTTE would frequently raise the stakes by moving in fairly large groups of cadres from its jungle bases for hit-and-run attacks to pin down troops who would otherwise have been withdrawn to support Government offensives in the *Vanni* and Jaffna peninsula. For Tamil civilians, conditions were indeed grim and grisly, with food shortages, subjection to indiscriminate brutality when troops went on the rampage (as they usually did in localities where a mine had exploded), the danger of getting caught in the crossfire of artillery duels between the combatants, and the menace of death squads on both sides.

Mostly in Colombo, Black Tiger (suicide) bomber attacks struck periodically at the economic life of the country and at individuals who were perceived as potential threats to LTTE interests. There was a succession of bombings of targets, including the oil refinery on the outskirts of the city, the Central Bank building in the Fort financial district, the Trade Centre and nearby tourist hotels, the airport and adjacent Air Force base and a packed commuter train, in nearly all of which civilians were killed and many injured. Moreover, several leading members of TULF, the moderate Tamil party were assassinated, including the MP for Batticaloa, two mayors of Jaffna and, in July 1999, Neelan Tiruchelvam. Modest to a finally fatal fault, this courageous and immensely civilized Sri Lankan thought that he was not important enough to justify the expenditure of a Black Tiger.

Ceasefires and peace processes

November 1994 to April 1995

In August 1994, Chandrika Bandaranaike Kumaratunga led the Peoples' Alliance to a narrow victory at the polls with a pledge to end the eleven-year-old war, and was sworn in as Prime Minister. In November, she won the Presidential election by a large majority.

Although there were high hopes on both sides when a cease-fire came into effect in November 1994, the modalities for the talks, as indeed of the ceasefire itself, were weak and otherwise inappropriate to deliver substantive negotiations on highly sensitive issues, especially when there were dauntingly high levels of mutual distrust and suspicion. Thus, progress to establish ways to enforce the ceasefire was so slow that the talks had already broken down irretrievably before the international chairmen of the monitoring committees could take up their duties. Even more importantly, the split-level structure for contacts between the parties – on the one hand face-to-face talks for a small number of relatively brief sessions, and on the other an ongoing exchange of correspondence – proved insufficiently sound to take the strain. Moreover, the tone of the written communications between the two sides was inappropriately contentious for a process of rapprochement on highly sensitive political issues.

The LTTE insisted on four preconditions to peace talks: lifting of the economic embargo in the north; an end to the restriction on fishing in the north east; removal of the Army camp at Poon-eryn; and free movement for its armed cadres to, from and within the east – and imposed a deadline of 28 March by which it expected compliance. In response, the Government conceded the first two demands, but deferred consideration of the last two until a subsequent meeting. The LTTE then extended its deadline by three weeks to 18 April, saying that it would withdraw from the peace process if by then the Government had not complied with its demands. In the early hours of 19 April the Tigers launched a series of devastating attacks, including the sinking of two Navy gungoats in Trincomalee harbour by frogmen. *Eelam War III* had commenced.

February 2002

In December 2001, Ranil Wickremesinghe led the United National Front (UNF) to victory in the parliamentary elections and formed an administration which made preliminary contacts with the LTTE. On 23 February 2002, the Government and the LTTE concluded a ceasefire agreement on appropriate modalities for the cessation of military operations; the separation of their forces; the introduction of measures to restore normalcy by putting an end to hostile acts against civilians of all communities, allowing the unimpeded flow of non-military goods, opening roads and railway lines and a gradual easing of restrictions on fishing; and establishment of the Sri Lanka Monitoring Mission (SLMM) – comprising personnel from Nordic countries, led by Norway, to conduct on-site monitoring of compliance with the agreement's provisions – and, in most districts in the north east, the appointment of local monitoring committees chaired by an international monitor.

At the third round of peace talks, held in Oslo in December 2002, the parties "agreed to explore a solution founded on the principle of internal-self-determination in areas of historical habitation of the Tamil-speaking peoples, based on a federal structure within a united Sri Lanka". In other words, for the LTTE, the establishment of Tamil Eelam as a sovereign socialist state – the battle cry of Tamil militancy since the Vaddukoddai Resolution of 1976 (Chapter 3, p. 39) – although not renounced, would not be pursued, while in the south, federalism, for long a dirty, word was acceptable. And at Tokyo in following June, the international donor conference pledged some US$ 4.5 billion, much of which was made conditional on progress in the peace process.

In April 2003, however, the LTTE suspended its participation in the peace talks, blaming the Government for neglecting the needs of the people in the north east, although according to its chief negotiator, Anton Balasingham, the movement had neither terminated the negotiating process nor walked away from talks. Moreover, in November, in response to proposals made by the Government, the Tigers published their own presentation on establishing the Interim Self Government Administration (ISGA), which provided for an authority to include Government and Muslim members but with an LTTE majority to control administrative and financial functions including taxation, powers to borrow internally and externally, to receive aid directly and to engage in trade both within and outside the country. Such an authority would control land, and natural and marine and offshore resources, and have power over law and order. Proposals were also made for a separate judiciary, which went outside Sri Lanka's constitutional framework. The proposals also included a separate human rights commission for the north east, which the LTTE would effectively control.[1] However, before the ISGA proposals could be discussed in detail, the country was plunged into crisis by President Kumaratunga's "constitutional coup", whereby she controversially – but in the event successfully – exercised her executive Presidential prerogative to take over the key ministries of Defence, the Interior and Information, and suspended Parliament.

The immediate effect of these moves was to destabilize the peace process, as both the President and the Prime Minister tried to wrong-foot each other in relation to their handling of it, while Norway initially withdrew its peace envoys pending clarification of the question of appropriate political authority. Then in February 2004, the President dissolved parliament more than four years before the end of its term, and announced general elections in April, which she went on to win decisively at the head of the United Peoples Front Alliance (UPFA), including the hardline Sinhalese nationalist People's Liberation Front, the Janatha Vimukti Peramuna (JVP). The JVP was vehemently opposed to the peace process and refused to moderate its position when it entered the new administration, while its strength reflected a resurgence in Sinhalese Buddhist nationalism that was also to be seen in the Jathika Hela Urumaya (JHU), the first ever political party of Buddhist monks (with nine seats in parliament), and increased political activity within the Buddhist clergy.

Meanwhile in the north east, the "eastern question" – essentially, the resentment by Tamils in the east of domination by northerners, particularly from Jaffna – came out into the open with a vengeance. A splittist movement within the ranks of the hitherto formidably monolithic LTTE emerged under the leadership of "Colonel Karuna" – the nom de guerre of Mulitharan Vinayagamoorthy – until then very much an up-and-coming easterner in the movement, who had distinguished himself as a commander on the battlefield and also played a prominent part in the peace negotiations. Historically, the authority of the LTTE central leadership had ever been weakest in the east, and consequently the primordial need to avoid a split has been one of its abiding concerns since early days.

Although by mid-April 2004, following decisive moves by the central leadership to re-assert its authority, the open revolt in the east appeared to have collapsed, this was far from the end of the matter, as killings by the LTTE and counter-killings from the by now underground Karuna faction continued.

Protection practice evolves

Over the past 15 years, UNHCR's practice in Sri Lanka has evolved in direct response to the cyclically recurrent challenges of civilian danger, displacement and destitution in the war zone at the source of an international exodus from this major country of refugee origin. This has been a dual function: on the one hand, the programme has been monitoring and facilitating returns and the reintegration both of repatriating refugees (almost entirely from South India) and IDPs going back to their home areas when conditions permitted; the other function has been protective neutral engagement during periods of fighting, not only on behalf of the returnees but also of the IDPs and locally endangered civilians among whom they were living at the source of the exodus. The interaction of these two elements, and their relation to the changing conditions and challenges in the war zone, has been the story of the agency's protection role throughout *Eelam War II*, the brief ceasefire and peace initiative in 1994–95, *Eelam War III* and the Norwegian-brokered ceasefire of 2002; it is likely to continue to be needed in the inevitably highly unstable years ahead, particularly as there are already intermittent outbursts of fighting and an early resumption of open warfare on a continuing basis is quite possible (see below pp. 227–9). Notable developments in protection practice are summarized below.

Repatriation of refugees, return of IDPs

The vexed question of the repatriation of Sri Lankan Tamil refugees from the camps in South India and the appropriateness of UNHCR's association with that programme was even more controversial at the end of 1991 than it had been when boatloads of returnees were organized under bilateral arrangements following the 1987 Peace Accord.

January 1992 saw the first of a series of new movements – but without the involvement of UNHCR, as the agency believed both that there was a significant element of coercion in their departure, and that conditions in the areas in north east Sri Lanka to which they were returning were insufficiently secure, as indeed did its ICRC colleagues. By June of that year, more than 23,000 refugees had repatriated, but owing to the ground situation, many were unable to return to their home villages and had to remain in Government-run reception or transit centres.

In July, however, UNHCR reached agreements with the authorities both in India and in Sri Lanka. The Indians agreed to permit a partial measure of verification of the voluntary nature of the repatriation prior to departure, and Sri Lanka gave assurances that returning refugees would not be unlawfully detained upon arrival but permitted to return to their home areas, even in LTTE-controlled territory. But the summary accounts of such measures in the High Commissioner's annual report to the General Assembly were less than entirely reassuring as regards both the refugees' decision to return from India and the security of conditions in Sri Lanka. Thus, although local and international NGOs were noted as saying that the establishment of a UNHCR presence in Madras had effectively eliminated instances of pressure by local officials on refugees to return, verification procedures comprised no more than sample interview checks and the examination of nominal rolls provided by the Indian authorities. Moreover, "the percentage of refugees expressing a willingness to return during interviews dropped to below two per cent."[2] Nonetheless, in order to strengthen its protection position and to supplement Government assistance, UNHCR expanded its relief programme to provide additional food, medical aid and domestic items, together with a range of micro-projects in sectors such as water supply, minor roads and education, to facilitate the reintegration of refugees into the communities to which they were returning. The agency was thereby enabled to enhance its field presence with the opening of two additional field offices, an increase in the number of staff and, most appropriately in view of the availability of additional funding, the extension of beneficiary entitlement to include conflict-affected groups of Muslims and Sinhalese in southern districts adjacent to the war zone. However, by May 1993, there were still some 6000 refugee returnees in the transit centres awaiting sufficient improvement in the ground situation to enable them to return home; and owing to the continuing conflict, the agency changed its repatriation policy from promotion to one of active assistance for those volunteering to return.

Whenever possible, UNHCR field staff monitored and facilitated the safe return of IDPs to their home areas, as for example, some 12,000 returning from LTTE controlled areas in the *Vanni* to the Jaffna peninsula.

Open relief centres

The open relief centres continued to perform their sustainable protection function in the war zone. In 1992, the "gentlemen's agreement", which hitherto had provided the basis for UNHCR staff to monitor military access to the centre at Pesalai, was formally accepted by the Ministry of Defence, although this centre was eventually to be eclipsed by the neighbouring Government-run welfare centre for refugee returnees in the context of repatriation from South India. At Madhu, when the population rose to 30,000, a satellite centre was opened in the vicinity to accommodate a further 4000 persons. However, towards the end of 1992, both combatant parties began to take an increasingly hard line towards Madhu, with the Army trying to restrict food supplies in order to compel Tamils from certain villages to return home to areas under its control, while there were violent demonstrations in the centre with threats to UNHCR personnel and property. Consequently, the operation there was suspended until February 1994, when satisfactory assurances were obtained from the LTTE on security.

There was a pragmatic development in the open relief centre concept on one occasion in *Eelam War III*, when the large numbers of civilians fleeing the fighting threatened to swamp the established facilities at Madhu. In response, UNHCR intervened with field staff and the civil administration to provide protective relief in a secure location en route on a temporary basis until the fugitives were able to move back to their home areas.[3] Both combatant parties continued largely to respect Madhu's neutrality, and many thousands of endangered and destitute civilians were thus able to use the centre as a practicable alternative to flight abroad, and eventually to return to their homes.

In 1995, it was noted that despite the intensity of the warfare, there had not been a single death in an open relief centre as a result of military action;[4] and Madhu carried on until near the end of the decade. During the Army offensive to clear the *Vanni* in 1999, there was an incident when two policemen were shot near Madhu, as a result of which the Defence Ministry closed the centre. But some civilians remained, and in November 38 were killed in fighting between the LTTE and Government forces at Madhu. When the LTTE regained control of large areas of the *Vanni*, some 16,000 IDPs sought shelter there and the centre reopened with the return of international field staff. It continued thereafter until IDPs were able to return to their home areas following the 2002 ceasefire.

Government welfare centres

After the closure of the open relief centre at Pesalai by the Army during *Eelam War III*, welfare centres provided the only accommodation available for IDPs and refugee returnees who were unable to return to their homes in Government-held areas. These centres were in effect camps and functioned very differently from the UNHCR centres. The differences were particularly noticeable in relation to exit procedures: the rationale of ORCs was for the individual on the move to decide whether to enter, how long to stay and when to move out; once someone had moved into a Government welfare centre, however, departure was not so easy. Indeed, an important protection function of UNHCR field staff was to intercede with the authorities on matters such as the freedom of movement and the issuance of travel documents. Conditions in these centres were monitored by UNHCR, but frequently criticized by NGOs.

Food convoys

During the five-month suspension of UNHCR activities in Madhu in 1994–95, the Government took over the organization of food convoys, an arrangement which continued after the agency resumed its programme in February 1995. Although UNHCR carried on with its convoys for non-food relief items, the cessation of its food convoy function seriously weakened its leverage to uphold the humanitarian neutrality of food in the war zone, as when food stocks were getting dangerously low it was no longer in a position to push its convoys through. This was of particular importance in *Eelam War III* when NGOs reported that conditions for thousands of IDPs were deteriorating as a result of complicated bureaucratic procedures, delays, and most importantly, the tendency on both sides to subordinate humanitarian principles to strategic objectives.[5]

Safe passage

Corridors for emergency supplies, medical evacuations, emergency food relief and safe passage for civilians are the stuff of humanitarian response in any civil war. In northern Sri Lanka in the early 1990s, except during military operations, UNHCR food convoys and individual Tamil civilians were regularly coming and going across no-man's-land outside Vavuniya. But crossings of the Jaffna lagoon from Kilali on the northern shore of the LTTE-held peninsula to Government-held Pooneryn on the southern side were much more problematic and dangerous. Consequently, UNHCR tried to negotiate with both combatants to establish an internationally supervised corridor. The talks broke down on the modalities of checks on persons crossing from Jaffna, with the LTTE refusing to accept searches by the Army and insisting that they be carried out by UN personnel. UNHCR rightly considered that such a function would require the presence of UN military or security personnel, but they would have been politically unacceptable to the Government, and so negotiations were abandoned in mid 1993. Although there was a very real humanitarian need, the question was acutely sensitive on both sides and, if adopted, would have probably been problematic to implement. However, UNHCR was on surer ground in May 2000 during the engagements in and around Jaffna, when it continued to intervene informally to ensure safe passage for civilians trapped by the fighting.

UN Guiding Principles

By the end of the 1990s, UNHCR was able to benefit from the UN Guiding Principles on Internal Displacement.[6] These provide a working tool of critical value in building a rights-based foundation for IDP protection, bringing together as they do in an authoritative presentation and convenient format the relevant provisions of humanitarian and human rights law. As such, they have provided the framework for initiating, discussing and promoting cooperation with national counterparts in Colombo. And they have been of particular effect outside the war zone, during stable ceasefires and most notably following the ceasefire of February 2002, when large numbers of IDPs started to return to their home areas. In the latter respect, Principle No. 15, which enunciates the right to return in safety and dignity, has been of key importance.

However, it is in the nature of the Principles that they cannot provide complete answers to the problems of IDP protection, either conceptually or operationally. First, they are not legally binding. Second, as argued below (Chapter 17, pp. 246–7), the problem with displacement as the touchstone of humanitarian concern in conflict is that it gives a special status to persons who have been displaced; however, there are usually also local inhabitants who for one reason or another have not been able to flee, and so may be in very similar conditions of danger and destitution. It is in practice virtually impossible to separate civilian victims in a war zone into two categories – not to mention the humanitarian unacceptability of any such discriminatory action in relation to persons in need. Moreover, the reality of complex conflicts, with their fragile ceasefires and faltering peace processes, means that headway towards peace or even substantially less insecure conditions is anything but a straight and steady progression. Indeed, on the contrary, ceasefires tend to be broken, peace negotiations to break down or even be abandoned, and relapses into open warfare cannot be excluded.

Thus, in a situation such as Sri Lanka's, which has been moving in and out of conflict over the last two decades, the Principles have inevitably been more relevant in some conditions, times and places than others. For fieldworkers in the frontline, their relevance turns largely on the current state of hostilities in the war zone: if the fighting is ongoing and the conditions highly volatile, the protection imperative then and there is the art of the possible – as far as circumstances permit, to engage pragmatically to ensure civilian safety: essentially protective neutral engagement with variations appropriate to the conditions. And practitioners have another need which has to be met outside the Principles, namely "a few humble, practical rules of thumb to help … with the extraordinary difficulties and complexities" of their daily work.[7]

Eelam War IV?

In a book which tries to maintain an outsider's objectivity, the fear of enflaming acute sensitivities becomes a major constraint, making it difficult to analyse the systemic weaknesses on both sides in the depth they intrinsically merit. Suffice it therefore at this stage to make no more than a passing allusion to their nature: in the south, there is a vibrant democracy, but one with serious deficiencies which numerous Sinhalese writers subject to searching analysis

(Chapter 14, note 1); in the north, a liberation movement with exceptional courage and tactical flair in combat, but which off the battlefield has as yet been unable to control the excesses of its mono-lithic position – which in view of the robustly pluralist outlook of many Tamils, points to fundamental tensions in the future.

During 2004–05, the drift of events had a disquieting similarity with mid 1990 immediately prior to the outbreak of *Eelam War II*. Then the LTTE was deeply frustrated with the peace process and neither side wanted war, but it came nevertheless. It was triggered by trivial chance events in the most volatile flashpoint in the north east – then, as now, Batticaloa – where there is both an abundance of combustible material and a high incidence of sparks to ignite it. With such continuing tension, the danger is not only that minor incidents can easily escalate to levels way above their intrinsic significance, but also that once they do, they activate war machine dynamics which, even with goodwill on both sides, can rapidly become too strong for the respective political leaderships to bring under control through the negotiation of ceasefires.

On 17 November 2005, the Presidential election was won by Prime Minister, Mahinda Rajapakse, with a narrow majority; there had been a largely effective boycott of the polls in Tamil areas in the north east, particularly the Jaffna peninsula, where there were reports of intimidation. 2006 thus opened with hardliners in the ascendant on both sides and a sharp rise in tension owing to a number of explosive incidents in the north east at the end of 2005. Brinkmanship? Probably not. Historically, Sri Lankans don't do brinkmanship: throughout the *Eelam Wars* the commencement of hostilities and their relentless continuation have reflected the way hardliners were overplaying their hands and were not averse to hard conditions which could be presented as justifying their grim prescriptions. Moreover, it is difficult to see how, with such an esca-lation in violence on the ground in the east, the temperature can be kept below the level of spontaneous combustion.

* * *

On 25 April 2006, a suicide bomber gravely wounded Lt General Fonseca, the Armed Services chief in Colombo and provoked Air Force retaliatory strikes and artillery bombardments on LTTE posi-tions in the east. To maintain that this is something less than civil war is too strenuously semantic: undeniably, it is serious warfare

[228]

and future historians may well come to note that *Eelam War IV* started with deadly attacks by both sides on clearly defined military targets, while at the same time each tried to put the blame for the resumption of hostilities on the other.

Meanwhile, the Norwegian-facilitated meeting between the parties to be held in Oslo in June never opened, as in the event the LTTE refused direct talks with the Government delegation. And the levels of both internal displacement within the north easy and external flight across the Palk Strait to India continue to rise rapidly.

16. Innovative concepts

Protection at source – protective neutral engagement – self-regulating refuge and open relief centres – humanitarian neutrality under the UN flag – absence of military – protection monitoring agreement – back-to-back agreements with combatants – small-scale protection with broad impact

Although UNHCR's role of protective neutral engagement during the first 18 months of *Eelam War II* was essentially a needs-driven response to its immediate mandatory responsibilities, it came at a time of tension between the humanitarian and the bureaucratically legalistic – rather than the legal – approaches to the protection responsibilities of the High Commissioner's mandate.[1] The validity of some long-established patterns of practice was called into question by the unusually complex configuration of events in northern Sri Lanka, both geopolitically and on the ground. The agency had a clear obligation to play an active protection role for all civilians connected with the international exodus at the source of the conflict in that major country of refugee origin. However, we had no models or precedent in relevant field practice to help shape appropriate modalities for response. There was therefore significant controversy as to whether indeed any action should be taken at all, which was also exacerbated by the then financial stringency.

All these pressures helped germinate the seeds of pragmatic field practice sown in the largely virgin but highly fertile soil of the northern war zone. The innovative concepts and modalities that emerged, and the often controversial questions they raised, produced a wide range of protection lessons which helped to establish the parameters of appropriate international humanitarian response in internal conflicts.

Protection at source

By the time *Eelam War II* erupted in north east Sri Lanka in mid 1990, UNHCR was no stranger to countries of refugee origin, nor was this the first time it had exercised protection functions within such a country rather than – in accordance with its traditional mandatory practice – in a country of asylum. From its early years, the agency had launched a number of operations in countries of origin under its "good offices" or otherwise, with due UN authorization on an operationally ad hoc basis; and it had become increasingly interested in developing a protection monitoring role in the context of voluntary repatriation (Chapter 5, pp. 70–3). In those ad hoc in-country operations, however, UNHCR activities were noted more for their delivery of material assistance than active protection practice. And although the Executive Committee Conclusions made it explicit that a monitoring role – including the High Commissioner's legitimate concern for and right of access to refugees whose repatriation he/she had assisted – was inherent in the traditional mandate, the protection functions involved had so far been passive and relatively weak (Chapter 5, pp. 70–1).

In Sri Lanka, however, the challenge on the ground was for an active protection role at the source of a conflict, to engage with the dynamics which were triggering the outflow. And in consequence, particularly in view of both the absence of prior methodology on how to deliver it and the operational necessity to include within the programme's benefit all conflict-affected civilians who were likely to seek asylum abroad, the response was a major landmark in the evolution of the concept and practice of protection in countries of origin, the nature and range of which is considered below.

Protective neutral engagement

Protective neutral engagement is a descriptive name for the objective, scope and modalities of the UNHCR programme in the complex ground situation in northern Sri Lanka in the early part of *Eelam War II*. The objective was to reduce pressures in the Mannar war zone from which Tamils were fleeing to seek asylum abroad. The scope was to protect and relieve not only refugee returnees, most of whom were concentrated in Mannar and for whom UNHCR had some legal responsibility, but also IDPs from elsewhere in the country, together with endangered and destitute local inhabitants who for one reason or another remained in their homes. Within the operational structure, the various pragmatic modalities were interactive, with each functioning according to a particular concept: the open relief centres on self-regulating refuge; the food convoys which provided the lifeline for the mainland centres, on the operationally neutral position of an agency delivering humanitarian relief under the UN flag in convoys without military involvement; and the protection monitoring of Sri

Lankan Army access to the centre on Mannar island, on hotline reporting for immediate intervention with top officials in Colombo – while throughout there was a concerted effort in field diplomacy to maintain working relations with both combatants in the war zone at all levels from the checkpoints in and out of no-man's-land and with patrols in the jungle at the bottom to the field command at the top.

Self-regulating refuge and open relief centres[2]

As a concept, self-regulating refuge – the rationale for open relief centres in the Sri Lankan conflict – derived from two sources. One was the realization that without the ready back-up of decisive military force, no international humanitarian organization could responsibly be associated with a guarantee of civilian security in a war zone, and that consequently a safe haven was not a workable proposition. Another was the observation that many civilians in the Mannar war zone (whether refugee returnees, persons displaced from elsewhere in the country or those at risk in the locality and contemplating flight) did not want to flee abroad. These people were shrewdly exercising their judgement to move to temporary places of refuge no further from their homes and for no longer than they considered the immediate situation demanded. In that respect, the open relief centres were the product of a field-driven initiative taken by an international humanitarian organization to conceptualise, organize and facilitate a local pattern of relief.

There had therefore been scope for developing a conceptually much less ambitious mechanism than a safe haven, which provided the essentials of humanitarian relief in centres monitored by outposted UNHCR international staff at key points in the mainland jungle and on Mannar island; the decision whether to stop there or to continue their flight or to stay temporarily or indefinitely, was left entirely to the individual family on the move. As such, the centres were to prove their worth as a mechanism which could provide a substantial number of endangered and destitute civilians with a viable alternative to flight abroad. Moreover, the rationale of self-regulation in refuge also corresponded with the need to take account of "spontaneous" repatriation – the trade name for when refugees decide individually to return home by their own means and at their own risk, rather than as part of an organized group movement. This occurs in every such situation from time to time when, for a wide variety of personal reasons, individual refugees cautiously begin to move back towards their home areas, initially to reconnoitre and take the security temperature and, if it is not too dangerous, to return for a while at least, with or without their families. The received wisdom was that from the outset of a refugee exodus, the High Commissioner should keep the possibility of voluntary repatriation for all or part of a group under active consideration.[3] This also strongly influenced the concept of the centre mechanism, in that it was envisaged that their location along the route out of the country should be able sooner or later to facilitate "spontaneous" returns.

Humanitarian neutrality under the UN flag

As the only UN agency working in the war zone at that time, we made full use of the UN and UNHCR flags, logo, banners and lettering wherever we were operational: at the approaches to the centres, on our own vehicles and on the convoy lorries traversing no-man's-land (where they were, as intended, an impressive sight); and the UN flag fluttered bravely in the breeze on the small boats in which we crossed to and from Mannar island.

Despite the fact that in comparison with the red cross, white background and black lettering of the ICRC, the pale blue flag and white logo of the UN was a good deal less clearly visible at a distance, we had to fly it in order to identify as best we could our areas of concern and activity, and indeed our presence. Moreover, flying the UN flag imparted a certain symbolic status which facilitated working relations with both sides and was a statement that an element of trust had been established in the intensely partisan environment of the war zone.

Beyond that, the significance of UN insignia in the war zone was more complex. Both sides appreciated the need to be seen to respect the flag in view of the importance of the United Nations as an arena in the struggle for support and sympathy worldwide and as a symbol in upholding universal humanitarian standards on the ground. Thus, as the Government was frequently under attack in the representative organs of the world body, in particular during annual sessions of the Human Rights Commission in Geneva, it was glad to be able to point to its support of UNHCR's humanitarian programme in the war zone. And, at least during a session of the Commission, the Government was mindful of the need to avoid action on the ground which would lay it open to criticism, as had been seen at a critical point during the Madhu crisis (Chapter 13). As regards the Tamil cause, lobbying through and by the diaspora was focused particularly on United Nations fora, where it was very much in the LTTE interest to be known to be cooperating constructively on the ground with the primary UN humanitarian agency.

In these ways the UN flag had come to have a quasi-totemic significance in the war zone which, together with both the absence of military support or back-up of any nature and the maintenance of strictly even-handed operational practice in running the food convoys through no-man's-land, helped establish the credibility of UNHCR's position of humanitarian neutrality – which in turn strengthened its capacity to protect Tamil civilians in the conflict.

* * *

As a go-between function, crossing and re-crossing no-man's-land twice weekly, the convoys were only feasible on the basis of strictly impartial professional relations with both sides. In the process, we were fortunate in not having to witness atrocities perpetrated by either side. Even if we had, however, to anything like the extent of our colleagues in Bosnia a few years later, we would still not have been able to sound off about them in the media without immediately imperilling continuation of the convoys which were the open relief centres' lifeline. Such constraints did not, however, preclude insistence on protection positions when the situation so demanded; they meant only that we had to state our case in accordance with acceptable professional forms. For example, in reporting the grave abuse of human rights at Talaimannar to the Presidential Advisor, the facts were set out an anonymous "non-document," enabling it to be circulated with less embarrassment (Chapter 11, p. 168). Similar principles were applied during repeated informal interventions with key officials participating in the closed sessions of the National Security Council during the Madhu crisis (Chapter 13), and in invoking the provisions of the "gentlemen's agreement" through the Ministry of Defence in order to counter unauthorized Army incursions into the open relief centre at Pesalai (Chapter 13).

Absence of military

In the range of international humanitarian action in conflict, the Sri Lankan model was at the opposite end of the scale to so-called humanitarian intervention, where the motivation of intervening governments was usually more geopolitical than humanitarian. Essentially, this was because there was never any risk of violating national sovereignty in Sri Lanka, as the competent officials with whom the programme had been discussed from very early days in the war were strongly supportive, and continued to be so throughout its implementation.

Despite the keen interest in the war among the international community, particularly in those Western countries that were hosting large numbers of Sri Lankan Tamil asylum seekers, the level of geopolitical pressure during *Eelam War II* was relatively low. Primarily, this was because Indian intervention between 1987 and 1990, which had involved deployment of the Indian Peace Keeping Force (IPKF) pursuant to the 1987 Peace Accord, had gone awry and was most unlikely to be repeated. Thereafter, there had never been any question of intervention by external military forces, even by UN "blue helmets" in one form or another. (If there had been, it would have been decisively opposed by both the Sri Lankan and Indian Governments.) In consequence, the UN response to the challenge of protecting Tamil civilians in the war zone took the minimalist form of a very small humanitarian programme, devised as a needs-driven initiative by seasoned professional fieldworkers.

In Geneva, the absence of military escorts and back-up even of a technical and logistical nature for a UNHCR programme in a war zone had initially been regarded by some as a serious operational shortcoming. Paradoxically, however, this ostensible weakness facilitated rather than hindered the development of a protective role for a number of reasons. First, as regards the combatants, there was no third military actor for them to try to manipulate to their respective tactical advantage. Even to those on both sides who were most suspicious of an international role in the war zone, the handful of UNHCR fieldworkers was manifestly devoid of military significance.

Second, the small agency team was spared the humanitarian–military misunderstandings arising from the role of the latter in implementing the former's mandate, such as those that subsequently occurred in former Yugoslavia between the UN Protection Force (UNPROFOR) and UNHCR.[4] Third, without the UN military, there was no conflict between the United Nations' political and impartial humanitarian roles: UNHCR had its own statutory definition of neutrality: humanitarian and social work "of an entirely non-political nature".[5] The Security Council was not seized of the Sri Lankan conflict, and consequently there were no loftily-worded resolutions to complicate the situation on the ground with their ambiguity, as subsequently occurred in Bosnia. Although, within the limits of its own competence, the Human Rights Commission was concerned with Sri Lanka, its interest indirectly enhanced the position of UNHCR fieldworkers, because both combatants were mindful of the need to be seen to avoid action which might reflect adversely on their respective causes in Geneva.

Protection monitoring agreement

The open relief centre at Pesalai on Government-controlled Mannar island was covered by the "gentlemen's agreement" agreement negotiated on the ground with the General Officer Commanding the North (Chapter 11, pp. 165–6). This established certain protective modalities enabling UNHCR international field staff to monitor and report by two-way radio to the Colombo office incidents when the local military personnel entered the centre. In this way a number of potentially ugly incidents were avoided by making immediate high-level interventions.

Back-to-back agreements with combatants

Back-to-back agreements are a mechanism commonly used in corporate legal practice where it is in the interest of two parties that a certain function is performed, but neither is prepared to entrust the other with it, and so each makes its own separate agreement with a third party to carry it out. As such, it was readily adaptable to the Mannar war zone in *Eelam War II*, where UNHCR had to feel its way forward with each combatant party in order to explore the potential humanitarian space between them, and then conclude separate agreements/understandings. Although such an arrangement was frowned upon in bureaucratic circles in Geneva, it worked well enough on the ground (Chapter 17, p. 247).

[236]

Small-scale protection with broad impact

With a budget of a meagre US$ 1.5 million and a staff of only seven internationals, the original Mannar relief programme was critically underfunded and understaffed. Such funding was almost a historical low for a country emergency programme, particularly one with such a demandingly active operational role. In effect, it prevented the extension of open relief centres to elsewhere within the war zone, where both Tamil civilians and some of the more enlightened elements in the Army were asking for them, and outside it for the Muslims who sought refuge in the south when they were expelled from the north in an act of ethnic cleansing LTTE-style (Chapter 10, pp. 151–2). Nonetheless, in view of the contrastingly colossal scale of UNHCR operations in subsequent conflicts, first in Northern Iraq and then in former Yugoslavia, one moral of the relatively diminutive Sri Lankan programme would seem to be that operational effectiveness did not always necessarily have to be achieved through massive expenditure.

UNHCR's institutional capacity to play a protection role in a specific situation has often been regarded as dependent largely on the financial leverage of its material assistance projects. However, it is pertinent to note that in the early part of *Eelam War II* the importance of its programme to the Government was not so much its monetary value – which was minimal – as the impact of the professional services upon which its protection-orientated role was based, which were not in themselves cost-intensive. And this would seem to point to another moral: that it was the protection input, the extent to which an understanding of universal humanitarian standards could be established and a certain moral influence exercised to uphold them in a war zone – even if it didn't always succeed – which was critical in determining the qualitative impact of international engagement in a conflict.

In passing, it might also be mentioned that, ironically, the constraint of stringent economy was not always entirely negative in effect, as sometimes there were intangible advantages in the tone of the programme and the way it was perceived by its beneficiaries. One such was that it precluded much of the resentment among programme beneficiaries at the contrasting lifestyles of international agency fieldworkers – especially those recruited locally – which has often been aroused by more generously funded operations.

As for staffing, with only seven internationals for rigorously functional protection-orientated duty, we were overstretched for much of the time – and sometimes exhausted – which in difficult conditions was in itself operationally unhealthy. But otherwise, there were a number of advantages in the smallness of such a team as regards the commitment and solidarity it created (we had to be a close, lean and keen team to survive); the interchange of ideas and information it facilitated; and the broader understanding of operational and situational problems which was caused by our having to stand in for one another from time to time in order to permit family leave and other essential absences. Moreover, individually, our faces were all more widely known throughout the war zone than they would have been in a less short-staffed operation, which helped in the vital ongoing task of maintaining relations with both sides at day-to-day working levels, most notably at the checkpoints on each side of no-man's-land.

As for the notable slowness of the personnel service in Geneva in recruiting or providing replacements for the colleagues who were later taken for higher profile operations – notably before, in and after the First Gulf War – whether this was contrived or merely bureaucratic lassitude, it eventually enabled us to recruit directly ourselves from fellow fieldworkers in international non-governmental organizations alongside whom we had already been working on the ground – a thoroughly healthy development, albeit one which has unfortunately seldom been repeated elsewhere.

The financial stringency in Sri Lanka was dictated by UNHCR's funding problems worldwide which were acute in 1990, but were fortunately remedied sufficiently to permit significant expansion of the Sri Lanka programme in 1992.

* * *

That this relatively small programme was able to punch way above the weight of its resources, might perhaps be thought likely to have made planners pause for thought. But in fact there is no evidence that it did so. Indeed the institutional trend thereafter was strongly in the opposite direction, towards mega-programmes of material assistance, most notably in Northern Iraq and former Yugoslavia, where the development of protection practice was not impressive. The message that more could be achieved by programmes of relatively small-scale but more active engagement in protection and protection-orientated activities was evidently one which for a variety of reasons, from bureaucratic style to institutional culture, the agency did not want to hear. Put another way, although the High Commissioner had accepted the Sri Lanka programme as a programme model, had it been digested by line bureaucrats and absorbed into institutional culture? Or was it, below the High Commissioner and outside the Protection Division, regarded as an implicit critique of the way the agency mandate was perceived, the extent to which its protection function was prioritized and how its strongly material assistance orientated programmes were put together (Chapter 17, pp. 243–4)? In this regard, it is interesting to note the conclusions of an authoritative joint review mission in September 2001, which found the Sri Lanka programme to be strong and effective – but also expressed disappointment that in view of its performance and importance, it had not been the subject of detailed analysis or assessment from UNHCR headquarters for nearly a decade. Consequently, the review team "felt strongly that UNHCR as an organization should endeavour to fully analyse and document its experience in Sri Lanka, learning and sharing (its) lessons". It also recommended that the agency as a whole should make greater efforts to utilize the knowledge and experience of its field staff in Sri Lanka.[6] The extent to which these recommendations were in fact followed is difficult to ascertain.

17. Controversial questions

Asylum: threat or viable alternative? – UNHCR: beyond the mandate? protection in institutional culture – displacement: responsibility for IDPs, primary criterion for international humanitarian response? – "talking to terrorists": a humanitarian viewpoint, governmental positions – security: safety of fieldworkers? – agency relations: overlap with the ICRC – Non-governmental organizations – humanitarian diplomacy? – humanitarianism versus human rights – "bottom-up"?

Asylum: threat or viable alternative?[1]

One of the more genuinely humanitarian rather than politically contrived doubts expressed about the role of protective neutral engagement at the source of a refugee outflow was that, at least potentially, it was a threat to the universal human right of persons in fear of persecution in their own country to seek asylum elsewhere.[2] How far was there such a threat in Sri Lanka at that time?

From the outset, when the concept of an active UNHCR protection role in the conflict was still on the drawing board in Colombo, the possibility of it prejudicing the right to seek asylum had always been a primary consideration, and the utmost care had been taken to ensure that the competent Sri Lankan authorities and the Indian High Commission were fully apprised of the extent of UNHCR preoccupations in that regard. Indeed the Indian authorities made no attempt to restrict, let alone stop, the landing of Sri Lankan Tamil refugees in Tamil Nadu, where they were mostly accommodated in camps along the coast, a practice which continued until late May 1991. At that time, however, as Rajiv Gandhi, the Congress party leader and former Indian Prime Minister who had signed the 1987 Peace Accord, was campaigning in the general elections in Tamil Nadu, a young Tamil woman bent down to touch his feet in a traditional gesture of supplication, thereby detonating the two kilos of plastic explosive strapped to her body.

Thereafter, it was not only much more difficult for Tamil asylum seekers to land in India, but also increasingly hard for those who were already there, as they felt what were in the circumstances understandable pressures on them to return home. This had led to some tension between the Indian High Commission and the UNHCR office in Colombo in that, while the former reflected the wish of their authorities for early repatriation of Sri Lankan Tamil refugees, the latter was insisting on the agency's fundamental position that any such repatriation had to be voluntary. The High Commission accepted this, but intimated nonetheless that the refugees were no longer welcome in India. And there were reports that Sri Lankan Tamil refugees in the camps in Tamil Nadu were feeling increasingly insecure. Meanwhile, UNHCR was firmly of the opinion that conditions in the north east were unsuitable for repatriation, as was the ICRC.

The threat to the right to seek asylum in India had not come from UNHCR's protection role at the source of the refugee outflow, but from the tidal wave of resentment against Sri Lankan Tamil refugees and asylum seekers caused by the assassination of Rajiv Gandhi. And, most importantly, the Indian authorities subsequently resumed their liberal asylum practices.[3]

* * *

In recent years, the view of the UNHCR office in Colombo has been that its involvement with IDPs does not appear to have prejudiced the right to seek asylum abroad or the decision-making practice of refugee receiving countries. Moreover, although it notes that some countries have been applying the "internal flight alternative" notion in relation to Sri Lanka, it is not aware of applicants for refugee status in those countries having been rejected on account of UNHCR's role in Sri Lanka.[4]

UNHCR

Beyond the mandate?

Initially, criticism of the innovative protection role in Sri Lanka had ranged from one end of the institutional spectrum to the other. Some dismissed it as no more than a bundle of expedients devoid of concept, and as such unworthy of the agency ("short-termism", "pure pragmatism" etc.); others claimed that it was either beyond the UNHCR mandate or did not constitute international protection – or both.

The volatility and diversity of conditions in which different conflicts are fought are such that a large element of pragmatism in international humanitarian response – providing it is focused to achieve appropriate protection objectives – is not only healthy, but essential. With the vast experience of the ICRC in conflict, it was doubtful that an ICRC chief delegate would have found it necessary to argue such a point. That a UNHCR representative had to was indicative of the agency's comparative lack of previous involvement in this particular field of protective practice. Moreover, far from being a number of random expedients, the UNHCR role of engagement comprised a coherent system of balanced and mutually supportive mechanisms (Chapter 16, p. 231–2). The charge that protective neutral engagement as practised in Sri Lanka was not international protection derived from its traditional function for the nationals of countries whose governments were unable or unwilling to protect them because they were beyond their frontiers. What had happened in Sri Lanka was that as a result of *Eelam War II*, the Government had been unable to protect its own nationals of Tamil origin, not because they were in another country, but because they were in an area controlled by insurgents within their own country. In this way, and with the Government's very willing agreement, UNHCR had undertaken the task of establishing open relief centres to protect and relieve them, of organizing neutral convoys across no-man's-land to supply the centres on the mainland and, in the case of Pesalai, of monitoring military access to the centre.

The contention that the mandate was being exceeded was more complex, as it involved an evaluation of the respective merits of the agency's statutory mandate on the one hand, and of its "good offices" or ad hoc responsibility for specific operations authorized by the UN on the other, as the basis for an active and inclusive protection role within a country of refugee origin. Although in normal times there would have been some advantages in launching a programme under "good offices", since the element of protection methodology in such operations was usually muted or non-existent, it was doubtful whether such an arrangement would have been suitable to support the active protection role which the ground situation in Sri Lanka demanded. Even more importantly, the times were not normal, and with the intense pressure on and within UNHCR to retrench, "good offices" for such a programme – with the large appeal for additional funds it would necessarily have entailed – was a non-starter.

In the circumstances, the High Commissioner's clear obligation to the refugee returnee group, which was laid upon him by the statutory mandate as authoritatively interpreted by the UNHCR Executive Committee in terms of his legitimate concern for the consequences of a return,[5] had provided a legal opening through which he could initiate action. Accordingly, High Commissioner Stoltenberg had approved the programme, and although his subsequent resignation seriously undermined its position in the internal politics of the agency, in no way did it impugn the validity of his mandatory decision.

* * *

Before the end of the first year of *Eelam War II*, the initial doubts about the programme in Sri Lanka had been disproved by the demonstrably effective ways in which it was responding to humanitarian challenges in the war zone. By then, it was also evident that sensitively applied pragmatism was essential for the delivery of protection and humanitarian relief in the midst of the highly volatile conditions of a war zone. And by 1992, despite its continuing unpopularity in some quarters in Geneva, UNHCR's role of protective engagement in Sri Lanka's civil war looked set to survive, essentially because it was performing a much needed humanitarian function which other relevant actors were either unable or unwilling to take over. And most importantly, after she had fully taken charge of the agency and had had time to consider the matter, Sadako Ogata, the new High Commissioner, decided in the Sri Lanka programme's favour: the agency would not withdraw from the country and its active protection role in the conflict at the source of the refugee outflow would continue. Rather than the "short-termist" expedient that some had feared it would be in 1990, protective neutral engagement had proved to be a constructive element in the long term perspective of humanitarian needs in conflict and the capacity of a UN agency to meet them.

Protection in institutional culture

International protection has been accepted as the primary function of UNHCR's mandate throughout its history and is ever formally reaffirmed as such at international conferences and in UN documents. In the agency's in-house politics and institutional culture, however, it has not always worked out that way. The experience in formulating an active protection role in the midst of the *Eelam* wars both illustrates the problem and helps to explain how it has come about. An ironically revealing exchange occurred at the outset of *Eelam War II* when Colombo's request for two field officers primarily for protection-orientated duty in Mannar was rebuffed by Geneva, initially on the ground that its programme was not big enough to justify protection staff: in other words, the material assistance cart was effectively being put before the protection horse. The institutional background to this bizarre development is that despite the key statutory role of the High Commissioner in protection, there is also a not always consonant bureaucratic attitude in which the delivery of UNHCR's primary function is seen as an operational incidental rather than the central purpose of the agency's existence.

In mandating the protection function to the High Commissioner rather than to the agency, the UNHCR statute reflects the thinking of the founding fathers, who considered that:

> there was no point in setting up just another unit in the United Nations Secretariat. What was needed was a High Commissioner who would carry weight with governments, and possess the attributes of impartiality and independence, including independence from the politically charged atmosphere of the UN and the Secretariat.[6]

Without exception, the High Commissioners have always taken their protection responsibilities very seriously. But with the progressive expansion of UNHCR activities in response to displacement-related needs, the extent to which heads of the agency could be directly involved in the resolution of protection crises was reduced.

Moreover, in the interdepartmental power game, protection tended to lose out to material assistance, primarily because of the dramatic escalation in the size and funding of UNHCR programmes and the bureaucratic muscle which this inevitably developed for those involved in assistance programming. This tendency was also part cause, part effect of the reduction in the status and function of the Division of International Protection as the vigilant guardian of protection in the life of the agency, a tendency which was indeed consolidated in the internal restructuring of 1986, when it was reorganized and re-designated as the Division of Refugee Law and Doctrine, and effectively downgraded.[7]

* * *

Unsurprisingly, some conclusions to be drawn from the institutional controversy over the Sri Lanka programme in the latter half of 1990 are in themselves controversial. One such is that sensitive decisions on the nature, direction and application of international protection are properly the preserve of High Commissioners who are duly elected, appointed and empowered to provide it – and nobody else. Accordingly, if during an interregnum there is a challenge to such a decision taken by the last High Commissioner, it is suggested that the appropriate course of action for an interim administration is to decline to entertain the matter and to refer it for eventual adjudication by the new High Commissioner when she or he takes office.

Displacement

Responsibility for IDPs

At that time, at least in some quarters, even refugee returnees were deemed to be barely on the fringe of the mandate, and the launching of a programme for a relatively small group of them in the midst of a conflict was therefore considered to be already stretching things to the limit or beyond. Thus, the reality on the ground that the UNHCR programme was benefiting not only returnees but also IDPs, and even endangered and destitute Tamil inhabitants in the war zone, was regarded with particular disfavour by some elements in Geneva. However, in a situation where they were suffering in the same conditions as the returnees, it would have been both unconscionable and operationally impractical to have excluded IDPs from the benefits of the UNHCR programme – and as regards endangered local inhabitants still in their homes in the war zone, any such attempt would have increased the pressure on them to flee.

It was thus unsurprising that High Commissioner Ogata followed up her decision in favour of the programme with a formal instruction on this topic to representatives in the field and officers in Geneva. The instruction considered the circumstances where "UNHCR should consider taking *primary* responsibility for the internally displaced, weighing in each case the additional benefit of its involvement in terms of protection and solutions."[8] Among these cases the High Commissioner specifically included situations where IDPs were mixed with refugees. And subsequently, she was to draw attention to "the direct linkage between internal displacement and refugee flows, as the causes of displacement may be indistinguishable … the only distinction being that the former have not crossed an international frontier".[9] This focus on the close interrelation of refugee and IDP dynamics at the source of an international exodus significantly broadened the agency's thinking on its due function in countries of refugee origin. Thereafter, the plight of endangered and destitute groups – at least in conditions where, as in Sri Lanka, returnees were involved – could not responsibly be ignored. Unfortunately, however, this did not always mean that there was sufficient institutional will to launch an active programme of protective relief in subsequent situations elsewhere.

Primary criterion for humanitarian response

Sri Lankan experience sometimes gave pause for thought on the relative priorities of displacement, destitution and danger in the establishing the case for humanitarian response, and the continuing validity of this long-established order in contemporary conditions of refugee exodus – particularly from conflict. Within the UNHCR mandate, prioritization of these criteria is tempered by the political interest of states in seeing that a bothersome problem of international disorder is addressed within an administratively manageable framework.

In reality, such prioritization is determined according to the extent to which the affected persons move: refugees have the first place, because they flee outside their own country; IDPs, who move within it, come second; and civilians normally living in the war zone and suffering the same conditions which cause the other groups to flee, but who for one reason or another have not yet abandoned their homes, are barely recognized in last place. Promotion up the hierarchy of entitlement from one category to another is also determined by movement, with the last group gaining IDP status if they leave their homes, and the IDPs acquiring the status of the first group – as refugees or asylum seekers – if they flee across an international frontier.

The effect is thus to put a premium on the degree of displacement, and external flight is in any event usually only possible for the relatively privileged, particularly those fortunate enough to find the wherewithal for international travel. The level of suffering, however, is often higher among those who cannot afford to get abroad, including local residents in the war zone who remain at home. But it is neither in the international humanitarian nor geopolitical interest to encourage and sustain an external exodus from a refugee-producing situation, particularly when, as in Sri Lanka, many persons affected by the conflict were likely to take the option of internal flight, if it was available. Such an analysis suggests that better criteria for international concern in conflict might be not so much displacement – a symptom rather than the cause of the problem – as destitution and danger. Although these are also not in themselves the root cause of the conflict, they nonetheless provide the substantive impetus for flight, and are therefore the most appropriate focus for response.

What, if any, is the moral? Of course the fundamental right to seek asylum must not be prejudiced in any way; but where substantial numbers of people do not want to flee any further than they feel constrained to, protection and relief should be provided for them as near to their home areas as sober professional assessment, international access, security and logistics in the war zone may permit.

"Talking to terrorists"?[10]

A humanitarian viewpoint

One aspect of the Sri Lanka programme's unpopularity in Geneva had been the dependence on cooperation by the LTTE, which was universally notorious for deadly ruthlessness and the perpetration of numerous acts of terrorism. In the circumstances, it was asked, was it prudent to have launched such a programme without having obtained the movement's written agreement, or at least acknowledgement? Was it appropriate, moreover, for a UN agency even to have dealings with such an unsavoury party?

The first question had been raised at a meeting in Geneva, when I explained that the signing of formal agreements played no part in LTTE practice, but that as a result of discussions in Jaffna at the leadership level, I was satisfied that there were sufficient elements of interest and trust to see the programme through the inevitably volatile events ahead. At that point, there had been silence in the room as the intent gaze of the critics present switched from me to the senior officer who was in the chair (and beside whom I was sitting) to see how he would react to such an admission of direct dealing with the LTTE. After a pause which was probably no more than 30 seconds but seemed much longer during which he was visibly reviewing the options, the chairman turned towards me and put his hand on my wrist, saying "You did well!" – whereafter the discussion moved on to less controversial matters. Such action was indeed within the statutory definition of the agency's work as "of an entirely non-political character … humanitarian and social",[11] and reflected its earlier operational relations with liberation movements in Africa during decolonization. Moreover, in a recent report to the Security Council, the Secretary General has advised that, given the nature of contemporary armed conflict, it is necessary to engage groups in a dialogue aimed at facilitating the provision of humanitarian assistance and protection.[12]

Governmental positions

However, from the perspective of national governments suffering terrorist attacks in furtherance of political agendas, the question of whether it is appropriate to "talk to terrorists" is different – and much more difficult. Both the Sri Lankan and the UK governments have had to face it, in relation to atrocities committed respectively by the LTTE and the IRA, and eventually decided that it was not so much a moral question of right and wrong, but of the art of the possible in finding a way out of a dangerous political impasse. In that respect, the case for initiating talks is that it can help loosen up somewhat the otherwise viciously circular process of tit-for-tat reactions from both parties. Contacts usually start as a dialogue of the deaf, and get nowhere fast. But the very fact of their having been initiated is in itself therapeutic in that it leads willy-nilly to both sides listening to each others' stories: inevitably a very slow and long-term process, and one that is chronically impeded by the fundamental corruption of values which terrorism foments. Nevertheless, initiation of the process facilitates a better appreciation of the essential fact that neither side can hope to entirely achieve its objectives. Without such critical perceptions, the IRA would not have declared its abandonment of traditional armed struggle against the UK government, nor would there have been the Oslo Declaration of 2002 in which the LTTE put aside the historic objective of achieving Tamil *Eelam* outside the Sri Lankan state.

It goes without saying that there can never be any question of giving in to terrorist blackmail. But in the current standoff between Islamist terrorists and the authorities in the UK, the vicious circle that has to be broken is between minds that, on the one hand, are sick literally to death and, on the other, the outlook of a government in dogged denial of the need to rethink a patently flawed foreign policy.

Security: safety of fieldworkers?

Any war zone is an unhealthy place for civilians of any sort at any time, and at the programme's conception in the early days of *Eelam War II* a significant part of the controversy and opposition which it aroused related to physical danger for UNHCR staff as fieldworkers as well as for the displaced Tamil civilians whom it was designed to protect and relieve.

There was always the possibility of the unpredictable event, such as getting caught in crossfire between the combatants (Chapter 2, pp. 15–16; Chapter 9, pp. 134; Chapter 12, pp. 182–4). Mines were a constant danger in view of the assiduous LTTE practice of mining stretches of track in the jungle and then systematically re-mining shortly after the Army had de-mined them (Chapter 10, p. 149–50). And there had been an attempt to scare us off, when an Air Force plane had shot up some parked and unmanned convoy lorries in the jungle (Chapter 11, pp. 169–71), although the sharp reaction of the diplomatic community in Colombo at the time rendered it abortive.

In comparison with subsequent conflicts, however, most notably in the Balkans and the Caucasus, the danger level in the Sri Lankan war zone where we were working, although of course never negligible, was relatively low. For this, there were several reasons. One was that after some ambiguity in attitudes during the programme's early months, both sides – or at least their more enlightened elements – had come to accept that UNHCR's neutral humanitarian role was in their respective, albeit of course very different, interests.

An incident on Mannar island is interesting in this context. An LTTE ambush party had fired a succession of submachine gun bursts at a passing UNHCR Landcruiser in which Pipat Greigarn, the Thai field officer, and his driver were travelling. At the first shots, they braked hard and kept their heads down, while the firing continued for ten seconds. Miraculously, neither of them was hit, although the windscreen had been shattered and the water pipe in the engine cut. However, this incident was exceptional and it served to illustrate both the relatively positive way in which both combatants had come to view the programme, and the tone of relations between UNHCR and the combatants. Pipat was convinced that it had been a mistake: there had been a white Army vehicle in the vicinity at that time and the (also white) UNHCR Landcruiser had been travelling at a speed which would have made it difficult to identify. (As he said, during his initial radio report, if the LTTE had wanted to kill him, it wouldn't have been necessary for them to go to the length of setting up an ambush on the road to Mannar town.) And on the following day, he was proved to be right when, by circuitous means, the LTTE – in an unprecedented move – expressed its regrets.

Later, when I discussed the incident at the Ministry of Defence in Colombo and said that in the circumstances UNHCR didn't intend taking the matter further, my interlocutor, the State Secretary for Defence, Air Chief Marshal Terence Fernando, gave me a long-suffering look and said, "But what a fuss you'd have made if the firing had been from our side!" before concluding with good-humoured resignation that nevertheless UNHCR was doing a good job.

In the war zone we kept our distance from both sides, neither of which liked us much, each suspecting that we were in cahoots with the other. But they were prepared to tolerate us as a necessary evil as long as we didn't get in the way – and in that regard it was advantageous for us to be seen to be operating as impeccably humanitarian fieldworkers without military support or even logistical or technical back-up, and therefore perforce impartial and even-handed in our dealings with them both.

Another reason for the relatively low danger level in Sri Lanka was the disciplined control which both sides maintained in their areas. There were no freebooting initiatives by criminalized irregulars, such as extortion at checkpoints or kidnappings which greatly increased the danger for UNHCR staff working in some subsequent conflicts elsewhere, most notoriously in the Caucasus.[13]

Evidently, we were lucky with security. But risks were reduced in daily working life not only by constant vigilance and the application of sober common sense, but by close contact with the people whom we were trying to protect, who were usually as well informed as they were shrewd. In that regard there is the dry comment of a former Sri Lanka colleague on his subsequent experience of UNHCR programmes elsewhere: noting the heavy personnel security measures of recent years, he said that the fact that in Sri Lanka we were living in the midst of those whom we were trying to protect had been a significant element in our own safety, yet in some programmes fears of possible attacks by refugees meant UNHCR international staff were now being protected to an extent which minimized their contact with the very people they were there to help.[14]

* * *

MSF, who had their own programme, but also implemented the health sector of the UNHCR programme, were not so fortunate with security as we were. They were first attacked in early February 1991, when an Air Force helicopter persistently fired on an ambulance, albeit without causing casualties. On 3 May 1991, there was another strike that was much higher in the scale of outrage, involving as it did a persistently pressed attack with both machine gunning and bombing in which the passengers travelling in the ambulance were wounded, some grievously so. It was, moreover, particularly disquieting that the attack continued over a period of two hours, during which MSF was repeatedly reporting the incident to the commander of the Air Force base and JOC, neither of whom stopped it.

Although this was primarily an MSF crisis, it was one in which UNHCR was directly concerned as a close operational partner – the ambulance had been travelling from the centre at Madhu when the incident occurred. We therefore coordinated our full support and solidarity throughout the intense crisis that followed, not least because we felt that MSF were probably in part serving as a proxy target for ourselves.

Shamefully, the Commission of Inquiry appointed by the Government duly heard evidence and then found that the incident was MSF's fault, on the ground that the ambulance had been on the wrong road. Although it had not followed the approved route, the finding implied that the Air Force had been justified in concluding that a white vehicle with a Red Cross logo and flashing emergency roof light belonged to the LTTE – and therefore in ordering and continuing the attack, even after it had been contacted by MSF. Altogether, it was a crude and unsuccessful attempt to whitewash an indelible stain on the otherwise largely clean record of Government relations with international relief agencies during that period of the conflict.

[251]

Agency relations

Overlap with the ICRC

That its innovative role was leading UNHCR into territory that was more properly the preserve of the ICRC was one of the charges levelled against the programme in 1990, and there were indeed some misunderstandings with the ICRC in the early days of *Eelam War II*. But these disappeared progressively as the nature of UNHCR's role in the war zone became clearer in the light of events, and appropriate coordination measures and relations of mutual trust were established on the ground. In Geneva, however, the issue of the programme allegedly duplicating ICRC functions had been kept alive, largely because the critics were still hoping that the Red Cross would agree to take over the UNHCR role, if not its programme.

The two agencies' roles of course were not identical. The ICRC had special responsibilities under the Geneva Red Cross conventions involving particular functions such as the protection of hospitals, the tracing of missing persons and visiting of prisoners, in which UNHCR was not normally involved.[15] It also had a large programme in the south of the country as a result of the entirely separate and unconnected JVP insurgency among the Sinhalese, which was outside the UN refugee agency's mandate. But both institutions had protection and relief concerns for civilians in the northern war zones, with UNHCR dealing with Mannar at the source of the refugee outflow, while the ICRC concentrated on the much larger numbers in the Jaffna peninsula.

Among the Western diplomatic community in Colombo, it was widely accepted that the roles of the two agencies in the northern war zone were constructively complementary. Notably, the UK and Canadian High Commissioners – both of whom were closely following events in the north – had expressed strong views on the matter, with the latter saying during the programme review that there was a good de facto division of responsibility, with UNHCR dealing with internally displaced persons and civilians who might be contemplating departure and the ICRC focusing on those who hadn't any intention of fleeing the country.

Beyond such a largely pragmatic division of responsibility, complementarity was notable in the difference in styles of interaction with the civil administration. Both agencies were, of course, apolitical and even-handed with the combatants in their operational practice. But because of its experience prior to *Eelam War II*, UNHCR was a good deal closer to the local authorities than was the ICRC – a position illustrated by a GA in Jaffna who, although extremely grateful to the ICRC for transporting food and other essential food supplies to the peninsula, nonetheless expressed his frustration at the relatively limited scope of their functions when he said "They will get you relief supplies from A to B – but that's it!" Of course, it wasn't: the ICRC did a great deal more than transporting relief supplies to and within the north.

Nonetheless, there was a notable difference in the degree to which the two agencies were prepared to interface with the local authorities. In Mannar, for example, largely because of UNHCR's close relationship with the *kachcheri*, it had been possible to adopt a more flexible approach, both in setting up the open relief centres and in negotiating arrangements for monitoring military access to them. Another example related to the use of radio communications systems: ICRC radio was strictly reserved for use by its own delegates, whereas the UNHCR system was made available for the ongoing dialogue about humanitarian needs and relief deliveries between the GAs in the northern *kachcheris* and CGES in Colombo, to facilitate the administration of education services (including examinations) in the north, and even on occasions to a limited extent to help the banking sector to continue functioning in Jaffna with all that this meant for living conditions during the conflict.

The ICRC position reflected its immense experience and role in wars and emergencies, while the corresponding UNHCR policy was determined largely by the need to relieve the suffering and pressures of the conflict on civilians. There was space enough and need enough in the northern war zones for both institutional takes on the international humanitarian role to protect and relieve civilians, which was strengthened by their complementarity.

The crunch on the delicate issue of the two agencies' relations in Sri Lanka had finally come during the review mission in April, when the ICRC had been asked if it would be prepared to take over the UNHCR role in the north. On that occasion, Pierre Wettach, the chief ICRC delegate, responded in habitually low-key but blunt style: the ICRC was not interested in taking over UNHCR's role in Mannar. It already had its hands more than full and considered that UNHCR was morally obliged to do what it was in fact doing. Moreover, the refugee agency also had clout with the Government, which was important, especially in relation to an issue such as repatriation, where it needed to advise that conditions for organized repatriation were not yet ready.

Far from being hostile to the programme – let alone wanting to take it over – the ICRC was supportive and wished us well.

Non-governmental organizations

Entirely apart from relations with the ICRC, there was the question whether UNHCR's innovative role might not have been more appropriately performed by one or more "international" (i.e. externally financed, managed and to a significant extent staffed) NGOs. This was considered by the Colombo office at the programme planning stage shortly after the outbreak of *Eelam War II*, but rejected for a number of reasons. The most important point was that the credibility of such an innovative function had to be earned and maintained with the combatants amidst the ongoing challenges and tensions of a highly volatile war zone – a task of particular sensitivity as regards presentation and relations, which required tight discipline and control over operational activities that was more in line with the field practice of UN agencies than of NGOs.

Again, there was the question of clout: as the only UN humanitarian agency on the ground, UNHCR had some international standing and influence with the Government and the separatist LTTE, both of which in their different ways tended to be suspicious of NGOs. Moreover, it was unlikely that the Government would have agreed to entrust the delivery of its food to a single NGO in the way it did to UNHCR, and a relief consortium of NGOs would have been even more problematic in that regard.[16] And as for protection, only UNHCR had the mandate.

Nevertheless, the decision to set up the programme alone and not to share leadership caused resentment among some NGOs, who regarded it as unnecessarily exclusive, although agencies such as MSF and subsequently SCF undertook functions within the overall framework it provided. However, in 1996, such misgivings were addressed by Neelan Tiruchelvam, the leading human rights activist, who was also director of the ICES – itself a Colombo-based NGO with an international mandate and board. Having reviewed the controversial background to the UNHCR initiative he concluded that while several NGOs were performing essential relief functions, they "were not capable of maintaining the complex relations with the military, the government and the LTTE that a UN agency could sustain".[17]

Humanitarian diplomacy?[18]

Wherever in the world, the primary task of a UNHCR representative is to ensure that the agency receives sufficient cooperation from the competent national authorities to enable it to discharge its mandatory responsibilities and programme objectives. Such quasi-diplomatic functions have evolved over the years as the agency adapted to the changing international challenges of displacement. In its early days in the aftermath of the Second World War, the first representatives were posted mostly in industrialized countries where their working relations were with competent national security and immigration authorities, officials in the embassies of the principal resettlement countries, and national and international NGOs. Later, when UNHCR established large programmes of material assistance to respond to the needs of refugees and asylum seekers in situations of mass influx in developing countries, there was a broadening in the range and a rise in the level of a representative's contacts, largely because of the political sensitivity of the refugee situations which the agency was addressing.

In a civil war situation in a country of refugee origin, the nature of a representative's functions developed still further in a number of ways. In Sri Lanka, this was because UNHCR was playing an active role in militarily contested areas, which essentially involved the management of sensitive relations with both combatants – the Army and the LTTE separatists – with day-to-day working contacts in the war zone and higher up the scale of government in Colombo, and occasionally when the situation demanded, the LTTE high command in Jaffna (Chapter 9, pp. 136–41).

Sri Lankan Army, central Government officials and diplomats

The innovative nature of UNHCR's role of protective neutral engage-ment in the war necessarily required a concerted and sustained effort to ease the naturally fairly tense relations at all levels of functional contact on both sides. In the war zone, there were the checkpoints on both sides of no-man's-land. Relations with security personnel could be problematic on the outward journey, when the relief-laden convoys were closely searched for prohibited items (Chapter 12,

p. 179), and particularly on return journeys during periods of anticipated hostilities (Chapter 12, p. 181). At unit commander levels,
contacts were more with the Army, which was holding key positions
on routes over which we had to pass, than with the LTTE, whose
patrols in the jungle were constantly on the move and usually kept
out of sight. Save on exceptional occasions, Army–UNHCR relations
were good.

In Colombo, central Government officials were not as well
informed of humanitarian conditions in the war zone as they
needed to be. Their own sources of information were the GAs and
their civil administration teams in the *kachcheris* and the Army
commands, both of which were of limited value in that respect.
This was because, on the one hand, the principal line of commu-
nication for the GAs with Colombo was the UNHCR radio, which
could only be used for brief requests for emergency relief supplies
from Essential Services in Colombo. And on the other hand, the
Army's professional tendency was to see the situation in strategic
rather than humanitarian terms, and so it was unlikely to report
sensitive conditions regarding civilians in areas where it was
operating.

In consequence, the UNHCR representative could speak in
Colombo with objective professional authority on humanitarian
conditions in the war zone, not only to the interested but largely
uninformed diplomatic community, whose members normally did
not go anywhere near the frontline, but much more importantly, to
key officials in the Government who needed to be better informed.
As regards the latter, relations stabilized when it appeared that the
UNHCR programme was succeeding in establishing a critical level
of trust at the humanitarian operational level in the midst of the
crudely partisan conditions of the war zone and, with flexibility and
pertinacity, was able to maintain its position through the ongoing
volatility of events and frequent crises.

Ironically, moreover, the UNHCR representative's position
was enhanced by the programme's chronic understaffing. This
meant that the representative had to travel to and within the war
zone much more often than would normally have been necessary.
That disadvantage was more than offset by his being all the
better informed, and so he could always be sure of ready access
to key competent officials, not to mention key players in the
diplomatic community, during the relatively little time he was in
Colombo.

Humanitarianism versus human rights?

As for tension between humanitarian and human rights approaches on the ground, the experience of Sri Lanka at this time was that, at least in the context of strongly protection-orientated relief, the variation was more the art of the protectively possible than a stark choice between different methods. This was not to say that there was no tension, but that it was one that could be managed within a sensitively pragmatic framework such as the UNHCR mandate, where protection was a unique combination of human rights and humanitarian practice: on the one hand, refugee rights were a specialized branch of the former delivered through negotiated procedures and interventions, and on the other, relief activities often helped achieve protection objectives by enhancing the influence of fieldworkers on the ground.

"Bottom-up"?

The small Sri Lanka programme was a prime example of a bottom-up initiative from the field, and one which vindicated such a method in the formulation of protective response in conflict – and at the same time, an illustration of why this concept is talked of so much in quasi-academic circles, but so little heard of in relation to actual programmes. Indeed "bottom-up" has long had an exceptional status in UN jargon as a universally lauded buzzword which is in constant use in seminars, papers, speeches and other presentations, one to which the right-minded invariably aspire – but so very rarely practise, for the simple reason that there is usually a well-established interest in keeping things going in the time-honoured way which, when it comes to the point, defends the status quo by all available means. Broadly, that was the experience of the Sri Lanka programme in the early days of *Eelam War II*. But even when it had been re-endorsed by the incoming High Commissioner, Sadako Ogata, the agency bureaucracy still seemed to have some difficulty in taking bottom-up principles into its working practice. For example, a decade later, the joint UK DFID/UNHCR review (Chapter 16, p. 239) identified bottom-up planning as one of the Sri Lanka programme's strengths – yet at the same time noted that despite the fact that it was the largest and strongest of the agency's IDP programmes, its staff had not been consulted in the preparation of UNHCR's new operational guidelines for IDP projects. Top-down practice dies hard in international bureaucracies. As someone in Colombo wryly observed when the Sri Lanka programme was being subjected to intense internal pressures in 1990, "bottom-up is a vulnerable position."

18. Improvisation – intervention – engagement

Improvisation: UNHCR "special operations" – military intervention: northern Iraq and Bosnia – neutral engagement in Tajikistan – "responsibility to protect" in Darfur? – operationalizing protection for IDPs?

Improvisation: UNHCR "special operations"

> The choice was to do nothing, or to improvise. (Sadruddin Aga Khan, 1975)[1]

In the early 1970s, there were several reasons why the international response to situations of post-conflict reconstruction – in the Asian subcontinent, Cyprus, Indochina and southern Sudan – was channelled through UNHCR "special operations" outside the agency's traditional competence and regular budget. The primary reason was UNHCR's responsibility to facilitate the voluntary repatriation of refugees under its statutory mandate.[2] Beyond that, there was the problem of UN institutional insufficiency. Other than for refugees, there was no agency which was competent or equipped to respond to the challenge of conflict-affected persons, particularly those displaced within their own countries. But as UNHCR had proximate experience and skills and a reputation of can-do operational flexibility, the High Commissioner, Sadruddin Aga Khan, thus came to play a leading role that was largely outside the agency's traditional mandate, through its "good offices" and pursuant to relevant General Assembly resolutions in "those humanitarian endeavours of the United Nations for which his Office has particular expertise and experience".[3] Moreover, Sadruddin saw clearly the connection between refugees and IDPs affected by long years of war. In southern Sudan, he emphasised the significance of the operation in enabling the UN to help both groups inside their own country.[4] And in Viet Nam, where the agency was providing humanitarian assistance in another post-conflict context, he stated that the situation of IDPs "affected by long years of war is similar in every respect to that of refugees covered by the activities of my Office".[5] Indeed, there and elsewhere, he saw such programmes as confidence-building measures to promote a climate which would be conducive to early voluntary repatriation.

However, as regards protection, UNHCR's role in post-conflict situations was slow to develop. It was not until the 1980s, that its Executive Committee adopted formal Conclusions on international protection in voluntary repatriation situations, spelling out a monitoring role including the right of access, which it declared to be inherent in the mandate.[6] But this was for refugees who had repatriated following amnesties and peace agreements, and did not extend to IDPs. Such protection benefit as the latter group might gain from UNHCR was therefore unlikely to be much more than a rub-off from the agency's operational assistance activities and its monitoring of refugees in the same conditions and localities. Nevertheless, it was a start, and was to help define the international protection dimension in the agency's repatriation activities, as in Cambodia and Sri Lanka.

Military intervention: northern Iraq and Bosnia

It was not until the early 1990s, that the force of events propelled UNHCR into protection roles in conflict situations in countries of origin, not only for refugee returnees, but de facto for all endangered civilians, including IDPs and local inhabitants at risk in war zones in ways which had not been foreseen, and in some institutional quarters, were even less welcome then than they are now. The circumstances occurred mostly in the aftermath of the geopolitically cataclysmic developments of the time: the First Gulf War, in northern Iraq; the disintegration of Former Yugoslavia, in Bosnia; and after the dissolution of the Soviet Union and its replacement by the Commonwealth of Independent States (CIS), in Tajikistan. As outlined below, in the first two situations UNHCR found itself working in humanitarian space which had either been created originally and guaranteed thereafter by force – as in Iraqi Kurdistan with the US-led military coalition – or which was to a significant extent dependent on UN forces – as in Bosnia, where the latter were also operationally involved in delivery of the humanitarian mandate.

Northern Iraq

Conflict in Kurdistan

Following the victory of the coalition powers in the First Gulf War – with their incitement but without their support – the Kurds in the north revolted against the surviving Saddamist forces of the central government, who soon gained the upper hand and thereafter carried out widespread brutal repression. Consequently, there was a mass flight of civilians towards the Iranian and Turkish frontiers, and as the Turkish authorities refused to let the fugitives enter their territory, or to stay if they managed to enter, some 400,000 mainly Kurdish refugees and IDPs were stranded in the mountainous frontier region in conditions of acute privation and exposure.

At that point John Major, the British prime minister, took a personal interest in their plight and pressed the case for establishing a protected enclave in Iraqi Kurdistan which would enable the Kurds to return home in safety. Initially, although endorsed by the European Community, this proposal was favoured neither by Washington, which wanted to avoid getting sucked into an internal Iraqi conflict, nor the United Nations secretariat, which feared that such a plan would infringe Iraqi national sovereignty and could lead to renewed hostilities. In the event, however, the leading coalition powers intervened forcibly to establish a safe haven and launched a massive humanitarian project, Operation Provide Comfort, within it. As a result, there was a large-scale return movement from the border areas, while the UN secured acceptance by the government of an international humanitarian operation in northern Iraq for which UNHCR had assumed responsibility by mid June 1991. Following the early withdrawal of coalition troops from the safe haven, its external security was guaranteed by Operation Poised Hammer, with the imminent threat of immediate air attacks if central government forces attempted to interfere.

UN protection response

The challenge – the need for the international community to protect endangered civilians within a civil war at the source of a refugee outflow from their own country, was the same as it had been in Sri

Lanka, as was the broad perception of appropriate response within an area of special protection. But UNHCR's operation in Iraqi Kurdistan differed sharply from the Sri Lankan model in a number of key respects, including the mandate, the nature of geopolitical pressure, operational scale, military involvement and protection methodology.

When *Eelam War II* broke out in mid 1990, UNHCR was already in Sri Lanka on account of prior responsibilities under its statutory mandate to monitor the reintegration of refugees who had previously repatriated voluntarily. It had therefore subsequently been able to develop a professional protection response, largely because the geopolitical situation was such as to exclude the possibility of external intervention.

In northern Iraq, however, there was military intervention by the coalition powers under cover of which they had launched Operation Provide Comfort. The agency was there because the Secretary General had been under intense pressure to ensure that the UN took over the humanitarian operation. In consequence, he had appealed to the international community for funds and asked UNHCR to take over humanitarian responsibility for IDPs – a role described in the relevant agency report as having been "dictated by the request of the Secretary General".[7]

The difference in the scale of the two operations was dramatic: in Sri Lanka there were seven professional staff and a mere US$1.5 million, while in northern Iraq there were more than 150 internationals and funding on a scale that was historically unprecedented. Yet it was on the sensitive question of military intervention and support that the two operations were most strikingly different. In Sri Lanka there was neither military intervention nor support of any nature; in northern Iraq, in contrast, not only was the agency there because of prior military intervention, but it was only able to remain because of the security net provided by the coalition powers.

Within UNHCR, there was no noticeable acknowledgement of the relevance of Sri Lankan experience in northern Iraq. Ironically, however, there were others outside the agency who were interested in its innovative practice, including in varying degrees a number of national diplomats – one UK diplomat came from London specifically to see how the programme was working out on the ground in early 1991 – and some senior UN officials. Thus initially, when the UK government was pressing the UN to launch a humanitarian programme within the enclave established by coalition forces and lawyers in the Secretariat in New York were demurring on the ground that it would violate Iraqi national sovereignty, a British diplomat drew attention to the precedent of the open relief centres in northern Sri Lanka which were being run by UNHCR without government interference.[8] Shortly afterwards, Sadruddin Aga Khan, as Executive Delegate of the Secretary General in Baghdad, was able to conclude a UN memorandum of understanding with the Iraqi authorities on the provision of humanitarian relief which preserved the form of respect for national sovereignty and non-interference in Iraq's internal affairs. Moreover, several of the working principles enunciated in that instrument had close analogies with the operational rationale and modalities already proved in Sri Lanka. They included the free access of UN staff with radio facilities, the establishment of UN sub-offices and humanitarian centres where relief assistance would be provided, and the setting up of way stations along the routes for the movement back home of returnees and IDPs. Nevertheless, the crucial element of protection in Northern Iraq was not so much the proactive role of international staff on the ground as the backing of decisive military power, together with the political will to use it.

Bosnia

Bosnian warfare

In November 1991, when UNHCR was first involved in Bosnia, it was still legally part of the disintegrating Yugoslav federal state, and so the agency again found itself assisting IDPs in a war zone within their own country. In early 1992, Bosnian independence was recognized internationally, and the civil war continued between government forces and the Bosnian Serb Army (BSA), with particular danger for Bosniac civilians in beleaguered locations. By April 1993, the Security Council was demanding that Srebrenica be treated as a safe area free from any armed attack or other hostile act, and in May, it insisted on full respect for the rights of the UNPROFOR and international humanitarian agencies to have free and unimpeded access to all safe areas; these it extended to include Sarajevo, Tuzla, Zepa, Goradze and Bihac. UNHCR's role included the delivery of humanitarian relief, and so involved close cooperation with UNPROFOR.

UN protection response

As in northern Iraq, the international response in Bosnia was delivered through areas of special protection, with military involvement and programmes of material assistance on a massive scale. And once again, UNHCR was made responsible for IDPs at request of the Secretary General. But the programme differed fundamentally in several respects. One was that the protection response had been duly channelled through the competent UN organs, with authorization by the Security Council, formulation and planning in the Secretariat and implementation on the ground by UNPROFOR under the political direction of a Special Representative of the Secretary General (SRSG). Another was the military position. The coalition forces in northern Iraq had overwhelming strength and few diplomatic inhibitions about exercising it. In Bosnia, however, there had been serious doubts about UN capability even at the planning stage, with the UNPROFOR commander opining that the safe area mandate was inherently incompatible with peacekeeping. He accordingly advised that protection of the areas was a job for a combat-capable peace enforcement operation.[9]. In the event, this advice was ignored which, in the words of the eventual UN report, led to the UNPROFOR mandate being "rhetorically more robust than the Force itself".[10] Acute geopolitical rivalry resulted in a high degree of uncertainty as to when and how force should be used,[11] with the result that the SRSG pursued a policy of extreme caution in which there was "relatively passive enforcement, the lowest common denominator on which all Council members more or less agreed".[12]

The role of UN forces had other negative repercussions in Bosnia. One was military involvement in implementing the humanitarian mandate. The operational problems this entailed from the UNHCR standpoint were indicated subsequently by its special envoy.[13] Another was that the neutral humanitarian credentials of UNHCR fieldworkers on the ground were prejudiced by having a UN force as an actor in the war zone.

The leadership of UNHCR's operation in Bosnia appeared to have been unaware of the prior Sri Lankan experience of protecting endangered civilians in conflict .[14]

Srebrenica

Why did UN efforts to protect beleaguered Bosnian civilians in areas which it had declared to be safe end in a massacre on a scale unknown in Europe since the Second World War? Largely because in the top-down process of forging UN policy through Security Council resolutions, the bottom-up experience of fieldworkers, both military and civil, had been ignored or discounted. The failure to heed the warning of the UNPROFOR commander mentioned above was a case in point. (Sadako Ogata, the High Commissioner for Refugees, also had reservations on the safe area concept.[15]) Moreover, the observation made in the Secretary General's subsequent report that safe or protected areas had to be either demilitarized and established by agreement with the belligerents or defended by a credible military deterrent[16] ignored the fact that such a view was far from being original thinking and indeed had been the reason why, in Sri Lanka six years earlier, the original proposal to establish a safe haven on Mannar island had been shelved in favour of setting up open relief centres (Chapter 9 pp. 131–3). This is not to suggest that areas of special protection on lines similar to the centres in Sri Lanka could have been successfully established in Bosnia. With the manifest war criminality of the BSA in "ethnically cleansing" the territory it controlled, there was insufficient humanitarian space within which a UN agency could have developed such a neutral humanitarian role. Moreover, unlike the Sri Lankan centres, the Bosnian areas were not neutral; in addition to civilians, they also contained government forces. But if the Sri Lankan rationale – which was no more than the applied common sense of fieldworkers in a war zone – had been more widely known at the time, the member states represented in the Security Council might have been more perceptive in seeing that the mechanism which they were setting up in Bosnia was a disaster in the making.

As it was, the results on the ground could hardly have been worse, as the Bosnians in the safe areas were given a false sense of security, while the BSA concluded accurately that with such evident ambiguity and lack of international political will in the UN position, it could implement its genocidal policy with impunity. After such a debacle, of course everyone vows that nothing like it must ever be permitted to happen again. Nonetheless, such is the nature of the current quintessentially lofty political process of decision making in the United Nations, untempered by professional evaluation from the field, that similar disasters in the future cannot be excluded.

[265]

Neutral engagement in Tajikistan

The protection theme of this book is largely about why and how protective neutral engagement evolved in the particular ground situation of northern Sri Lanka in 1990–91. However, another situational variation on humanitarian engagement without military involvement or back-up developed between 1993 and 1996 in the new CIS republic of Tajikistan.

Intermittent hostilities

In May 1992, civil war broke out between rebels from areas where people had mostly been excluded from power under the Soviet *ancien régime* – mostly Garm and Pamiris – and groups who traditionally had been politically dominant and wielded economic power – the Khojandis, Kulyabis and to a lesser extent the Uzbeks – who were now supported by Russian troops. During the war, some 20,000 persons were estimated to have lost their lives, 600,000 persons were displaced internally and more than 60,000 refugees fled across the frontier to Afghanistan, where the rebels had set up a base. The war ended in November 1992, with the rebels having failed in their attempt to change the status quo.

UN protection response

By the time UNHCR arrived in Tajikistan in January 1993, the war was officially over, so that rather than devising pragmatic mechanisms to protect endangered civilians in a war zone, such as variations on the areas of special protection set up in Sri Lanka in 1990, northern Iraq in 1991 and Bosnia in 1993, the primary need was to enable displaced civilians – whether refugees who had fled abroad, mostly to Afghanistan, or IDPs who had remained within the country – to return to their homes, and help them reintegrate. But in the reality of the ground situation – with unresolved conflict issues, intermittent hostilities and volatile insecurity – for much of the time, the situation was on the borderline between conflict and post-conflict.

With funding of US$ 9 million and international staff of 15, the UNHCR operation in Tajikistan was of medium size, nearer the Sri Lankan programme from 1992 onwards than the massive interventions in northern Iraq and Bosnia. Although the original plan had been for an integrated inter-agency response which included a major role for UN Peacekeeping (UNPK) forces, in the event this did not materialize, and by default UNHCR became the lead agency. At the same time, there were strongly positive perceptions of the UN on both sides, with UNHCR in particular being widely regarded as having the field skills and resources to be able to help the country back to peace and stability. Both these conditions provided the humanitarian space where an active protection role could develop on the basis of UN humanitarian impartiality – one which bore a closer resemblance to the model of protective neutral engagement in Sri Lanka than to the operations in northern Iraq and Bosnia where, as has been noted, in different ways the relief programmes could not have functioned without the military. On the ground, security was frequently fragile and relations with the local authorities highly sensitive as the returnees were mostly the Garm and Pamiris who had lost the war, while officials including the police were part of the traditional Kulyabi, Kojandi and Uzbek establishment which had won it. However, UNHCR insisted that all returnees, whether refugees or IDPs, be treated in the same way and succeeded in playing an active and highly mobile protection role in both monitoring the rights of the returnees and intervening, some-times quite forcefully, to uphold them. When crimes were commit-ted against returnees, the victims often complained in the first instance to the UNHCR field officers who then coordinated with the competent authorities to ensure that there was full and fair investi-gation. Moreover, such staff working through the local authorities helped returnees regain possession of homes which had been illegally occupied during the war.

All this was a major step in the evolution of in-country protection methodology in conditions of conflict. There was also a shelter proj-ect, within the wider perceptions of the so-called "preventive protection" policy of the time, assistance to strengthen the legal and judicial systems and other capacity and confidence building meas-ures and, in response to the manifest needs of the situation, an unprecedented diplomatic mediatory role in conflict resolution. There were indeed several other similarities with the Sri Lanka programme in *Eelam War II*, including the notable cost-effectiveness on the ground, the qualitative contribution of protection in that regard, the emergency procedures to monitor unauthorized mili-tary activity and control it through immediate intervention with the central government in Dushanbe, and particularly governmental support and cooperation.[17] Moreover, there was the same reality of the indispensability of such a UN agency role in and between conflict, as demonstrated by UNHCR's largely unsuccessful attempts to find other bodies to which it could hand over its functions to enable it to phase out. In 2006, the agency continues to be needed in both countries.

"Responsibility to protect" in Darfur?

> We are prepared to take collective action, in a timely and decisive manner, through the Security Council, in accordance with the Charter, including Chapter VII, on a case-by-case-basis and in cooperation with relevant regional organizations as appropriate, should peaceful means be inadequate and national authorities are manifestly failing to protect their populations from genocide, war crimes, ethnic cleansing and crimes against humanity.[18]

It is difficult to imagine any civil war which is not highly complex in its causes and evolution, does not cause immense suffering among civilian populations affected by it, does not contribute to insecurity in neighbouring countries and even globally, is not problematic as regards methodology for humanitarian engagement, and does not defy regional and international efforts to bring it to an end. But in such respects, the current conflict in Darfur in the Sudan – the world's biggest displacement emergency with 1.8 million IDPs and 200,000 refugees – has it all in spades. However, since the World Summit in September 2005, the UN now has its "responsibility to protect" – a trump card, albeit one which can only be played in the last resort and with exceptional finesse if it is not to create more problems than it would hope to solve by prejudicing the peace settlement in the south and increasing the dangers of spreading regional conflict along one of the world's most sensitive divides.

Origins

The present (second) war started with an eruption of fighting in West Darfur in early 2003 when the killing and raping by militias triggered massive displacement of civilians, both as refugees into neighbouring Chad and as IDPs within Darfur.[19] The present conflict is distinguishable from the southern civil war – brought to an end by the Comprehensive Peace Agreement (CPA) in January 2005 – in several respects. These include its geographical location (the three Darfur states are in the north, on the border with Chad), the absence of a religious element (both warring tribal groups, the "Arab" nomadic herdsmen and "Black African" farmers,[20] are Muslim), and socio-economic rivalry (the combatants are competing for resources increasingly under pressure owing to encroaching desertification and recurrent periods of drought).

The conflict in Darfur and the south nonetheless have common features, and despite the conclusion of the CPA, continue to impact on one another. The deep-rooted grievances, although different in degree, are similar and derive from analogous marginalization, neglect and discriminatory racial identification, predominantly of non-Arab groups.[21] The type of warfare waged and its humanitarian consequences – the use of Arab and other tribal militias to fight proxy wars with the rebels, involving the killing of civilians, burning of villages, abduction of children and women, destruction and looting of property and massive displacement of people from their land – is also analogous.[22] Moreover, the Sudan People's Liberation Movement and Army (SPLM/A) was implicated in the first Darfur revolt in 1991 and was widely believed to have been involved in the current rebellion.[23]

The African Union

At the regional level, the African Union (AU) initiated peace talks between the parties in Abuja within its Peace and Security Council. It made progress with a protocol guaranteeing humanitarian agencies "unimpeded access" and making commitments to the protection of civilians,[24] and expanded the strength and mandate of its Mission in Sudan (AMIS) to monitor the ceasefire and humanitarian agreements, thereby enabling it to exert some influence on security and protection in certain areas. However, hopes that the expanded AMIS force might have been able to establish a workable security framework have not materialized owing to both funding problems and the lack of rapid tactical mobility of its units on the ground.

"Protection by presence"

Meanwhile, the United Nations Mission in Sudan (UNMIS) and UNHCR adopted a strategy which they called "protection by presence". Putting unarmed humanitarian fieldworkers in any war zone can never be entirely without danger, both for the workers themselves and the civilians they are trying to protect, and is only justified when the risks are soberly assessed to be manageable and heavily outweighed by the benefits of deployment. In Darfur, there are questions about the appropriateness and risks of such a strategy regarding both operational principles and methodology, as indeed in relation to the political and security conditions.

As to principles, although in any situation the establishing of an international presence on the ground is the first operational move towards providing protection, presence alone is usually insufficient to deliver it. As this book argues on the basis of experience in Sri Lanka's *Eelam Wars*, fieldworkers need to play an *active* role by operating mechanisms which respond effectively to the protection needs of civilians in the war zone. Without such focused and clearly relevant activities, they cannot hope to win from the combatants the minimum level of grudging acceptance as actors in their own right whose role has to be taken account of; and sooner rather than later, events are likely to overtake them.

As to methodology, UNMIS protection strategy included the establishment of safe areas and the deployment of mobile teams. From the outset, the former ran into serious problems and soon had to be abandoned, while the feasibility and value of the latter has been increasingly open to question in the light of deteriorating security. Safe areas in most previous conflicts elsewhere have been supported by outside military forces or, exceptionally as in Sri Lanka, negotiated by the relevant UN agency with each of the combatants on the basis of back-to-back agreements.[25] But in Darfur, they were arranged bilaterally between UNMIS and the government – itself a combatant – which was to be responsible for providing security within them. Unsurprisingly in such conditions, they became a pawn in the fighting and had to be shelved.[26] (At some future stage, it is perhaps possible that an appropriate variation of the safe area concept might help in Darfur, but not as perceived and negotiated in the UN Plan of Action.)

As mentioned earlier, mobile protection teams were deployed by UNRWA to good effect in the Palestinian Occupied Territories during the first *intifada* (Chapter 5, pp. 64–6) and the free movement of UNHCR staff in the northern war zone was a key element in UNHCR's strategy of protective neutral engagement in Sri Lanka in

Eelam War II (Chapter 10 pp. 67). But in neither situation was the required scale of operations nor the vastness of the terrain comparable and, most importantly, government forces in both cases were more sensitive to international criticism than in Darfur. The government of Sudan appears to have avoided the substance of the undertaking to disarm the *Janjaweed*, its proxy militia responsible for most of the atrocities, by incorporating many of its personnel into forces such as the Border Intelligence Guard.[27] Owing to deteriorating security, UNHCR has withdrawn staff from the most exposed areas, with the result that many endangered civilians have been left to look after themselves. At that point, whatever confidence "protection by presence" may have been able to impart mutates into a delusion, primarily for the civilians who are supposed to be protected by it, but also for the international community which likes to think that it is doing more than in fact it is. The harsh reality is that ground conditions in Darfur are too rough and volatile for fieldworkers to be able to function effectively and safely outside a strong framework of military security; and now that the AMIS cannot provide it, it is for the UN to provide a peacekeeping force of sufficient size and capacity.

UN "responsibility to protect"

In May 2006, the negotiations in Abuja succeeded to the extent that both the Government and the SLM, the principal rebel group, signed an agreement to end the fighting. Of course it is fragile and could well be eclipsed by misunderstandings between the combatant parties, infighting between the rebel groups and a collapse in security on the ground. However, now that the UN holds the trump card of forcible intervention in the last resort, the hope is that the operationally effective peacekeeping force which the situation demands will eventually be accepted by the government in Khartoum, even if in the process the Security Council is likely to involved in some daunting rounds of brinkmanship.[28]

Operationalizing protection for IDPs?

In various forms and with varying degrees of concern, frustration, justification and civility, the question " Where the hell's UNHCR?" has been asked many times since the 1980s by actors in a range of conflicts as widely apart as the Sudan, the South Caucasus and the Balkans.

When in 1994, UNHCR's own Protection Division reviewed its worldwide experience with IDPs, it readily admitted that in Sudan the agency had not always been playing as active a protection role as might have been expected, either for refugee returnees or IDPs.[29] Then there was the South Caucasus – the turbulent region comprising Armenia, Azerbaijan and Georgia, now newly independent republics in CIS, which in view of their problems of conflict and displaced populations, felt that they deserved better of the UN refugee agency in the early years of their independence. In 1992, their position was well put by Eduard Schevardnadze, the President of Georgia, when he said that he had heard very good things of the agency in other parts of the world, but although his region had many refugees, UNHCR had yet to start work there – a frustration fully shared by the author as its regional representative in Moscow at that time.[30] Eventually, UNHCR did establish small programmes in all South Caucasian countries, as well as play a vital humanitarian engagement role in Tajikistan (pp. 266–8). Nevertheless, it has too often been reluctant and sluggish, if not slothful in its response to the challenge of conflict and post-conflict situations, and in particular of the IDPs and other civilian victims within them. And the experience in Sri Lanka at the outset of *Eelam War II*, which this book describes, shows that even in an exceptional situation when UNHCR was present at the start of a civil war, elements within its bureaucracy went to remarkable lengths to prevent it playing any role in the conflict.

Why did an agency which had been so willing and able to face the challenge of effective humanitarian innovation to help heal the wounds of conflicts in the early 1970s fail to live up to such promise in subsequent decades? One reason was that from 1977, when Sadruddin Aga Khan resigned as High Commissioner, UNHCR no longer had the benefit of his driving vision of a more active UN role, nor his entrepreneurial flair with field operations to address global problems of displacement and return to peace in developing countries. Another was the trend for conflicts to increase in number and complexity. In particular, after the dissolution of the Soviet Union, many latent inter-ethnic tensions could not be easily contained within the new successor states of the CIS; and in a long-running civil war such as the southern Sudan, as already noted, the conflict intensified and extended further the longer it continued. With such widely expanding needs for its attention, but without correspondingly augmented resources, UNHCR could not have been expected to face such challenges alone.

Yes – but when all allowances and excuses are made, there are still serious problems in UNHCR's own position towards international needs for protection in the twenty-first century, of which its inadequate response to the challenge of IDP protection is but one aspect. Some see the problem as lack of vision; others as inadequate methods for gathering and analysing information on changing situations. There is also the reality of cultural ambiguity towards its primary function of international protection, as mentioned in the previous chapter. And there is the top-heavy establishment in Geneva: costly, complacent and too often indifferent to protection needs: a big problem, albeit one for which it must be said the donor community is partly to blame owing, on the one hand to its overly generous funding in the past, which started in the First Gulf War and continued in Former Yugoslavia, and on the other, to its increasing demands for more information on agency programmes.

Does it matter to the international community whether or not UNHCR rises to the challenge of broadening and operationalizing its protection mandate? Conversely, why should the agency itself be worried if it loses its leading role in protection? First, for the international community: historically, for all its bureaucratic faults, UNHCR has been a success story for the United Nations in bringing committed idealism to bear in sensitive situations which are beyond national governments acting alone or in concert, and thereby making a worthwhile difference for many millions of suffering humanity. And in so doing over the years, its High Commissioners have vindicated the judgement of the founding fathers that such a post was essential for the effectiveness of the international protection function; its Protection Division has developed impressive professional capacity for setting, maintaining and promoting the extension of international standards within the instrumental refugee definitions; and on the ground, its field staff have gained practical skills and know-how which enable them to perform effectively in rough and problematic conditions. These are notable *acquis* of international humanitarian practice which cannot responsibly be weakened, as they very probably would be if UNHCR were to be reorganized within a larger and more composite humanitarian and rights organization.

Second, should UNHCR itself be worried if it loses its leading role in international protection by failing to rise to the occasion of broadening and operationalizing its mandate, particularly for IDPs? It should recall that in significant part, its formidable reputation was originally built up in the 1970s through a readiness and ability to respond effectively to international needs in forced migration. With all the developments in this field in recent years, more than ever the challenge now is to adapt, or face diminishing relevance. Those within the agency who for various reasons do not welcome change should face the reality that the international community will be unlikely to continue to pay for an institutional regime that continues to benefit only a relatively privileged category among the displaced, and one whose numbers are indeed decreasing.[31]

UNHCR's indifferent response to the IDP challenge led to the so-called "collaborative response" under the aegis of the Inter-Agency Steering Committee (IASC), a heavily bureaucratic mechanism for international agency cooperation more suited to taking note of problems than to getting to grips with them. But from mid 2005, protection prospects in the UN began to improve. Despite its lack of critical detail, the World Summit opened up the road to more and better international protection with its endorsement of both the responsibility to protect (pp. 268 above) and the proposed Peace-building Commission.[32] The former is a historic step forward, while the new commission – 30 years after Sadruddin Aga Khan's above-quoted comment (p. 259 above) – will help fill a debilitating organic gap in the UN system.

Then there were indications that UNHCR was at last beginning to get its act together to respond to contemporary protection challenges, particularly in relation to IDPs. There were measures to mainstream protection in the life of the agency, and even some enthusiasm expressed about operationalizing it in the field.[33] Most important was the statement to all staff members by Antonio Guterres, the newly appointed High Commissioner, that protection was primarily what the agency was about, including its broadened role for IDPs, and that they had better get on with it.[34] This is a critical leadership initiative which, if sustained, promises to bring about something of a cultural revolution in the agency's bureaucratic life, with its preference for massive programmes of material assistance in which protection has too often been no more than a sideline. Moreover, Jan Egeland, the UN Emergency Relief Coordinator and head of the Office for the Coordination of Humanitarian Affairs (OCHA), outlined improvements in the inter-agency collaborative approach in which UNHCR would be leading clusters of agencies in protection, emergency shelter and camp management for IDPs. However, "leading clusters" is different from being the "lead agency" which UNHCR was in the Balkans in the 1990s, involving as it does answering at the country level to the Humanitarian Coordinator, and ultimately the Emergency Relief Coordinator – a procedurally complex reporting network.

So, it's plain sailing towards more and better UN protection for IDPs? Unfortunately not. Although nothing should be done to dampen the current much belated but widespread enthusiasm to protect IDPs, serious concerns remain over appropriate capacity at the institutional and operational levels. First, UNHCR – whose professional role is critical in developing professional practice – is still a lot less than the bureaucratically leaner and operationally keener-on-protection agency which the situation demands. And second, it has to be asked how far the revised Collaborative Response modalities will improve IDP protection on the ground? Although probably substantially so in areas far removed from active hostilities and in the less unstable conditions of post-conflict, within the highly volatile and fast-moving situations in war zones – which are mostly responsible for triggering massive displacement in the first place – insufficient attention is being paid to the funda-mental problems of physical safety of fieldworkers, leadership capacity and the structure for crisis management.

* * *

With the current deadly drift of events in the north east, the situa-tion in Sri Lanka will soon put the integrity of United Nations' commitment and the soundness of its operational protection struc-tures to the most stringent of tests – one which the international community cannot afford to let the UN fail.

Notes

1.   UN crisis, dangers and opportunity

1. During the critical first year and a half of *Eelam War II*, there were never more than seven international staff members – sometimes fewer. In financially less stringent circumstances, UNHCR would very probably have launched an appeal for a large special humanitarian operation endorsed by the Secretary General, which could have specifically included internally displaced persons (IDPs) as well as the refugee returnees whose reintegration it had been monitoring. But this was not a valid option at that time.

2. "Power tends to corrupt, and absolute power corrupts absolutely," Lord Acton, Victorian historian, in a letter to Bishop Mandell Creighton, 3 April 1887.

3. To name but a couple, Ralph Bunche (1903–1971), UN peacemaker and Nobel Prize laureate, and Oscar Schachter (1915–2003), a Secretariat lawyer who made an outstanding contribution to shaping the rule of law and in particular the legal framework of UN peacekeeping,.

4. In Sri Lanka, the nature of hostilities and conditions in the war zones differed markedly between the *Vanni* (including Mannar), the Jaffna peninsula to the north and Batticaloa in the east. Notably, an independent analyst recommended a partial adaptation of the UNHCR role in Mannar for Batticaloa, where the agency was not present, and suggested that an ICRC delegate might play a role in the Government welfare centres there similar to that of the UNHCR field officer's protection monitoring function in the open relief centre at Pesalai. (See Court Robinson, "Sri Lanka: Island of Refugees", US Committee on Refugees issue paper November 1991, p. 36, VII Recommendations No. 2). In the event, the proposal was not favoured by the ICRC. But even if some such mechanism might have been put in place, it is doubtful if it would have worked altogether satisfactorily in the different ground conditions in the east.

5. Predecessor of the Office of the Coordinator for Humanitarian Affairs (OCHA).

6. W. Clarance, "Field Strategy for the Protection of Human Rights", *International Journal of Refugee Law*, vol. 9, 1997, p. 248, note 31.

7. In 1998, Vincent Cochetel, a UNHCR staff member in charge of cross-border assistance in Chechenya, was kidnapped and held for eleven months.

8. Fortunately, this was dropped because of German and Swedish objections.

9. See "Safe Areas: A Substitute for Asylum", *The State of the World's Refugees*, 1995, p. 128.

10. *Guardian*, 4 September 2002.

11. *Guardian*, 11 July 2006.

12. In August 1999, the Secretary General, Kofi Annan, advised the Security Council that the international protection of civilians in war would be the principal challenge facing the UN in the twenty-first century. Although there have been four reports, in view of the recognition of the scale of the problem, the response as regards the development of protective methodology has been disappointing.

2. International protection in a civil war

1. The pearl fishery lasted until the early twentieth century, when it was closed as a result of overfishing; its open season in 1906 was supervised by Leonard Woolf, fresh from Cambridge as a cadet in the Ceylon Civil Service (*Growing: An Autobiography of the Years 1904 to 1911*, Leonard Woolf, 1961; *Woolf in Ceylon: An Imperial Journey in the Shadow of Leonard Woolf 1904–1911*, Christopher Ondaatje, Toronto, 2005, pp. 115–18).
2. The funding crisis both reflected and contributed to the agency's exceptional instability during this period. (During his three and a half year term in Sri Lanka, the author represented three High Commissioners and served through two interregnums between departure of the outgoing incumbents and election of their successors.)
3. UNHCR Executive Committee Conclusions on International Protection (Voluntary Repatriation) nos 18(XXXI) and 40(XXXVI) para. (l): "The High Commissioner must be entitled to insist on his legitimate concern over the outcome of any return that he has assisted. … [H]e should be given direct and unhindered access to returnees so that he is in a position to monitor fulfilment of the amnesties, guarantees or assurances on the basis of which the refugees have returned. This should be considered as inherent in his mandate."
4. UNHCR Press Release, 21 February 2006.

3. Roots of militancy, seeds of terrorism

1. C.R. de Silva, *Sri Lanka, a History*, Vikas, Delhi, 1987, p. 27; Devanesan Nesiah, *Tamil Nationalism*, Marga Institute, Colombo, 2001, pp. 7–8.
2. Nesiah, p. 7.
3. de Silva, p. 27.
4. Nesiah in correspondence with the author.
5. Nesiah, p. 9.
6. Government of Ceylon, *Report of the Special Commission on the Ceylon Constitution*, Colombo, 1928, p. 39.
7. Sir Ivor Jennings, constitutional lawyer, Vice Chancellor of the University of Ceylon and subsequently Cambridge.
8. All-Ceylon Tamil Congress representation to the Soulbury Commission quoted in *Ceylon: Report on the Commission on Constitutional Reform*, Cmd. 6677, Colonial Office, London, 1945, para. 177.
9. The French, for their part, were equally determined, albeit ultimately unsuccessful in their objective to keep Trincomalee out of British hands, as otherwise they feared their rivals would become "l'arbitre de toute l'Inde", see Gerard de Rayneval to the Comte de Vergennes, 4 December 1782, in *Archives des Affaires Etrangeres: Correspondence Politique, Angleterre*, vol. 539, f. 155.
10. Pierre Albertini, a teacher of British imperial history in Paris writes: "My students are quick to compare British imperialism to its French counterpart – and the comparison doesn't turn in favour of their country" (*Guardian*, 7 July 2003).
11. de Silva, p. 201.
12. de Silva. p. 247.
13. Jane Russell, "Communal Politics under the Donoughmore Constitution 1931", *Ceylon Historical Journal*, vol. 26, 1982.
14. A. Jeyaratnam Wilson, *Sri Lankan Tamil Nationalism*, Hurst, London, 1999, p.73.

15. "It will behove the Sinhalese majority to take the utmost care to avoid giving cause for any suspicion of unfairness or partiality". Cmd. 6677, para. 177
16. African Governors' Conference paper AGC 17 November 1947, referred to in *Oxford History of British Empire, Twentieth Century*, S.R. Ashton, Ceylon, p. 448.
17. Nigeria, Sudan and Uganda, all well-administered dependent territories, suffered similar ethnically driven separatist problems after independence.
18. de Silva, p. 237.
19. National State Assembly Debates, vol. 2, 3 October 1972, p. 731.
20. See Jeyaratnam Wilson, op. cit., p.110.
21. A. Jeyaratnam Wilson, *S.J.V. Chelvanayakam and the Crisis of Sri Lankan Tamil Nationalism 1947–1977*, Hurst, London, 1994, pp. 80–81, notes 2 and 3, in which it is asserted that the police had specific instructions from the prime minister not to intervene.
22. See Jeyaratnam Wilson, *Sri Lankan Tamil Nationalism*, p.125, and Rohan Gunaratna, *Indian Intervention in Sri Lanka*, South Asian Network on Conflict Research, Colombo, 1994, p. 71–72.
23. M.R. Narayan Swamy, *Tigers of Lanka: From Boys to Guerrillas*, Vijitha Yapa, Colombo, 1996, p. 51.
24. Dagmar Hellmann-Rajanayagam, *Tamil Tigers' Armed Struggle for Identity*, Franz Steiner Verlag, Stuttgart, 1994, p. 38.
25. I.G.P. Stanley Senanayake, reported in the *Indian Express* of 10 May 1981 and quoted in Narayan Swamy, p. 40.
26. R. Gunaratna, *Indian Intervention*, pp.135–136.
27. Jeyaratnam Wilson, p.131.
28. Hellmann-Rajanayagam, p.140.
29. Jeyaratnam Wilson, p. 20.
30. Hellmann-Rajanayagam, p.29.
31. Jeyaratnam Wilson, p. 24.
32. Neelan Tiruchelvam, "Devolution and the Elusive Quest for Peace", p. 192, in *Creating Peace in Sri Lanka, Civil War and Reconciliation*, Robert I. Rotberg (ed.), Brookings Institution, Washington, 1999.
33. *New Oxford English Dictionary*, 1998.

4. Ironies of a peacemaking protectorate

1. J.N. Dixit, Indian High Commissioner in Colombo at the United Services Institution of India, 10 March 1989, see R. Gunaratna, p. 575.
2. J.N. Dixit, *Assignment in Colombo*, Konark, Delhi, 1998, pp. 210–11. The Indian High Commissioner recalled his anguish over the incident and what he considered to be the excessively procedural position taken by the IPKF commander in refusing to accept instructions from him to prevent the group being moved to Colombo, and insisting on waiting for confirmation through the regular chain of command.
3. R. Gunaratna, p. 236.
4. Lt. General Depinder Singh, *The IPKF in Sri Lanka*, Trishul Publications, Bangalore, 1991.
5 Dixit, p. 339.
6. Ibid., p. 350.
7. Rajesh Kadian, *India's Sri Lanka Fiasco*, Vision Books, Delhi, 1990, p. 136, cites the total IPKF losses as "1155 dead, with three times as many wounded".

8. Research and Analysis Wing, the Indian intelligence agency.
9. Thomas Abraham, Colombo, 18 May 1989.
10. UN document A/AC.96/751(Part II)/Corr.1 made a discreet reference to the matter and included a probably conservative estimate of the numbers involved.
11. Inscription on IPKF memorial in Mannar district.
12. See Annexure to the Peace Accord 1987, clause 6), which provided that: "an Indian Peacekeeping contingent may be invited by the President of Sri Lanka to guarantee and enforce the cessation of hostilities if so required."
13. Nor were they during the next wave of repatriation from South India in 1992–93 when, although UNHCR international staff were allowed access to refugees in the camps in India prior to repatriation from July 1992, results of the convoluted procedures adopted were sometimes less than reassuring. See UNHCR Executive Committee document A/AC.96/808(Part II), paras. 2.0.25/ 2.0.27.
14. Tom Barnes, Head of Organization and Management in UNHCR headquarters, mission report quoted in *Refugees* nos 63 (1989) and 130 (2003).

5. UNRWA and UNHCR protective practice

1. Quoted in M. Viorst, *Reaching for the Olive Branch: UNRWA and Peace in the Middle East*, Washington DC, Indiana University Press, 1989, p. 10.
2. UN document s/19443.
3. Viorst, p. 21.
4. A. Williams, "UNRWA and the Occupied Territories", *Journal of Refugee Studies*, vol.2, no.1 1989, p.160.
5. Viorst, p. 10.
6. UNRWA briefing memo to field staff by former legal advisor, S. Sinha, quoted in L Takkenberg, *Status of Palestinian Refugees in International Law*, Oxford University Press, p. 295.
7. With the partial redeployment of Israeli forces and establishment of the Palestinian Authority pursuant to the Declaration of Principles between Israel and the Palestine Liberation Organization (the "Oslo Accord"), UNRWA's RAO programme was suspended in Gaza in May 1994 and finally officially terminated in April 1996.
8. Although para. 9 of the UNHCR Statute requires the High Commissioner to engage in such additional activities as the General Assembly may determine, the various General Assembly resolutions which have extended UNHCR competence over the years, mostly on an ad hoc situation-by-situation basis, have made no specific reference to it.
9. Although only adopted by a colloquium, and as such "soft law" of non-binding effect, the Cartagena declaration has nevertheless strongly influenced the practice of UNHCR and states in the region.
10. Some, however, have claimed on the contrary that it has been part of the problem in perpetuating certain situations (notably in the Great Lakes region of Africa).
11. ECOSOC resolution 1741(LIV).
12. "Special operations" was an internal UNHCR bureaucratic term for programmes funded by voluntary contributions outside the regular budget. "Special humanitarian tasks" was eventually used by the General Assembly to describe the ad hoc good offices functions of the High Commissioner. (See GA resolutions 3271(XXIX), 10 December 1974 and 3454(XXX), 9 December 1975).

13. See also Chapter 18, pp. 259–60.
14. See Categories of persons to whom the High Commissioner is competent to extend international protection, UNHCR branch office memorandum no.49/81 of August 1981.
15. See Conclusion No. 40 (XXXVI), para (I) .
16. Ibid, para (e)

6. Hopes for peace, fears of war: December 1989 to June 1990

1. The field officers were Solomon Abebe and Tariq Shahjada.

7. Flux in Geneva, forebodings on the ground

1. *The Year 1989/90: The Premadasa–LTTE Talks – Why they Failed – and What Really Happened in Negotiating Peace in Sri Lanka: Efforts, Failures & Lessons*, Kumar Rupesinghe (ed.), International Alert, London, 1998, pp. 173–85.
2. Rohan Gunaratna in conversation with the author.
3. Particularly *Negotiating Peace in Sri Lanka* (note 1 above).

8. National implosion, international indifference: June 1990

1. At that stage, exact figures were unobtainable. But when conditions stabilized somewhat, the *kachcheri* estimated that of a total population in the centres and sub-centres of over 70,000, nearly 15,000 were refugee returnees. (See Mannar *kachcheri* document "Population in ORCs and ORSCs in Mannar", dated 23 May 1991).

9. The war zone and the LTTE

1. Later in *Eelam War II*, Yogi was permitted to retire to the very Sri Lankan position of cricket coach to the Jaffna schools.

10. Engagement in Mannar, controversy in Geneva

1. Exchange between one of the programme's critics and the author in Geneva in November 1990.

11. Rising tension on Mannar island

1. Literally, the "jungle", usually used in reference to the mainland areas in the north south of the Jaffna peninsula and north of Vavuniya.
2. "The paramount consideration in the employment of the staff ... shall be the necessity of securing the highest standards of efficiency, competence and integrity" (UN Charter, Article 101). Staff "shall be chosen from persons devoted to the purposes of the Office of the High Commissioner" (UNHCR Statute, para.15(b)).

12. Food is neutral

1. For an account of UNHCR's relief convoys for non-food items at a later stage in the war, see Kilean Kleinschmidt, "Death, Despair and Hope", *Refugees*, vol. 1, no. 130, 2003, pp. 20–1.

14. "Open relief centres are working"

1. Including Rohan Gunaratna (*Indian Intervention in Sri Lanka*, Colombo, 1993, p. 485), Adrian Wijemanne (*War and Peace in Post-Colonial Ceylon 1948–1991*, Longman Orient, New Delhi, 1996, pp. 18–20) and Godfrey Gunatilleka (See S.D. Karunakharan, "Voices in the Open Forum", *The Island*, Colombo, 2–3 June 2001).
2. Alan Simmance, a former senior UNHCR officer, was brought in to deal with this matter.
3. *Island of Refugees*, Court Robinson, US Committee for Refugees, Washington, October 1991.
4. UNHCR Executive Committee 1991, document A/AC.96/776, paras 30–32.
5. *Servitude et Grandeur Militaire*, by Alfred de Vigny, soldier and French romantic poet in the early nineteenth century, gave an idealized picture of hardship yet humble commitment in military life.

15. In and between Sri Lankan warfare

1. V. Nesiah and S. Nanthikesan "From ISGA to Eternity: The Light at the End of the Tunnel has been Shut Out until Further Notice", *Tamil Times*, London, December 2003, vol. 22, no. 12, pp. 15–20.
2. UN doct. A/AC.96/808 (Part II), para. 2.0.27.
3. *Manual on Field Practice on Internal Displacement*: examples from UN agencies and partner organizations of field-based initiatives supporting internally displaced persons, OCHA, Inter-Agency Steering Committee Policy Paper Series, no.1,1999, para.18.
4. *The State of the World's Refugees: The Challenge of Protection*, UNHCR-Penguin, 1993, p. 135, and *In Search of Solutions*, UNHCR-Oxford University Press, 1995, p. 128.
5. "UN Refugee Warning", *Sri Lanka Monitor*, British Refugee Council, London. no. 98, March 1996.
6. UN doc. E/CN.4/1998/53/Add.2 adopted by the Commission on Human Rights on the basis of the report submitted by Francis Deng, the Representative of the Secretary General. See the explanatory note of Walter Kalin, the present Representative, in *International Journal of Refugee Law*, vol. 10, no. 3, 1998.
7. See Edward Benson "Sri Lanka, Internally Displaced Persons and the Guiding Principles: A Critique", an unpublished MSc dissertation in Development Studies at the School of Oriental and African Studies, London University, 2001, p. 51, cited with permission of the author.

16. Innovative concepts

1. Although the Division of International Protection did not formally take a position on the Sri Lankan programme and open relief centres during October 1991, some of its senior leadership were strongly supportive of the Colombo position in the controversy in Geneva at that time, notably the late Shun Chetty.
2. W.D. Clarance: "Open Relief Centres: A Pragmatic Approach to Emergency Relief and Monitoring during Conflict in a Country of Origin", and "Protective Structure, Strategy and Tactics: International Protection in Ethnic Conflicts", in *International Journal of Refugee Law*, Oxford University Press, respectively vol. 3 1991 and vol. 5 1993.

3. UNHCR Executive Committee Conclusion on International Protection 40 (XXXVI), para (e).
4. J.-M. Mendiluce, *War and Disaster in the Former Yugoslavia: The Limits of Humanitarian Action*, World Refugee Survey 1994, US Committee for Refugees, p.16.
5. UNHCR Statute, art. 2.
6. *Sri Lanka: Report of the Joint Appraisal Mission*, UK DFID and UNHCR (ref EPAU/2002/04)

17. Controversial questions

1. This and other issues relating to the open relief centres were considered in UNHCR's *Operational Experience with Internally Displaced Persons*, paras 149–154, Geneva, September 1994. However, such a potted format was unsuitable for the treatment of a highly complex situation, and in consequence some of the comments made in passing were open to question.
2. Universal Declaration of Human Rights, 14(1).
3. "India allows NGOs into refugee camps", *Sri Lanka Monitor*, no. 122, March 1998.
4. UNHCR Sri Lanka 2004 Annual Protection Report, p.19.
5. UNHCR Executive Committee, op. cit., para. (l).
6. G. Goodwin-Gill, *International Journal of Refugee Law*, vol. 3, no. 1, 1991, p. 122, summarizing the debate on drafting the UNHCR statute (see GAOR, 4 Session, Summary Records, Third Committee, 262 meeting).
7. G. Loescher, *UNHCR and World Politics, a Perilous Path*, Oxford University Press, 2001, pp. 249 and 266. Subsequently, High Commissioner Stoltenberg restored the title and some of the functions of the former Division of International Protection, albeit without overall authority and responsibility for protection in the field.
8. *UNHCR's Role with Internally Displaced Persons*, para. 8 (a), IOM-BOM/33/93 of 8 April 1993 (High Commissioner's emphasis).
9. S. Ogata, *World Order, Internal Conflict and Refugees*, address to John F. Kennedy School of Government, 28 October 1996.
10. Robin Soans, *Talking to Terrorists*: a docudrama play with powerful testimonies both from terrorists in various parts of the world and from those who have tried to deal with them sensitively, which played to full houses in London around the time of the terrorist attacks in mid-2005.
11. UNHCR Statute para. 2.
12. Report of the Secretary General to the Security Council on the Protection of Civilians in Armed Conflict of 30 March 2001, para. 50, recommendation 9 (S/2001/331).
13. UNHCR staff member Vincent Cochetel was kidnapped in Chechenya and held for eleven months.
14. Binod Sijapati in conversation with the author.
15. For a concise description of the variety of ICRC tasks in the field, see J.-P. Lavoyer "Guiding Principles on Internal Displacement: A Few Comments on the Contribution of International Law", *International Review of the Red Cross*, no. 14, 1998.
16. The opinion of a senior official in the competent ministry, in discussion with the author at the time.
17. Neelan Tiruchelvam, "Sri Lanka's Ethnic Conflict and Preventive Action: The Role of NGOs", in Robert Rotberg, (ed.), *Vigilance and Vengeance: NGOs Preventing Ethnic Conflict in Divided Societies*, Brookings Institution, Washington, 1996.

See also Law Society and Trust, *Sri Lanka, State of Human Rights, 1994*, Colombo, 1994, pp. 228–268.

18. UNHCR's Operational Experience With Internally Displaced Persons, para. 153.

18. Improvisation – intervention – engagement

1. High Commissioner's Statement to Executive Committee, 8 October 1975, GAOR, Thirtieth Session, Supplement 12A, Annex III, p.36 (A/10012/Add.).
2. UNHCR Statute, chapter I.1.
3. General Assembly resolution 2956(XXVII).
4. UNHCR Bulletin, No 1, July 1972, quoted in L.W. Holborn, *Refugees: A Problem of Our Time*, Scarecrow Press, New Jersey, 1975, p. 1352.
5. High Commissioner's Statement, p.42.
6. UNHCR Executive Committee Conclusions on International Protection, no. 40 (XXXVI), para. (l).
7. UNHCR Report on Northern Iraq, 1 September 1992, para. 1.18.
8. Reuter Library report, 10 April 1991.
9. *The Fall of Srebrenica*, Report of the Secretary General, para. 43, UNGA doct A/54/549 of 15 November 1999, para 51.
10. *Srebrenica*, para. 43.
11. Adam Roberts, *Humanitarian Action in War*, International Institute for Strategic Studies, Adelphi paper no. 305, London, 1996, p. 43.
12. Wolfgang Bierman and Martin Vadset, eds, *UN Peacekeeping in Trouble: Lessons Learned from the Former Yugoslavia*, Ashgate, London, 1999, quoted in *The Fall of Srebrenica*, para. 44.
13. J.-M. Mendiluce, *War and Disaster in the Former Yugoslavia: The Limits of Humanitarian Action*, World Refugee Survey, US Committee for Refugees, Washington, 1994, p. 16.
14. Ibid, p. 13.
15. Sadako Ogata, letter to Secretary General, 17 December 1992, quoted in *Srebrenica*, para 49.
16. *Srebrenica*, para. 499.
17. UNHCR Report on Tajikistan, 1993–1996, p. 26, citing an incident where a rogue unit of troops with a tank established itself in a transit centre and began robbing and beating up returnees, when the problem had to be referred to the UNHCR office in Dushanbe for resolution at the national level.
18. *2005 World Summit Outcome*, A/res/60/1, 24 October 2005, para 139.
19. As at end October 2005, UNHCR figures for refugees in Chad were some 220,000 and an estimated 1.8 million IDPs in Darfur.
20. Francis Deng, UN Secretary General's first Representative on Internally Displaced Persons, a southern Sudanese and a distinguished advocate of international standards, in *Mission to the Sudan: The Darfur Crisis*, E/CN.4/2005/8, 27 September 2004, p. 5, where it is noted that despite such identity labels there is considerable racial mixture between the tribes.
21. Ibid. p. 3.
22. Ibid. para. 16.
23. Ibid. para. 33.
24. "Protocol on the improvement of the humanitarian situation in Darfur", African Union press release Abuja, 1 September 2004, quoted in H. Slim "Dithering over Darfur?", *International Affairs*, vol. 80, no. 5, 2004, p. 820.

25. Adam Roberts, op. cit., pp. 40–41.
26. International Crisis Group (ICG), Africa report no. 89, pp. 6–7.
27. ICG Africa report no. 89, p. 8.
28. "UN Calls for Major International Force to Go Darfur", *Guardian*, 11 March 2006.
29. *UNHCR's Operational Experience With Internally Displaced Persons*, op. cit., para. 163.
30. *The State of the World's Refugees: Fifty Years of Humanitarian Action*, UNHCR, Oxford University Press, 2000, p. 192, note 16.
31. During 2005, the number of refugees being assisted or protected by UNHCR dropped from 9.2 to 8.4 million – a 26-year low – although persons living in a refugee-like situation within their own country rose to 6.6 million and the overall numbers of concern to the agency increased by 1.3 million to 20.8 million. *Global Refugee Trends*, UNHCR, Geneva, 9 June 2006.
32. *2005 World Summit Outcome*, General Assembly resolution A/60/L.1, 20 September 2005, paras 97–105; Security Council resolution, S/res/1645(2005).
33. Note on International Protection (EC/55/SC/CRP.12, 7 June 2005) and Director of International Protection statement, 5 October 2005.
34. UNHCR press release on opening of 56th session of its Executive Committee, 3 October 2005.

Sources and reading

The narrative relies on a personal journal kept day-by-day from 1989 to 1992, the historical background is based on a number of leading works by national authors from both communities and the analytical references both within and outside that time and place relate largely to substantive UN and UNHCR documents. A minimal selection of published works is given below.

Origins of Sri Lanka's conflict

C.R. de Silva, *Sri Lanka: a history*, Vikas, Delhi, 1987.

K.M. de Silva, *Reaping the whirlwind*, Penguin, Delhi, 1998.

S.R. Ashton, *Ceylon*, in W. R. Louis (ed.), *Dissolution of the British Empire*, Oxford History of British Empire "Twentieth Century", 1999.

J. Manor, *The expedient Utopian: Bandaranaike and Ceylon*, Cambridge University Press, Cambridge, 1989.

M. Roberts, G. Gunatilleka and D. Nesiah (eds), *A history of ethnic conflict in Sri Lanka* (Marga Monograph Series), Marga Institute, Colombo, 2001.

Tamil militancy

A. Jeyaratnam Wilson, *S.J.V. Chelvanayakam and the crisis of Sri Lankan Tamil nationalism*, Hurst, London, 1993.

——*Sri Lankan Tamil nationalism*, University of British Columbia Press, 1999.

D. Nesiah, *Tamil nationalism*, Marga Monograph Series (as above).

R. Gunaratna, *War and peace in Sri Lanka*, IFS, Colombo, 1987.

——*Indian intervention in Sri Lanka*, South Asian Network on Conflict Research, Colombo, 1993.

——*Sri Lanka's ethnic crisis and national security*, South Asian Network on Conflict Research, Colombo, 1998.

M. Narayan Swamy, *Tigers of Lanka*, Vijitha Yapa, Colombo, 1996.

Indian intervention

J.N. Dixit, *Assignment in Colombo*, Konark, Delhi, 1998.

Lt. General Depinder Singh, *The IPKF in Sri Lanka*, South Asia Books, Bangalore, 1991.

Rajesh Kadian, *India's Sri Lanka fiasco*, Vision Books, Delhi,1990.

R. Gunaratna (as above).

The *Eelam wars* and peace processes

R. Hoole, *Sri Lanka: the arrogance of power – myths, decadence and murder*, University Teachers for Human Rights, Jaffna, 2001.

K. Rupesinghe (ed.), *Negotiating peace in Sri Lanka: efforts, failures and lessons*, International Alert, London, 1998.

Sri Lanka Monitor: regular informative briefings on the conflict during 1988–2002 under the aegis of the British Refugee Council.

Tamil Times, London: monthly coverage of events and issues.

For those dissatisfied by meagre coverage in the Western press, online service is provided by the leading Colombo dailies: *The Island, Daily Mirror/Sunday Times, Daily News* and *Sunday Leader*, and *The Hindu* in Madras.

UNRWA

M. Viorst, *Reaching for the olive branch: UNRWA and peace in the Middle East,* Indiana University Press, Bloomington, Ind., 1989.

L. Takkenberg, *Status of Palestinian refugees in international law,* Clarendon Press, Oxford, 1998.

International protection, refugees, IDPs and UNHCR

L.W. Holborn, *Refugees: a problem of our time,* Scarecrow Press, Metuchen, N.J., 1975.

G.S. Goodwin-Gill, *The refugee in international law,* Oxford, 1996.

G. Loescher, *UNHCR and world politics: a perilous path,* Oxford University Press, Oxford, 2001.

Francis M. Deng: key reports, papers and articles both as the Secretary General's first Representative for Internally Displaced Persons and co-director of the Brookings-SAIS Project on Internal Displacement.

Walter Kalin: similar authoritative publications; currently Secretary General's Representative on the Human Rights of Internally Displaced Persons and co-director of the Brookings-Berne project.

Roberta Cohen: similar leading work both as co-director of the above project and otherwise.

Forced Migration Review (FMR), RSC, Oxford.

Danesh Jayatilaka and Robert Muggah, "IDP vulnerability assessments in Sri Lanka", *FMR* 20, May 2004.

Protection-in-conflict elsewhere

J.-M. Mendiluce, *War and disaster in the former Yugoslavia: the limits of humanitarian action,* US Committee for Refugees World Refugee Survey 1994.

Adam Roberts, 'Humanitarian action in war', International Institute of Strategic Studies, London, Adelphi paper no 305, 1996.

Index